JEWS AND MEDICINE
Religion, Culture, Science

"THEREFORE CHOOSE LIFE..."

DEUT. 30:19

דברים ל' י"ט

JEWS AND MEDICINE
Religion, Culture, Science

EDITED BY NATALIA BERGER

BASED ON THE EXHIBIT AT BETH HATEFUTSOTH
THE NAHUM GOLDMANN MUSEUM OF THE JEWISH DIASPORA

THE JEWISH PUBLICATION SOCIETY
Philadelphia • Jerusalem

PUBLICATION OF THIS VOLUME WAS ASSISTED BY A GRANT FROM THE AMERICAN PHYSICIANS FELLOWSHIP FOR MEDICINE IN ISRAEL.

Design: Yael Bogen-Gerald, David Tartakover

Production: Tartakover Design

Photo research: Natalia Berger

Editorial Coordinator and text production: Susy Rosenbloom

Publishing Coordinator: Yossi Avner

English editor: Chaya Amir

English translations: Chaya Amir, Chaya Galay

Photography: Jacob Brill

Reproduction of photographs: Ronit Abramovich, Lea Weidenfeld

Typesetting: Rami Livneh - Total Graphics

Color separation: Shva Ltd.

Plates: Kav-Or Ltd.

The book has been published on the occasion of the exhibition *Therefore Choose Life ... Jews and Medicine: Religion Culture Science* organized by Beth Hatefutsoth, The Nahum Goldmann Museum of the Jewish Diaspora, Tel Aviv, June 1995 - December 1995.

Opposite:

Scenes from the life cycle birth, marriage and burial.

Title page of Selihoth (Penitential prayers) for the Hevra Kadisha of Frankfurt am Main. Handwritten in square Ashkenazi script and decorated on vellum, 1740. Private Collection.

Front Cover:

Bloodletting Man.

Bibliothèque Nationale de France, Paris, Ms. hebr. 1181, folio 264v.

Jews and medicine : religion, culture, science / edited by Natalia Berger.

    p. cm.

    Originally published: Tel Aviv, Israel : Beth Hatefutsoth, 1995.

    Includes bibliographical references.

    ISBN 0-8276-0644-3

    1. Jews—Medicine. I. Berger, Natalia.

R135.5.J49 1997

610'.89'924—dc21   97-26717

                       CIP

Ruth Reed of Johannesburg dedicates this book to the memory of her son Arthur Ralph Kaplan (1953-1990) whose special qualities touched so many people in his short life.

ACKNOWLEDGMENTS

First and foremost I would like to thank Zelda and Leon Street whose idea, initiative and generosity made this project possible. They accompanied the project in all its stages with interest, enthusiasm and support. Sincere thanks must also go to Aaron Feingold for his help and encouragement during the many difficult hours.

Jews and Medicine was not an easy undertaking for the simple reason that Jewish physicians lived in many countries and the documentation of their lives and work is dispersed in institutions and private collections around the world. This is evident from the long list of institutions and individuals who have given us material for the exhibition and the book. But even their assistance would not have been possible were it not for the basis provided by the pioneers of research in this field, many of whom are no longer alive.

The most important figure in the field was Harry Friedenwald (1864-1950), who collected medical manuscripts and books and wrote on medical history for more than fifty years. In his will he bequeathed his huge collection to the Jewish National and University Library in Jerusalem. Solomon Kagan (1889-1955) was another important scholar in the field. His work is still today the most comprehensive source for material on Jewish physicians in modern times. In Israel, research on Jewish physicians was begun by Suessman Muntner (1897-1973) and was closely connected with the revival of the Hebrew language. With the establishment of the Faculty of Medicine of the Hebrew University of Jerusalem he militated for the creation of a research institute, an idea that was realized by Joshua Leibovitz (1895-1993), co-founder in 1947 of the Israel Society for the History of Medicine and Science, and in 1952 of the journal of medical history *Korot*. In 1957 Leibowitz initiated the first formal course in the history of medicine at the Hebrew University-Hadassah Medical School. His successor, Samuel Kottek, the present head of the Division of the History of Medicime, has been an invaluable consultant and historical advisor for us in everything connected with the exhibition and book. Special thanks are also due to Gerhard Baader, whose knowledge and guidance contributed to the realization of this project.

I am more than grateful to Chaya Amir who helped me immensely with the book.

There are numerous other people without whose help Jews and Medicine would never have reached fruition, among them, Michel Garel of the Bibliothèque Nationale de France; Nigel Allen of the Wellcome Institute for the History of Medicine in London; Giselle Lawrence of the Science Museum, London; Bernard Purin of the Jewish Museum in Vienna; Amnon Barzel of the Jewish Museum in Berlin; Stephanie Schüler-Springorum and Inka Bentz of the Stiftung Topographie des Terrors, Berlin; Marek Webb and Fruma Mohrer of YIVO, New York; Shari Segal and Esther Brumberg of the Museum for Jewish Heritage, New York; Richard Steele of the Mount Sinai Hospital Archives; Genya Markon of the United States Holocaust Memorial Museum, Washington D.C.; Steven Martin of the Albert Einstein College of Medicine, New York; Francesco Moreno and Chava Noverstein of the Jewish National and University Library, Jerusalem; Ely Ben-Gal of the "Florilege MBB", Tel Aviv and Nina Springer of Yad Vashem, Jerusalem.

Special thanks are due to David Gal for the inspired design of the exhibition and my colleagues at Beth Hatefutsoth, especially to Susy Rosenbloom, Zippi Rosenne, Gila Woolf, Orit Uziel, Debbie Furst, Ilana Ruskay and Peleg Tamir for their dedication above and beyond the call of duty.

Natalia Berger

Overleaf:

Ma'aseh Tuviyah by Tobias Ben Moses Cohen.

Venice, 1707.

Tobias Cohen (1652-1729) was born in Metz (France), graduated at Padua and later practiced in Turkey. His book is an encyclopedia. The author was well aware of "modern" advances in medicine and adhered to Harvey's scheme of circulation. He compares the human body to a house with foundations (legs), floors and roof (head). This work passed through five editions, the first one (1707) being by far the most finely printed and illustrated.

Aaron Feingold Collection, New Jersey.

Contents

PREFACE

One of the basic tenets of Judaism can be summed up in the saying: "He who saves one soul, saves a whole world". In the Torah and in the Halacha, the saving of life and the healing of the ill are considered the noblest of all the commandments. Medicine and physicians have always been central in the promulgation of this aspect of Judaism.

There were social and historical reasons for the disproportionately high number of Jewish doctors in almost all the Muslim and Christian countries from the Middle Ages on, and their contributions to the development of medicine were of unusual significance.

The special relation between Judaism and medicine can also be discerned in the kindred field of ethics. In medicine, perhaps more than any other scientific discipline, questions of ethical behavior constantly surface - with regard to the duty of the physician in treating the indigent and the stranger. Nowadays great technological advances are challenging the physician in another direction: to what extent is the physician allowed to intervene in the artificial creation, prolongation or shortening of life, questions which have not yet been resolved universally.

The proud record of medical achievement in the State of Israel cannot be considered except as a continuation of the age-old tradition of the Jewish people in the Diaspora. Furthermore, world Jewry has always been more than generous in contributing to the foundation and expansion of medical centers and facilities. Israel, for its part, has been as generous in sharing its medical know-how and facilities with distant countries racked by earthquakes, epidemics and periodical starvation, as well as in offering its services to some of its close neighbors, even before the era of peace negotiations.

Jews and Medicine: Religion, Culture and Science looks at its subjects from the time of the Bible, down through history until the modern era. Both the book and exhibition are a salute to a profession, hallowed in the annals of the Jewish people. We are grateful to Leon and Zelda Street who initiated the exhibition and through whose generosity it was possible to realize.

I would also like to express my appreciation for the great effort made by Natalia Berger, curator of the exhibition and editor of the book, and to thank all those individuals and institutions who have contributed to this important project.

Giora Goren

Director General of Beth Hatefutsoth

NATALIA BERGER

WHY MEDICINE?

*A Jewish mother is walking down the
street with her two young sons.
A passerby asks her how old the boys
are. "The doctor is three," the mother
answers, "and the lawyer is two."[1]*

The relation of this joke to real life
needs no explanation. Since the Middle Ages Jews have regarded medicine as
one of the most honorable professions to pursue and have, since then, been
represented in it in much greater numbers than their percentage of the
population would seem to warrant. Moritz Steinschneider (1816-1907), the
famous bibliographer who laid the foundations, among other things, for
research into Jewish history in general and Jewish medical history, wrote in his
classic article on "The History of Hebrew Literature": "The Jewish
contribution in the field of medicine belongs to those activities in the field of
culture and literature that are taken for granted everywhere but have never
been the subject of research."[2] Since then, a great deal of research has been
conducted, but peculiar as it may seem, only two exhibitions on the subject
have ever been held. The first was organized by Harry Friedenwald
(1854-1950), a noted ophthalmologist, medical historian and collector, at
Johns Hopkins University in Baltimore in 1943, and the second by Samuel
Kottek from the Division of the History of Medicine at the Hebrew University
of Jerusalem in 1977. Both exhibitions were comprised mainly of manuscripts
and prints from Dr. Friedenwald's collection.

The present exhibition and companion book are more ambitious. They are an
attempt to examine the special relationship between Jews and medicine both

Diploma of Coppillia Pictor.

Padua, 30 December, 1695.

25 x 17 cm.

*This diploma was granted to Coppillia
Pictor, the Latinized name of Jacob
Maler. While the Christians' diplomas
began with the invocation In Christi
Nomine Amen, Pictor's begins with the
words In Nomine Dei aeterni (In the
Name of the Eternal God). This was
evidently done in consideration of the
fact that Pictor was a Jew. Jacob Maler
was a member of a distinguished
family. He practiced his profession in
Bingen and also served as an official of
the Jewish community until his death in
1720.*

*Jewish National and University
Library, Jerusalem, Fr 789.*

The tablets of the Ten Commandments among sanctuary vessels.

From a Bible transcribed and possibly illuminated by Solomon ben Raphael in Perpignan, Aragon, Spain, early 14th century.

36 x 27 cm.

The opening Hebrew words of each of the Ten Commandments are given (Exodus 20 and Deuteronomy 5). The opening word of the Fourth Commandment varies in the two versions: zakhor [זכור] (remember the Sabbath, Exodus 20: 8) and shamor [שמור] (observe the Sabbath, Deuteronomy 5:12) both are inserted. Bibliothèque Nationale de France, Paris, Ms. Hébr 7. folio 12v.

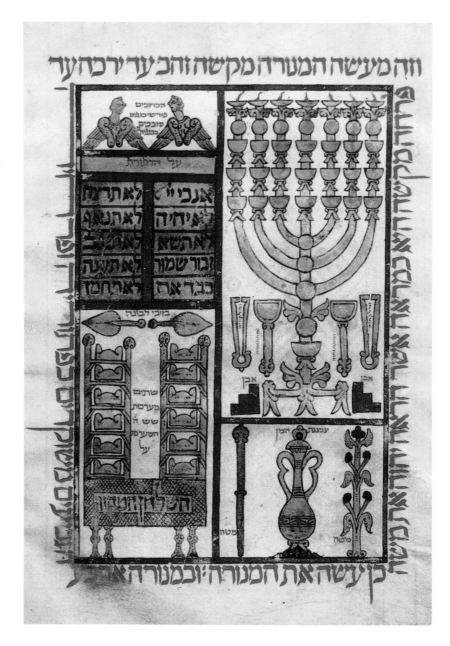

intrinsically, from within, and historically, from without. We have posed two overall questions: firstly, does Judaism in itself foster a special attitude towards medicine and, secondly, to what extent did life in the Diaspora influence the Jewish contribution to medicine? Both exhibition and book follow chronological lines tracing the most significant points of encounter between the history of the Jewish people and the history of medicine, beginning with the Bible and ending with the modern world and the State of Israel.

The motto of both the exhibition and the book, taken from Deuteronomy

(30:19), "Therefore choose life...," establishes the basis of the Jewish attitude towards medicine, while the title *Jews and Medicine: Religion, Culture, Science* conveys the idea that there has never been a "Jewish medicine" per se. Jews have always adopted the medical teachings of the prevailing cultures in which they lived, and proceeded to enhance them through their own significant contributions. The exhibition and book also illustrate the special interest of Jewish physicians in medical ethics and concomitant social behavior as well as the role of the Hebrew language in the history of medical writing.

The subject of "Jews and Medicine" has never yet been dealt with in such an all-embracing manner. True, every single chapter could probably be the subject of a separate exhibition or book, and I hope it will be in the future. Yet I believe that this attempt to portray the complex relationship between "Jews and Medicine" in its entirety is not only a valuable contribution to one particular aspect of Jewish history: it is also a most fascinating undertaking.

Medicine is closely related to philosophy, religion and culture. This perhaps explains why medicine was one of the few free professions that allowed Jews to live both in the Jewish world and general society and why it was so popular amongst the Jews. The subject is also fascinating because it touches on the lives of Jewish physicians whose contributions to medicine were often closely related to their being Jews.

In 1915 Harry Friedenwald wrote:

It is amazing to read of the trials and tribulations of Jewish physicians...and to see how much they accomplished in spite of it. I have lately acquired a book by David de Pomis published in 1588 – a wonderful defense of the Jewish doctor – 327 years ago.[4]

Religion, culture, science – this triple thread passes through the different periods in the history of "Jews and Medicine." As we shall see, a different aspect predominates in each period: religion in antiquity; culture in the Middle Ages; and science in the modern era. Yet all are united in one commandment: "Therefore choose life."

Harry Friedenwald.

Harry (1864-1950) was a member of Hebras Zion in Baltimore, probably the first American Zionist society. In 1911 and 1914 he visited Palestine where he served as a consultant for eye diseases in several Jerusalem hospitals. Friedenwald wrote on medical history with special emphasis on medieval Jewish doctors and the use of the Hebrew language in medical literature. In 1944 his collected and expanded historico-medical writings The Jews and Medicine (three volumes) were published. He donated his prestigious collections of books incunabula and manuscripts to the Hebrew University where they are stored and displayed.
National Library of Medicine, Bethesda.

A woman taking a ritual bath before rejoining her husband.

From a Siddur of Ashkenazi rite, Germany, early 15th century.

33 x 22.4 cm.

The only known Jewish illumination that shows the rite of immersion. The characteristic details are all depicted: complete nudity, vertical immersion, the arms outstretched to avoid touching the body. The only detail which does not strictly follow the accepted rite is that the hair is not totally immersed.

Staats-und Universitätsbibliothek, Hamburg, Cod. Hebr. 37, folio 122r.

Medicine and Religion

The fascination of the Jews with medicine has its roots in the Jewish attitude towards life and death as reflected in the Bible. Man was created in God's image and life, therefore, is sacred. Since life is the highest good, man is obliged to cherish it and preserve his state of health. Death came to the world through the fault of man and once it appeared there was no escape from it. There is no other life. There are passages in the Bible which have been interpreted differently, but they are not commensurate with the dominant view that there is no life after death.

In the Bible the attitude to healing and to the role of the physician is closely related to the interpretation of life and death. However, in a world created by God the right to heal could not be taken for granted and the dispute as to the propriety of human interference in sickness, regarded as divine retribution, is well-known and was not easily resolved. Nevertheless, the basic attitude was that healing was in the hands of God and the role of the physicians was that of helpers or instruments of God.

The Hebrews were influenced in their medical concepts and practice by the surrounding nations, particularly Egypt, where medical knowledge was highly developed. However, the uniqueness of Biblical "medicine" lies in its prophylactic nature, regulations for social and personal hygiene and a weekly day of rest. It has been contended that hygiene and prophylaxis were made into religious rules. Of the 613 commandments, 213 may be considered as having some connection with "medicine," including the strict dietary and sanitary directives pertaining to cleanliness, sexual life and quarantine during illness. The observance of a weekly day of rest – the Sabbath – is unique; there is no mention of it in the Hammurabi laws nor in Greek or Roman medicine.

The Talmudic attitude towards the sanctity of human life and the importance of health is expressed in numerous statements, and the saving of life (*piku'ah nefesh*) is considered the highest value. The Talmud contains a large number of references to doctors and healing. It is recommended in Sanhedrin 17b that no wise person should reside in a town that does not have

a physician and a "surgeon." Patients are required, not merely permitted, to seek medical help when needed, and all restrictions should be set aside.

The Karaites, opponents of Rabbinic Judaism, held that "God alone should be sought as a physician and no human medicine should be resorted to." But the Talmud does not regard calling upon a physician for medical aid as a failure to rely upon God to restore health: "Whoever is in pain, let him go to a physician" (Baba Kamma 46b). From this statement it may also be concluded that the number of practicing physicians was relatively high. A physician had to receive adequate fees. Free medical service was not approved since "a physician who takes nothing is worth nothing" (Baba Kamma 85a). At the same time, Jewish physicians had to show special consideration for the poor and the needy – a tradition that was maintained through the centuries. Nevertheless, there was another view of the physician. An epigram that has led

Circumcision in Naples.

From a Siddur of Spanish rite, late 15th century.

12.9 x 11.1 cm.

On the left the sandaq [godfather] and the mohel [circumciser] prepare to carry out the operation; on the right the mohel is shown after the operation with a cup in his hand pronouncing the blessings associated with the ceremony. Carré Art Bibliothèque, Nîmes, Ms. 13, folio 181 verso.

to endless discussion is: "The best of physicians is fit for *Gehenna*" (Mishna Kiddushin IV 14). According to Rashi (Rabbi Shlomo Itzhaqi, 11th century), whose explanation was accepted by most commentators, the Mishnah censures physicians for two reasons: for their overconfidence in their craft and for commercializing their profession to the extent that they sometimes fail to attend to the poor. The death of the neglected poor is tantamount to homicide committed by the physicians, a sin which is rightly punished with the pains of *Gehenna*.

This epigram is the subject of one of Joseph Zabara's stories in his *Book of Entertainments*.[5]

A philosopher, says Zabara, was sick unto death, and his doctor gave him up; yet the patient recovered. The convalescent was walking in the street when the doctor met him. "You come," said he, "from another world." "Yes," rejoined the patient, "I come from there and I saw the awful retribution that befalls doctors, for they kill their patients yet do not feel alarmed. You will not suffer. I told them on my oath that you are no doctor."

The tradition of rabbi-physician began during this period and continued until relatively recently. Since teaching or studying the word of God for reward was not considered ethical at least in principal, the practice of medicine was often chosen as a means of livelihood.

Medicine and Culture

The contribution of Jewish doctors in the Middle Ages lay mainly in their work as translators. Jewish physicians constituted an important link in the transmission of Arab medicine to Europe. In this way, they were crucial to the emergence of modern science. During this period we witness a revival of Hebrew as the language of scientific writing. Hebrew medical works were important in preserving and spreading medical knowledge until the beginning of the 16th century. Nothing illustrates this more clearly than the immense number of Hebrew manuscripts. According to Friedenwald, there are about 15,000 Hebrew manuscripts listed in the catalogues of the libraries around the world.[6]

Knowledge of Hebrew was considered extremely important in the study of medicine. In 1518 the rector of the University of Leipzig, Mosellanus, said in his inauguration speech:

In the libraries of the Jews a treasure of medical science lies hidden, a treasure as scarce as is to be found in any other language.

Nobody...will be able to get access to this treasure without intimate knowledge of the Hebrew grammar.[7]

One of the outstanding features of this period was the constant emphasis on ethical and social behavior. Medical aphorisms concerning ethical behavior were composed by every major medical writer from Asaph to Maimonides. An interesting glimpse into this world is given in the ethical will of Judah ibn Tibbon (c.1120-1190), an eminent physician and translator, to his son:

My son let thy countenance shine upon the sins of man: visit the sick, and let thy

Kiddush.

Woodcut illustration from Seder Zemirot u-Birkat ha-Mazon. One of the first Hebrew books printed in Prague, 1514. This woodcut illustrates the section from Genesis regarding God's resting on the seventh day of Creation. The Jewish Museum, Prague.

Diploma of Coppillia Pictor. Padua,

30 December, 1695.

Jewish National and University

Library, Jerusalem, Fr 789.

tongue be a cure to them; and if thou receivest payment from the rich, attend gratuitously on the poor.[8]

The most important aspect of the physician's activity, however, was the care of the sick. In the Middle Ages and until the late 18th century, sick people were usually treated at home. Stress was laid on the commandment of visiting the sick and of strengthening family ties. For these reasons the necessity for a hospital was not felt among the Jewish community. The *hekdesh* was a kind of hospice that served as a shelter for wandering peddlers and for poor sick Jews. It was administered by the *hevra kaddisha*, a brotherhood that cared for the sick and the dead. Servants had a right to special status as a kind of social insurance. In Krakow in 1595, for example, there was a communal ordinance which stated that whenever a maid-servant fell ill, her employer had to pay for her stay in the *hekdesh*.[9]

As merchants and travelers, the Jews met the best scholars of their time and became acquainted with drugs, plants and remedies from many parts of the world. The large number of Jewish physicians during the Middle Ages may be explained by the fact that scholars could turn to the practice of medicine to earn their living, and indeed many Jewish physicians were also rabbis, philosophers, or poets. As men of wide general knowledge, Jewish physicians attained high positions in the countries in which they lived. In spite of renewed ecclesiastical opposition, bishops and popes, kings and sultans all summoned Jewish physicians to their courts.

The most renowned Jewish physician in the Middle Ages, who was also a distinguished rabbi and philosopher, was Moses Maimonides (the Rambam) (1137-1204). Born in Cordoba, he fled to Fez. Later he went to Palestine and then to Cairo, where he became physician at the court of Saladin and his sons. Maimonides had a prodigious literary output, including extensive writing on medical matters. These were written at the end of his life, after his monumental Halakhic and philosophical works. Maimonides strongly believed in prophylactic medicine. In his *Guide to the Perplexed* he wrote: "Among a thousand persons only one dies a natural death: the rest succumb early in life owing to ignorant or irregular behavior." Maimonides considered the study of medicine (in *Mishne Torah, Hilkhot Deot IV, 1*) a very important factor of Jewish ethics:

Medicine teaches man to restrict his boundless lust which undermines his health and to choose the manner of living. It helps to maintain the fitness of the body and enables him to purify and raise his strength to an uplifted ethical plane.

However, not all physicians were venerated in the Middle Ages and in the Hebrew literature of that period we find many satirical poems and maxims bearing upon the physician. Some of them were found in a number of different manuscripts, an indication that they must have enjoyed wide popularity. In the book *Sefer ha-Pardes* of the poet Jedaiah Bedersi (13th century), we find the following medical maxim:

When you are in need of a physician, you esteem him like a god; when he has brought you out of danger, consider him a king; when you have been cured he becomes human like yourself; when he sends his bill you think of him as a devil.[10]

The 16th century was a period of immense exploration, discovery and progress – the century of Paracelsus, Servetus and Fallopius. In 1543, Andreas Vesalius, the twenty-nine year old Flemish professor of anatomy in Padua, published *De humani corporis fabrica* [The fabric of the human body]. His great work showed for the first time how nerves penetrated muscles, the relationship among the abdominal organs and the structure of the brain. Vesalius gave Hebrew names together with Greek and Latin equivalents for the anatomical structures, demonstrating the importance of medieval Hebrew medical literature. Vesalius did not know Hebrew, but the information was furnished to him by a learned Jewish scholar, Lazaro de Frigeis (1514-1564). The Hebrew anatomical terms used are for the most part taken from the Hebrew translation of the *Canon of Avicenna* and in some cases directly from the Talmud.

The beginning of the medical renaissance had tragic consequences for the Jews of Europe. At the Church Council of Basel (1437-1447) a catalogue of restrictions was drawn up for Jews, among them a decree that no Jew could

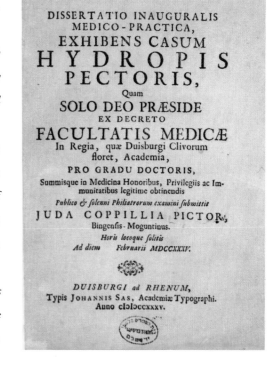

Exhibers Casum Hydropis Pectoris [On watery secretions in the chest].
Doctoral thesis of Coppillia Pictor, alias Maler, a Jewish graduate of medicine from the University of Padua.
Padua, December 30, 1695.
Jewish National and University Library, Jerusalem, Fr 789.

Diploma of medicine awarded to Lazarus de Mordis. Padua, 1699.

The diploma, as in Pictor's diploma, begins with the invocation In Nomine Dei Aeterni. In making these changes from the prescribed Christian formula, the University showed considerable consideration and tolerance.
Jewish National and University Library, Jerusalem, Fr. 789.

receive a university degree. These regulations emphasized the Christian character of the universities. Thus even when Jews were admitted to universities they were subject to special rules, charged special fees and forced to listen to conversional lectures. After graduation they were generally forbidden to treat Christian patients.

At the end of the 15th century, Spain and Portugal compelled the Jews to embrace Christianity. Many Jews became Marranos, and others emigrated. As a result, during the 16th, 17th, and 18th centuries a very high proportion of noted physicians, scientists and scholars in Europe were of Spanish or Portuguese origin. The Marranos continued to practice medicine in Spain and Portugal until the 18th century despite their precarious position in those countries, where they were continually persecuted by the Inquisition.

A particularly horrifying example is that of Garcia da Orta, a physician who had left Portugal for Goa, India (then a Portuguese colony) in 1534. There he completed a pioneer scientific work on Oriental medicinal plants, *Coloquios dos simples e drogas e cousas medicinaes da India* (1563). Da Orta died in 1568, but his work had already attracted great attention. A Latin abstract was published in 1567 followed by Italian, French, Spanish and English versions based upon it. But da Orta was a Marrano and various members of his family, among them his sister, were tried by the Inquisition and sentenced to be burned at the stake. In 1580, following da Orta's posthumous conviction on the charge of having lived as a Jew, his body was exhumed and burned.

In spite of the limitations, continuous persecutions and peregrinations, many Jewish physicians who distinguished themselves in medical practice and literature were also concerned with the moral responsibility which their profession placed upon them, and redefined the Hippocratic oath, including it in their prayers. Among them were Amatus Lusitanus, Zacutus Lusitanus and Jacob Zahalon. Amatus Lusitanus, one of the most prominent physicians of the 16th century, who lived a life of persecution as a Marrano and later as a Jew, was deeply concerned with the ethical aspects of his profession and his oath reads, i.a.:

"I have given my services in equal manner to all, to Hebrews, Christians and Muslims."

In Renaissance Italy there was evidence of a more liberal spirit. Some Italian universities, mainly those of Padua and Perugia, were among the few that allowed Jews to enter the medical faculties at a time when most other European universities were closed to them. During the period from 1517-1619, 80 Jewish students were accepted in Padua for medical studies and from 1619-1721, 149 Jews obtained the degree of doctor of medicine. Many Jews from Germany, Poland and the Levant consequently came to study in Padua. An evident sign of tolerance was the fact that the invocation "In Christi nomine amen" of the Christians' diplomas was changed to "In nomine dei aeterni" for the Jewish graduates.

Relative tolerance was only one aspect of the physicians' life in that period. In the extensive anti-Semitic literature published at the time, physicians were not spared. Successful Jewish physicians usually attracted the jealousy of their Christian counterparts, and they were subject to bitter attacks and innumerable calumnies. It is not surprising that Jewish physicians took to their own defense and published several books containing scholarly defenses of Jewish physicians. Among them were David de Pomis, Benedict de Castro and Isaac Cardozo. Cardozo (1604-1681) was born in Portugal. At the age of twenty-eight, after studying medicine and philosophy, he became court physician in Madrid to Philip IV and published several medical works. Persecuted by the Inquisition, Cardozo fled to Venice, and later settled in Verona and worked as a physician to the poor Sephardi community. There he published his apologia, *Las Excelencias y Caluminias de los Hebreos*. In ten chapters he emphasizes the distinguishing features of the Jews, their selection by God, their separation from all other peoples by special laws, and their compassion for the suffering of others; and in ten other chapters he refutes the calumnies brought against them, namely, that they worship false gods, smell bad, are hard and unfeeling toward other people, kill Christian children and use their blood for ritual purposes. He also responds to the accusation that the Jews caused the Black Plague in France by poisoning the wells of the Christians: "Physicians testified that it was not poison but a natural disease."[11]

The 18th century marked the beginning of the Haskalah (Enlightenment), whose aspirations matched those of enlightened gentiles for the moral and social betterment of the Jews and the abolishment of all social and legal discrimination. This period marked the beginning of the movement of Jews into German universities and the increase in the number of Jewish physicians. Marcus Herz is a good example of the change which took place in the status of the Jewish physician in the Modern Era. Born in Berlin, he studied in Halle and was a favorite of Kant. After graduation Herz lectured on Kantian philosophy and physics. At the same time he worked at the Jewish Hospital in Berlin and was reputed to be one of the best doctors of his time. As his illustrious predecessors, Herz was concerned with the ethical aspects of his profession and in 1783 published "The Physician's Prayer." It was similar to those which had come before, but Herz added a section about the thirst for knowledge, which reflected the spirit of the times:

May I be moderate in everything except in the pursuit of the knowledge of science. Grant me the strength and opportunity always to correct what I have learned ... for knowledge is boundless.

It is perhaps more than symbolic that for a long time the prayer was attributed to Maimonides.

Medicine and Science

The first half of the 19th century was characterized by a progressively increasing interest in the natural sciences. During the second half of the 19th century medical research was strongly dominated by the microscope and the concept of microbiology. The first, the microscope, advanced the knowledge of anatomy, histology and pathology considerably. The second resulted in a revolution of medical thought and modified the methods of diagnosis and therapy in most diseases. Development was rapid and brought with it a great subdivision of medical science into a myriad of disciplines, and steady progress toward the ideal of an exact science.[12] This period coincided with the

Emancipation and the opening of the doors of the universities, hospitals and scientific research institutes to Central European Jews. Jewish physicians were thus able to take an active part in this development, and there is scarcely an area in the broad domain of medicine in which they were not prominent as pioneers.

For many years, nonetheless, Jewish physicians were not accepted as university professors unless they converted. Furthermore they were unwelcome in the central fields of surgery and internal medicine. As a result, they worked primarily in private clinics and hospitals, where they did their research. They developed new fields of medicine that did not attract their non-Jewish colleagues, such as dermatology-venerology, immunology, hematology and psychiatry. Freud, who was not only a physician but a gifted writer, formulated the reason for this trend with great perceptiveness:

Soon there was the insight that I had only my Jewish nature to thank for two of the qualities that had become indispensable on my difficult path through life. Because I was a Jew, I found myself free from many prejudices that limit others in the use of their intellect; as a Jew I was prepared to go into opposition and forgo the acceptance of the "compact majority."[13]

Up until the 1930s the main development of medicine took place in Europe, mainly in Vienna and Berlin, cities with the largest concentrations of Jewish physicians, and to a lesser extent in Paris. In Vienna about 60 percent of the physicians were Jews and in Berlin about 30 percent. Among them were many women who had joined the profession as soon as they were allowed into the universities at the beginning of the century. Jewish women made up a disproportionately large percentage of the female physicians in Central Europe. At the University of Vienna Jewish women constituted nearly 60 percent of women studying medicine and in Berlin about 30 percent.

Emancipation brought with it many changes, among them the pattern of sick care within the community. With the improvement of the general hospital, the Jewish hospital too changed its character from a social to a medical institution. By the second half of the 19th century new Jewish hospitals were founded in Paris, Metz, London, Budapest and New York. This acceleration in the creation of modern Jewish hospitals continued in the 20th century, and by 1933 there were in Poland alone forty-eight such institutions. Some of them continued their activity in the ghettos even after the German occupation. The racial laws introduced into Germany at the beginning of the 1930s and, subsequently, into all of occupied Europe, severed the careers of Jewish physicians in Europe. Many of them succeeded in emigrating, the majority to the United States. Thus mainstream Jewish medical activity was transferred from Europe to the United States and coincided with the rise of American medicine. Jewish physicians in the United States greatly outnumber those in other countries and they occupy positions all along the professional and scientific spectrum. The highest percentages are in internal medicine (20 percent) and psychiatry (30 percent). "Every Jew is either in therapy, has just finished therapy, is about to enter therapy or is a therapist," claims a current witticism. It is not surprising then that there are so many Jewish jokes about psychoanalysis – like the following:

Goldstein has been in analysis for ten years, seeing his doctor four times a week. Finally, the analyst tells him that they've achieved their goals, he doesn't have to come back anymore. The man is terrified. "Doctor," he says, "I've grown very dependent on these meetings. I can't just stop." The doctor gives Goldstein his phone number. "If you ever need to," he says, "call me any time." Two weeks later, Sunday morning, six a.m., the phone rings in the doctor's house. It's Goldstein. "Doctor," he says, "I just had a terrible nightmare. I dreamt you were my mother, and I woke up in a terrible sweat." "So what did you do?" "I analyzed the dream the way you taught me in analysis." "Yes?" "Well I couldn't fall back to sleep. So I went downstairs to have some breakfast." "What did you have?" "Just a cup of coffee." "You call that breakfast?"[14]

The last section of the exhibition and the book takes us back to Israel. In mid-19th century Palestine there was not one qualified physician in the country, Jewish or non-Jewish. In 1843 Sir Moses Montefiore brought Simon Frankel, the first Jewish physician, to Jerusalem. A rapid development in medical care followed, and by the end of World War I there were already ten Jewish hospitals in Jerusalem. The first step towards the building of the health

מִשְׂרַד הַחִנּוּךְ וְהַתַּרְבּוּת • מִבְצַע הַנְחָלַת-הַלָּשׁוֹן לָעָם

בַּמִּרְפָּאָה

דַּבֵּר עִבְרִית וְהַבְרֵאתָ

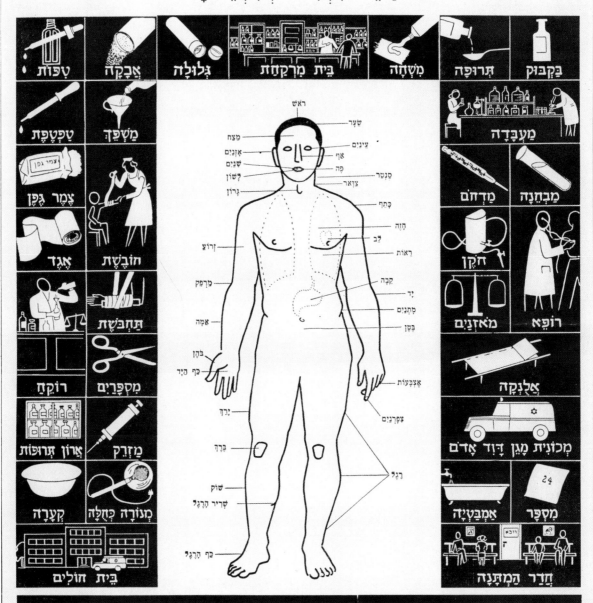

בְּהִתְיַעֲצוּת עִם הָאֲקַדֶּמְיָה לַלָּשׁוֹן הָעִבְרִית.

הַחוֹבֶשֶׁת מָרְחָה אֶת הַפֶּצַע בְּמִשְׁחָה.
בְּבַקָּשָׁה לְהַחֲלִיף לִי אֶת הַתַּחְבֹּשֶׁת.
הַחוֹבֶשֶׁת הַגִּישָׁה עֶזְרָה רִאשׁוֹנָה לַפָּצוּעַ
הִיא מְסִירָה אֶת הַתַּחְבֹּשֶׁת מֵעַל הַפֶּצַע.
הָאָחוֹת מוֹדֶדֶת אֶת הַחֹם וְנוֹתֶנֶת תְּרוּפָה.
נֶפֶשׁ בְּרִיאָה – בְּגוּף בָּרִיא.
עָלֶיךָ לִפְנוֹת אֶל הָרוֹפֵא בְּעִנְיַן כְּאֵב הַגָּרוֹן.

תֵּן לִי מִסְפָּר לְרוֹפֵא הַשִּׁנַּיִם.
מִי הָרוֹפֵא הַתּוֹרָן בְּשַׁבָּת ?
לַחוֹלָה יֵשׁ חֹם. אֲנִי מְבַקֵּשׁ בִּקּוּר בַּיִת.
כְּבָר חִלְּקוּ כָּל הַמִּסְפָּרִים לָרוֹפֵא הַפְּנִימִי.
חָלִיתִי שָׁבוּעַ. אֲנִי זָקוּק לִתְעוּדַת מַחֲלָה.
אֵינִי מַרְגִּישׁ בְּטוֹב, הַאִם אוּכַל לְהִתְקַבֵּל מִיָּד ?
בִּגְלַל הַכְּאֵבִים לֹא עָצַמְתִּי עַיִן כָּל הַלַּיְלָה.

הַחוֹלָה סוֹבֵל מֵעֲצִירוּת.
יֵשׁ לַיֶּלֶד בְּחִילָה וְשִׁלְשׁוּל.
הַפֶּצַע מְכֻסֶּה מֻגְלָה.
הָרוֹפֵא בָּדַק אֶת הָאֹזֶן וּמָצָא דַּלֶּקֶת.
הַצִּלּוּם מַרְאֶה נֶקַע וְלֹא שֶׁבֶר.
עֲדַיִן אִי-אֶפְשָׁר לִקְבֹּעַ אֶת סִבַּת הַפְּרִיחָה.
הַטִּפּוֹת הֵן נֶגֶד הַשִּׁעוּל וְהַמִּשְׁחָה – נֶגֶד הַנַּזֶּלֶת.

הֻדְפַּס עַל יְדֵי הַמַּדְפִּיס הַמֶּמְשַׁלְתִּי בְּצֵרוּף קְלִישָׁאוֹת יְדֵי "אַגַּת" יְרוּשָׁלַיִם. 6000—373/2# 6.55/

Dr. Aaron Mazie.

The Izakson Family, Herzliya.

care system in Israel was taken in 1911 with the creation of the worker's sick fund, later known as Kupat Holim. At the same time Hebrew, forsaken by the Jews since the Emancipation, was being revived as a scientific language. The main figures involved in this process were Aaron Meir Mazie and Sussman Muntner. Mazie (1858-1930), who was one of the founders of the Association of Jewish Physicians in Eretz Israel and the president of the "Hebrew Language Committee," gathered material for the preparation of a Hebrew medical dictionary. When he died his family invited the poet and physician Saul Tchernichovsky, who lived at that time in Berlin, to edit the dictionary. In 1934 the *Book of Medical and Scientific Terms* was published and Tchernichovsky was appointed physician of the municipal schools in Tel Aviv. Muntner (1897-1973) was a physician who dedicated his life to the revival of the Hebrew medical language. He compiled a *Hebrew-Medical Lexicon* which included 80,000 entries in Hebrew, Latin and English. He also edited and published medical writings of famous ancient and medieval physicians, particularly Maimonides. In the introduction to his book *The History of the Hebrew Medical Language*, published in 1940, on the occasion of the opening of the Hadassah Medical Center in Jerusalem, he writes:

The Hebrew medical literary language, the predominance of which in former times cannot be denied, with its enormous number of still existent manuscripts, could not continue. Having no home, scattered about among foreigners in an inimical environment, driven from country to country... it had no possibility of persisting. Now that it has returned to its home it may take root in its country once more.

It was only natural then that in May 1952, on the occasion of the graduation ceremony of the first medical course of the Hebrew University-Hadassah Medical School, the physicians' oath would be reformulated. The new oath echoed the sentiments of all those other oaths formulated by Jewish physicians down through the centuries:

You are charged night and day to be custodians at the side of the sick man at all times of his need . . . You shall help the sick, base or honourable, stranger or alien or citizen, because he is sick. Be true to him who puts his trust in you. Reveal not his secrets and go not about as a tale-bearer... Increase wisdom, and weaken not, for wisdom is your life and out of it are issues of life.

~

NOTES

1. Rabbi Joseph Telushkin, *Jewish Humor*, William Morrow and Company, New York, 1992.

2. J.S. Ersch und J.G. Gruber, *Allgemeine Enzyklopaedie der Wissenschaft und Kuenste*, Leipzig, 1850.

3. I am indebted to Marlyn Magen for suggesting the name.

4. Harry Friedenwald, *The Jews and Medicine*, volume 1, Johns Hopkins University Press, 1944, pp. xvii.

5. Ibid., pp. 70.

6. Ibid., pp. 165.

7. Suessmann Muntner, *The History of Hebrew Medicine*, Jerusalem, 1940, p.ix.

8. Friedenwald, *Jews and Medicine*, pp. 26.

9. M. Balaban, *Die Kracauer Judengemeinde – Ordung von 1595 und ihre Nachtädge* (in Hebrew), Jahrbuch der Jüdisch-Litterarischen Gesellschaft, Frankfurt am Main, 11:101.

10. Friedenwald, *Jews and Medicine*, pp. 71-75.

11. Ibid., pp. 67-68.

12. Solomon R. Kagan M.D., *Jewish Medicine*, Medico-Historical Press, Boston, 1952, pp. 142.

13. Rachel Salamandar, *The Jewish World of Yesterday,* Rizzoli, New York, 1990.

14. Telushkin, *Jewish Humor*, pp. 31.

BIBLIOGRAPHY

Encyclopedia Judaica, Jerusalem, Keter Publishing House, 1972.

FRIEDENWALD, HARRY, M.D., The *Jews and Medicine*, 3 volumes, Johns Hopkins University Press, 1944.

GAREL MICHEL, *D'une main forte*, Bibliothèque Nationale de France, Paris, 1991.

JAKOBOWITZ, RABBI (LORD) IMMANUEL, *Jewish Medical Ethics*, Bloch Publishing Co., New York (1959).

KAGAN, SOLOMON, R., M.D., *Jewish Medicine*, Medico-Historical Press, Boston, 1952.

LEVY, B. BARRY, *Planets, Potions and Parchments*, Jewish Public Library, Montreal, 1990.

METZGER, THERESE AND MENDEL, *Jewish Life in the Middle Ages*, Office du Livre 1982, Fribourg.

MUNTNER, SUESSMANN, *The History of Hebrew Medicine*, Jerusalem, 1940.

Jews in the History of Medicine, Exhibition Catalogue, Division of the History of Medicine of the Faculty of Medicine, The Hebrew University of Jerusalem, 1976.

TAMANI, GUILIANO, *Il Canon medicinal di Avicenna*, Editoriale Programma, Venezia, 1988.

SAMUEL S. KOTTEK

HEALING IN JEWISH LAW AND LORE

*Every religious system has
recognized the conflict between
the essentially divine (and
therefore providential) character
of disease, and the human efforts
– through medical treatment –
to mitigate or, if possible, to
frustrate its effect.*[1]

The conflict between the divine and the human aspects of healing in Jewish thought has been reflected in the Bible, in the Talmud, the Midrash and in the works of several medieval rabbinical authorities. This conflict was not easily resolved. There was a constant tension between those who tried to "prove" that the Lord expressly granted man the right to heal and those who considered all disease to be a visitation from the Lord which had to be suffered. The latter approach, often called – somewhat shortsightedly – fatalistic, seems to have been rather marginal compared to the former. In any case, there was never, throughout Jewish history, a legal code which imposed a prohibition on healing.

According to the Biblical outlook, health and disease are to be considered in the context of the Covenant between the Lord and His People. If the duties of the Law are fulfilled, "I will take sickness away from the midst of you." (Exodus 23:25) If they are violated, "I will appoint over you sudden terror, consumption, and fever that waste the eyes and cause life to pine away." (Leviticus 26:16)[2] There seems to be little room in this approach for human intervention.

Painting for the Rothschild Hospital, Haifa, 1940.

By Zeev Raban.

Yitzhak Einhorn Collection, Tel Aviv.

Yet the Bible features a number of episodes in which the prophets acted as healers. Perhaps they were considered ideal intermediaries between the divine and human healer. Elijah, for example, heals - or brings back to life - the son of the widow from Zarfath (1 Kings: 17), and Elisha revives the child of the Shunamite woman (2 Kings: 4). Elisha is also instrumental in curing the Syrian general Naaman of his skin disease (2 Kings: 5). King Hezekiah is cured of a boil by taking the advice of Isaiah (38:21) to rub it with a cake of figs.

In all of these cases, the prophet is, as it were, endowed with the power to heal. Occasional healing activity is not, however, central in prophetic writings - as it is in the Christian gospels, where healing is a most telling sign of the authority of the Nazarene preacher and his disciples.

The priests were another category of healers, mediating between the Lord and His People. They were supposed to have a comprehensive knowledge of the Law and were, further, required to maintain a higher degree of purity than others. The question that could be asked is: Did they also possess "medical" knowledge, as was the case in many ancient civilizations. The priest was entrusted with the duty of diagnosing what was called "leprosy" in the Bible and determining whether or not quarantine was required. In these cases, he was merely acting as a kind of health officer.

There were also physicians in the Bible. The first time *rof'im* are mentioned is in Genesis (50:1-3), where they are busy embalming the patriarch Jacob, hardly a healing procedure! Physicians and healing are mentioned, metaphorically, in the prophetical writings, particularly in Jeremiah, but in this context it is not surprising that they are considered of no avail. One frequently quoted passage in this respect is that of King Asa (2 Chronicles 16:12) who was frowned upon for having sought the help of physicians instead of praying to the Lord. Later commentators have interpreted this statement in two ways. Either King Asa should have first prayed to the Lord and then seen a doctor; or, as a king, he should not have consulted a physician, something permitted to ordinary people. In later texts of Hebrew and Jewish lore the problem of healing is considered in a more pragmatic way. We shall

nem leib viel·dz teten die diener·
vnd da ſy es getan hetten da für
ten ſy in zů ſeinen 3waien brüde
ren vnd legten in auch zů in in dē
kercker·Darnach an dem andern
tag ward dem richter geſaget es
wären zwů frawen die glaubten
auch an Jeſum criſtū·do warde
er zoznig vnd hieſ ſi für in prin
gen das tet man·Do ſprach er zů
in·Jr frawen jr ſölt euren vnge
lauben laſſen vnd ſölt den abgöt
teren opffcren ob jr müſte groſſe
pein vnd marter darumb leyden
vnd zů letſt den tod·die dzo half
nit dauon kund ſy nyemād prin
gen·do ward er zoznig vñ hieſ
einen roſt machen vnd glüent ko
len darunder thůn·vnd hieſſe die
zwů frawen darauff legen·dz te
ten die diener·Vnd da ſy darauff
kamen·do lobten ſy got vnd wa
ren gedultig in jrem leiden·vñ in
dem gabent ſy jr leben auff·Vnd
füren jr ſelen zů den ewigen freü
den·Darnach nam mā Neas wi
der auſ dem kercker vnd leget in
auch auff die glůt vnd prennet in
ſo lang das er auch ſtarb·do füre
ſein ſel zů den ewigen freüde·dar
nach nam man Claudium vnd
Caſtorium auſ dem kercker vnd
marteret ſy ſo lang biſ das ſy ge
ſturben·da füre jr ſelen zů dē ewi
gen freüden·Darnach hieſ d rich
ter die heilige leichnā in ein waſ
ſer werffen das ſy die criſten nitt
fünden vnd ſy nitt begrůben·das
teten die diener·vnd darnach do

funden die criſten jre heilig leich
nam vnd begrůben ſy alle dzeye
heimlichē mit groſſer andacht vñ
wirdigkeyt·Nun bitten wir die
heyligen drey brůder das ſy gott
für vns bitten vñ vnſ vmb got
erwerbe das wir auch kůmen zů
den ewigen freüden Amen

Von ſant Baſilio·

Ant Baſilius der waz
ein criſten vñ het gott
lieb vñ dienet jm mitt
fleiſ tag vnnd nachte
mit beten·vaſten·wachen·vñ mit
vil andern gůten übungen·vnnd
was ein biſchof vnd tet ſei ampt
got zů lobe vnd was demütig vñ
lebet ſeliklichen·Nun wz ein altt
uater zů der zeit der hieſ Effrem
dem tet got ſant Baſilius heylig·
keyt kunt·   Eines mals betet
Effrem mit andacht do ward er
entzuckt vñ ſahe ein feurine ſaul
die wz als lang vnd als groſ dz

The Jewish physician Ephraim, wearing a medieval Jewish hat, attending St. Basil.
From Plenarium by Hanns Schobsser, Augsburg, 1487.
The Jews and Medicine by H. Friedenwald, the Johns Hopkins Press, 1944.

A doctor bleeding a patient.

Cambridge Medical Miscellany.

Northern Italy, 15th century.

29 x 22 cm.

One of seven miniatures illustrating the text of a treatise by an unknown author on the "Days when bleeding is prohibited according to the wise men of the Gentiles."

Cambridge University Library, Ms. Dd.10.68, folio 211.

ימים שמונעין חכמי האומות להקיז

try here to examine how this conflict between the divine and the human aspects of healing is dealt with in the various texts. The scriptural passage that sanctions medical practice is, according to most commentators, that mentioned in Exodus 21:18-19:

When men quarrel and one strikes the other with a stone or with his fist and the man does not die but keeps his bed; then if the man rises again and walks abroad with his staff, he that struck him shall be clear; only he shall pay for the loss of his time, and shall have him thoroughly healed.

This is stated in a context of legal rulings related to all kinds of assaults and injuries and seems, therefore, of unquestionable accuracy. But we shall see that the question of whether or not healing is unswervingly put into the hands of a human healer was far from universally accepted in later Jewish lore.

Two 4th century Talmudic authorities held differing opinions on the subject. According to one of them, Rabbi Acha, a Palestinian *amora*, or interpreter, whoever is undergoing bloodletting (a common medical practice in antiquity and throughout the Middle Ages) should first beseech the Lord asking him for protection and praying that this procedure be of help, "for You, O Lord, art a trustworthy physician and your medications are true: it is not the way (or prevalence) of men to cure, only they took to it."

The other distinguished rabbi, Abbaye, a Babylonian amora, ruled that such a prayer was unbecoming since it had been clearly established by the school of Rabbi Ishmael (2nd century) that the right had been given to heal, on the basis of the scriptural verse cited above. It would thus appear that a rule established in the 2nd century was still questioned two centuries later. Nonetheless, Abbaye's authority being superior to that of Acha, the question was apparently settled. But only apparently.

Much later, in the 12th and 13th centuries, challenging questions were again raised regarding the license of medical practice. Abraham Ibn Ezra, a 12th-century Spanish rabbi, polymath and biblical commentator, argued that the passage taken as a basis for granting permission to heal (Exodus 21:19) features a case of external trauma. Who could know if internal, that is, "mysterious" diseases were included. For Ibn Ezra internal diseases were inflicted and cured by the Lord (Exodus 23:25). It was, however, in the power of man to prevent disease. The individual whose life was conducted according to the Law would need no physician, as the Lord would "bless his bread and water." In this way the Lord would protect him from environmental blights, considered in ancient times the chief contributing causes of disease.

Moses ben Nachman, Nachmanides, another Spanish rabbi who also practiced medicine – though not as extensively as his earlier compatriot, Maimonides – used similar language: If the Jews would act in full accordance with the Law, they would be perfect and their lives would be above nature's laws. (It should be pointed out that this statement does not appear in one of Nachmanides's medical tracts but in a biblical commentary on the Lord's protection.)

Nachmanides goes on to mention the case of the righteous King Asa who "was diseased in his feet, and his disease became severe; yet even in his disease he did not seek the Lord, but sought help from physicians." (2 Chron. 16:12)

Here he notes the opinion of Rabbi Acha that medicine is nothing but a habit or custom, adding the provocative question: "If it is granted that the Law has given license to heal, can we affirm that it has given license to the sick man to go to a doctor as well?" (Exodus 21:19) In other words, healing is a temporary expedient. In an ideal society where all people live in a state of perfection, there is no place for either medicine or physicians.

Yet the same Nachmanides, in a work called *Sefer Torath Ha-Adam* [The study of man], which provides much of the material for the chapter on medicine and Jewish law in the 16th-century *Shulhan Arukh*, Judaism's authoritative legal code, wrote that it was perfectly lawful "in our days" to cure and to get cured. It is not only permitted to cure according to Exodus 21:19: This permission is at once transformed by Nachmanides into a legal obligation which falls into the category of saving life. Therefore, according to Nachmanides and subsequent Jewish law, a physician has not only the license but the obligation to heal. As for the patient, Nachmanides is of the opinion that he should trust in the physician's treatment, provided, of course, that the physician is properly trained and acknowledged, and the most knowledgeable available for the specific ailment. If the physican acts in conformity with professional norms, the Lord will, hopefully, see to it that the treatment is successful.[3]

In other words, once Nachmanides puts himself in day-to-day reality, he readily accepts human healing as lawful. Ideally, there should be no need for physicians. Practically, there is. Judaism does not tend to rely on miracles or adopt a fatalistic view of life. As expressed by the 18th century scholar, Chayyim Joseph David Azulay, in his commentary on the *Shulchan Arukh:* "Nowadays one should not rely on miracles, and a sick person is required to conduct himself according to the natural order by calling a physician to heal him." This approach can be illustrated by two frequently cited texts, one Talmudic (Mishnaic), the other Midrashic.

The first notes that King Hezekiah hid a certain *Book of Medicines* and the rabbis praised him for that action. No reason is given in the Mishnah. In trying to understand why, later scholars offered certain explanations. Rashi (Rabbi Solomon Itzhaki, 11th century) thought that people would look into the book in case of illness and get cured without first making atonement to the Lord. Maimonides (12th century) opposes this as harboring a negative relation to medicine, much like saying: "I will eat no more bread and the Lord will see to it that I live." For this illustrious rabbi and physician, the reason for concealing the book was, firstly, that it also contained magical devices and/or astrological prescriptions, and, secondly, that people began to use the poisons mentioned in the book rather than their antidotes. At the core of this controversy, obviously, is the question whether or not healing can be left freely in man's hands. Theological reasons are posited against professional and ethical ones. Is healing akin to nature or is it metaphysical in essence?

The second text, by the 2nd to 3rd century Babylonian *amora* Samuel, refers to two noted rabbis of the 2nd century, Rabbi Ishmael and Rabbi Akiba, walking in the company of a farmer. A sick person approaches them and asks for medical advice – which the sages readily provide. The farmer then asks them why they have intervened. Was it not the Lord's will that this individual be smitten by disease? The rabbis point out that the trees, groves and fields are tended by the farmer although they are part of nature, as created by the Lord. In the same way, they explain, the body of man, planted in nature, is tended by physicians in order to remain healthy.

In one of his non-medical writings, Maimonides compares physicians – the healers of the body – to rabbis (or sages) – the healers of the soul. What he terms diseases of the soul, however, are moral perversions or insufficiencies. But as he himself exemplified, there were sages who were also experienced healers who could combine physical and moral healing (we are not referring here to faith-healing). The archetype of such a sage-physician was the Talmudic *amora* Samuel, mentioned above. Samuel was a trained and practicing physician who even performed experiments on himself. He was also an astronomer and one of the outstanding scholars of Jewish law of his time.

The Talmud provides us with numerous cases in which the sages ask for the practical advice of physicians or experts. Nevertheless, there were tensions and even clashes between the two groups and they were duly recorded. A sage of

Job.

Woodcut, 1537.

Job was "full of sores" and seen by Christian authors as the patron saint of lepers. This woodcut depicts his lesions much like those of small pox and syphilis, during that time. Job is the symbol of the righteous "sufferer" in Jewish lore.

Kupferstichkabinett Staatliche Museen Preussischer Kulturbesitz, Berlin.

the Mishnah once exclaimed: "The best of physicians – to Gehenna!" This rather excessive pronouncement was commented upon by generations of rabbis. True, haughtiness and pride have often been ascribed to physicians, but the contemptuousness of the sage was probably directed against the physician who relied exclusively on his own expertise, refusing to accept divine authority.[4]

One might ask if religious individuals refrained from entering the medical profession from fear of being – at least in some cases – intruders in the divine scheme. In fact, quite a number of sages are addressed in the Talmud as "trained healers", and there is good reason to think that physicians were generally respected by the sages. This can be ascertained by the way they were treated in the event of a medical mishap. When a physician causes injury to his patient, the sages rule, he will not be considered guilty or taken to court if he has acted in accordance with the prescribed ways of his profession. This was deemed fitting "for the sake of social order". The physician, however, would have to account for himself before the tribunal in Heaven. Only the Lord could know to what extent he had been negligent. This lenient (and realistic) rule was valid only for physicians licensed by the rabbinical court. Furthermore, if the physician has treated the patient according to the accepted professional means and the patient dies, no punishment is imposed on the physician: it is assumed that the Lord had decided that this patient would die of his disease.

The Book of Ben Sira, known in Christian sources under the name of *Ecclesiasticus*, was not accepted into the Jewish biblical canon although it was included in the Septuagint (the oldest Greek translation of the Hebrew Bible). It was, however, often cited by Talmudic sages. Ben Sira most probably lived in the 3rd century B.C.E., before the Hasmonean period.[5] The work, ethical in content and poetical in form, deals with daily life, including health and healing. Ben Sira's attitude towards physicians is pragmatic though subservient to the scriptural outlook. Just before Chapter 38 (see below) in which he gives advice on what to do in case of illness, Ben Sira offers some preventive recommendations: avoid gluttony and overeating. "Through lack

of virtue many have died, and through self-control man prolongs his life."

38. 1. Honor the physician before he is needed

He too is a creation of the Lord.

2. From Him does he acquire his wisdom

And from the king he will receive gifts....

4. And the Lord brings out medicines from the earth

And an intelligent man will not despise them....

7. By them the physician will alleviate pain

And the apothecary will prepare a confection.

8. So that the works (of the Lord) will not halt

Nor advantage (be withheld) from mankind.

9. My son, in case of sickness do not tarry:

Pray unto the Lord, for He will heal....

12. But also to the physician give a place

Let him not move for he is needed as well.

13. At times his help is successful

For he too will entreat the Lord....

15. He who withstands the physician

Is a sinner against his Creator.

Ben Sira, we would like to argue, provides a positive well-balanced outlook on healing in Judaism, or rather in ancient Jewish sources. Sure enough, the Lord strikes and heals. He is indeed the absolute, all-knowing Healer. He has offered a preventive panacea for keeping one's health, that is, wholeness and integrity, which may be attained by living in accordance with the law. The Lord, however, remains immanently involved in the world he created, and the physician will be "instrumental" in the healing process insofar as he recognizes that he is an instrument. Both the physician and the sick person pray to the Lord in their daily prayer, asking for divine sanction of human healing. The divine is called in as a kind of catalyzer of the physician-patient encounter. It is, therefore, a moral duty to honor the physician. But the physician must be fully aware of the fact that he too is a creation of the Lord.

In medical matters as in other aspects of Judaism, the relationship between the divine and the human spheres is both transcendent and immanent.

~

NOTES

1. Jakobovits, Rabbi (Lord) Immanuel, *Jewish Medical Ethics*, Bloch Publishing Co., New York, 1967 (1959), p. 2.

2. See also *Deut. 28*: 20-22, 27-29, 35, 59-61.

3. See author's study "Medical Practices and Jewish Law", focusing on Nahmanides's *Sefer Torath Ha-Adam*, forthcoming.

4. See author's study *Tov she-bi-rof'im le-gehinom* (Hebrew) [The best of physicians to purgatory], *Assia*, 1976, 4 (15), pp. 5-12.

5. See Segal, Zwi, *Sefer Ben Sira Hashalem* (Hebrew) [The complete works of Ben Sira] Keter, Jerusalem, 1972. Fragments of the work of Ben Sira have been found in caves at Qumran and Masada.

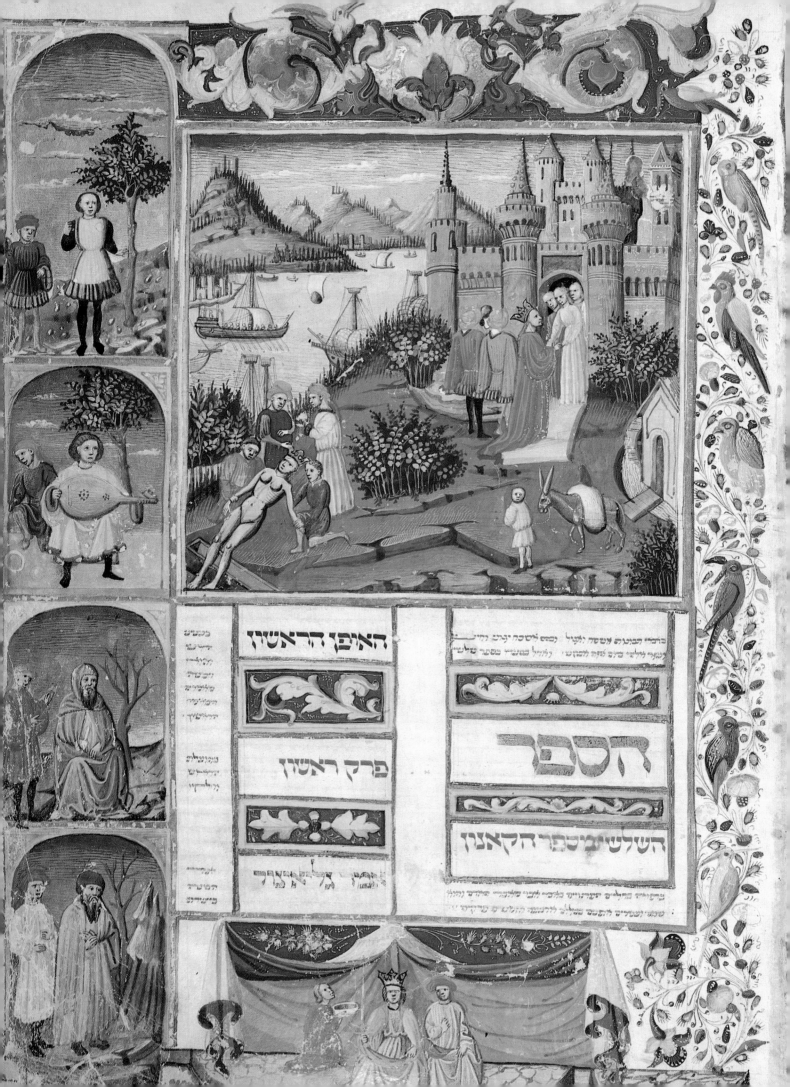

RON BARKAI

JEWISH MEDICAL TREATISES IN THE MIDDLE AGES

"He shall pay for the loss of his time and shall cause him to be thoroughly healed" (Exodus 21:19). This verse from the biblical penal code was the guiding principle of Jewish physicians in the Middle Ages and at the beginning of the modern era. It not only prescribed the religious duty of healing, but eliminated the difficulty of assimilating into Jewish life medical practices rooted in a pagan culture. For it must be emphasized from the first that the term "Jewish medicine" is misleading. Medieval Jewish physicians based their work primarily on Greek medical theories, and their methods of treatment were identical to those of non-Jewish doctors. The distinguishing feature of medieval Jewish medical texts was their language: they were written in Hebrew, Judeo-Arabic (Arabic transliterated into Hebrew script) or Yiddish.

Like other areas of science, medieval medicine as practiced by the three monotheistic cultures inherited its theory and practice from Greek scientific literature, which had in turn been influenced by eastern, particularly Egyptian, medicine. This literature was translated into Arabic in the 8th and 9th centuries, and adapted and assimilated into Arabic-Muslim culture. These works were translated into Latin from the Arabic in the 12th and 13th centuries. Broadly speaking, there were three major schools of thought in Greek medicine, each influenced by a different philosophical outlook.

The first, called "dogmatic" by its rivals and "optimistic" by modern historians, was the scientific-rationalist school. Their outstanding proponents were Hippocrates and Galen. It was their conviction that human reason was capable of deciphering the secrets of nature and the universe, among them

Salerno as depicted in the 15th century.
Illuminated manuscript of Avicenna's
Canon of Medicine.
Translated by Nathan ha-Meati.
43 x 29 cm.
Biblioteca Universitaria di Bologna,
Ms. 2197, detail of folio 210a.

those of the human body. The study of anatomy and physiology, together with observation and experience, would result in the formulation of a theory capable of accurately defining states of sickness and health, diagnosing illnesses and proposing effective treatments. Since rational thinking was essential for practitioners of medical science, Galen contended that the best of physicians must of necessity be a philosopher. Seven–hundred years later, this view was adopted by Rhazes, one of the most prominent and influential of Muslim physicians.

The second, essentially skeptical school of thought, known as the "experimental" school, doubted the ability of the human mind to uncover the secrets of the universe and of the human body. They argued that only the accumulated experience of generations could supply the physician with reliable data on the essence of diseases and ways of curing them. Knowledge rather than understanding should be the principle underlying the theory and practice of medicine. They were, for example, more interested in the healing properties of plants and other substances than in the connection between these properties and the nature of the disease. Naturally enough in the Middle Ages as well, many physicians, or rather "healers," employed empirical methods of healing rather than applying logical and scientific analysis.

The rivalry between these two schools in the Middle Ages was dramatically illustrated by Maimonides, one of the great rationalist Jewish physicians, who wrote:

First page of Omnia Opera Isaac,

illustrating Isaac Israeli with Haly Abbas

and Constantinus Africanus.

Lyon, 1515.

Jewish National and University Library,

Jerusalem.

Most men know that [medicine] is a craft which requires experience and scientific study... It is also an error to believe that a man may be skilled in medical practice without knowledge, but it is possible and true for a man to be learned in medicine, familiar with its roots and its branches, without being skilled in medical practice. This is possible if he learned from books and did not serve an apprenticeship with the knowledgeable practitioners of this craft and did not engage in it. But for a man to become skilled by observing the practices without having acquired knowledge of them, that is impossible, since the physician's craft does not resemble the crafts of carpentry and weaving.[1]

The third group, the "methodist" school, totally rejected the medical theories of the other two groups, contending that proper medical treatment had nothing to do with anatomical knowledge, comprehensive theories of the human body or knowledge based on experience. In their view, the physician had to discover whether the body was limp or contracted when the disease attacked. The disease itself might be either "acute" or "chronic." A third principle advocated by some members of the methodist school was the avoidance of violent intervention in the patient's body: Treatment should be confined to external measures. The most prominent representative of this school, Soranus, was remembered in the Middle Ages mainly for his gynecological treatises which, as we shall see below, had a strong impact on Jewish practices in this field. Of the three schools, Muslim-Arab medicine was influenced most by the rationalists, and in particular by their most disting-

Galen's four humors.

Manuscript, c.1472.

Galen did not ascribe personality types to the four humors governing human health and disease, but his Arabic commentators did. This western manuscript illustrates men dominated by the humors. From top left, clockwise: black bile (melancholic), phlegm (phlegmatic), yellow bile (choleric), and blood (sanguine).

The personality of women was not of interest.

Zentralbibliothek, Zurich, Ms. C. 54.

uished representative, Galen. Modern historians have pointed out that medieval Arab medicine was "Galenized," although it had other characteristics too. According to scientific Arabic texts (written mostly by Muslims, but also by Christians and Jews) there was a parallel between the structure of the cosmos and that of the human body, which they perceived as a microcosm. At its base were four elements, comprising two pairs of oppositions: earth and wind, and water and fire. These elements were closely connected to the four elemental fluids (or humors) of the body: black (bile), red (blood), white (phlegm) and yellow (bile), whose proportional composition differed from one individual to another. A state of health was defined as an equilibrium among them and disease was seen, accordingly, as a disturbance of this equilibrium. Further, the dominant humor in each individual determined his or her temperament: melancholy, sanguine, phlegmatic or choleric. Each of the humors had two natural qualities: the black was dry and cold; the red, hot and wet; the white, cold and wet; and the yellow, dry and hot; and each originated in one of the body's vital organs: the black in the spleen (or kidneys); the red in the heart (or liver); the white in the brain, and the yellow in the liver (or heart). This division paralleled the four seasons of the year, and each season dominated one of the humors and the organ from which it originated. Autumn was dry and cold, spring hot and wet, winter cold and wet and summer dry and hot. Altogether it created a rational order with a perfect geometrical structure, as shown in the following illustration:

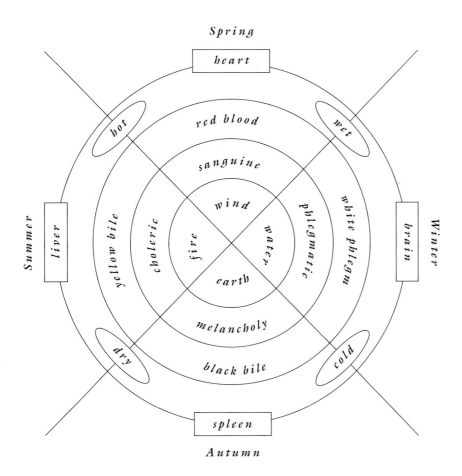

The Jews who lived under Muslim rule after the establishment of the caliphate, which extended from Persia to Spain, were assimilated into the dominant Arab culture and took an active part in its development. Hence, the medical tracts written by Jews up to the 12th century were composed in Arabic and were an integral part of Arab Galenism. There were two important exceptions written in Hebrew. The first, *Sefer ha-Refu'ot* [Book of remedies], is attributed to Asaph ha-Rofe [Asaph the physian], referred to in some manuscripts as "the astrologer," although there is no clearcut evidence as to the identity of the author or the date of composition. The book is unique

Sefer ha-Yakar.

Manuscript, Italy, 13th-14th century.
Sefer ha-Yakar, medical miscellany
written by Shabbtai Ben Avraham Ben
Yoel Donnolo.
Jewish National and University
Library, Jerusalem, Fr. 95, folio 75v.

in its blending of the principles of Greek medicine, as propounded primarily by Hippocrates and Galen, with Jewish, mainly Talmudic, tradition, and this is evident in that it contains a "physician's oath." Asaph's book consists of four parts: Aggadic tradition on the transmission of medical knowledge from God to mankind; a general survey of medicine; a lexicon of medical materials; and, finally, medical aphorisms. The second was the work of Shabbtai Ben Avraham Ben Yoel Donnolo, who is known to have lived in Oria in the province of Brindisi in Italy in the 10th century (913-983). Shabbtai Donnolo's medical writings are of prime importance not only for the history of Jewish medicine but also in the annals of European medicine before the establishment of the medical school at Salerno in the 12th century. In this period, the bulk of literature on medicine and other fields of study was composed in monasteries, particularly by the Benedictines. Donnolo's writings, like other medical works disseminated and translated into Latin in this period, derived from authors who wrote during the period of the Roman Empire, who in turn were influenced by Greek medicine, particularly Hippocratic and Galenic. It is one of the few works written outside the monasteries and provides evidence that medical treatises were in fact disseminated beyond their walls in the early Middle Ages.

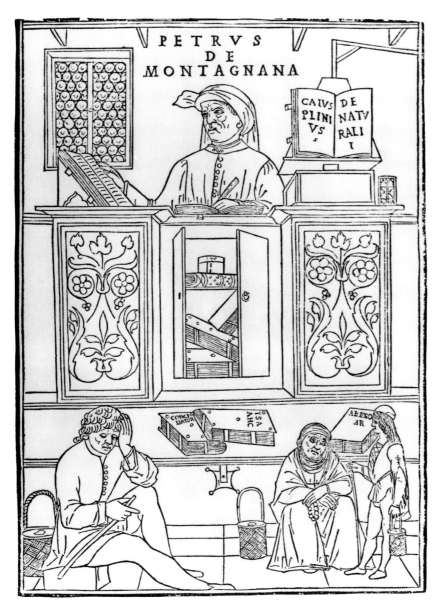

PETRVS
DE
MONTAGNANA

CAIVS PLINI VS | DE NATV RALI

Petrus de Montagnana.

Illustration by Gentile Bellini.

Petrus de Montagnana, in his lecture

chair, surrounded by the works of Isaac

Israeli, Avenzoar, Pliny and Peter of

Abano.

From the Venice edition of John of

Ketham, 1522.

National Library of Medicine,

Bethesda.

As noted, almost all the medical works written by Jews in the early Middle Ages were composed in Arabic or Judeo-Arabic. Jewish writers played a part in the scientific activity of their day and were involved in the discussions which engrossed their Muslim colleagues. Their Judaism played no role in their scientific work, and their writings were almost indistinguishable from those written in Arabic by Muslims and Christians. Two outstanding examples illustrate this phenomenon. One of the most influential physicians in both the Muslim and the Latin world was Isaac ben Solomon ha-Israeli (850-932?), better known by his Arabic name – Ishaq al-Israili, or his Latin name – Isaac Judaeus. Unlike most of the great Muslim physicians who won renown by publishing comprehensive medical encyclopedias, Isaac Israeli gained his reputation on the basis of a number of treatises devoted to specific subjects.

Isaac Israeli was born in Egypt, but most of his scientific work was apparently carried out in Cyrenaica in North Africa. There he wrote medical tracts on

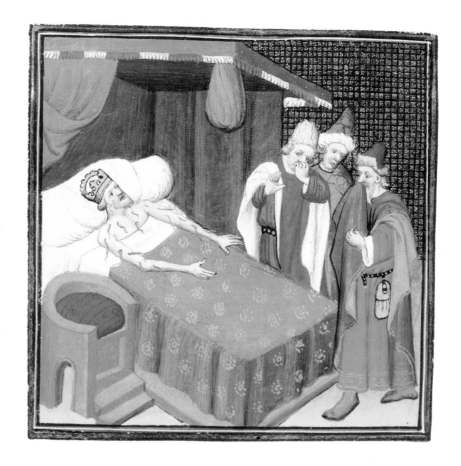

The use of leeches in the treatment of disease in the Middle Ages.

The patient is the Roman Emperor Galerius, pictured, with numerous leeches on his body. Three physicians are standing at the bedside.

A page from a French manuscript of Boccaccio's Decameron.

Science Photo Library, London.

fevers; urine and urine analysis; food; healing potions; and medical ethics. Most of these tracts were translated into Latin from the 11th century on as part of the great translation project of Constantine the African, a Benedictine monk, who lived in Italy. Later they were translated into other European languages. Israeli's Judaism is evident only in his work on medical ethics, where he combines Greek tradition, particularly that of Hippocrates, with Talmudic approaches.

Even more significant is the case of Maimonides, who was not only a renowned physician and author of medical works of major importance, but also a distinguished teacher of Halakha. In his philosophical and medical writings, he used Arabic, thereby continuing a long tradition which regarded this language as the ideal instrument for expressing scientific ideas. In his halakhic works he wrote in biblical and post-biblical Hebrew. In his Arabic *Kitab Sharh asmaí al-Uqqar* [Treatise on asthma], for example, a lexicon of plants and other substances used in the preparation of medicines, Maimonides gives parallel terms in Castillian, Persian, Greek and Syrian but not in Hebrew, despite the fact that biblical and post-biblical Hebrew contain almost 500 such terms and Maimonides was unquestionably familiar with them. (We know this because he used them in his monumental Hebrew work, *The Code of Maimonides.* Moreover, perusal of his commentary on the Mishnah, written in Arabic, shows clearly that he was acquainted with the Arabic counterparts of these terms.)

In contrast to well known Arab authors like Avicenna, al-Majusi, and Rhazes, who composed medical works of an encyclopedic character, Maimonides focused primarily but extensively on single subjects: health management, asthma, poisons and antidotes, hemorrhoids, and the restoration of potency. To these should be added the *Aphorisms of Moses*, a synopsis of the main principles of medicine and his commentaries in the medical aphorisms attributed to Hippocrates.

Most of Maimonides's medical works were translated from Arabic into

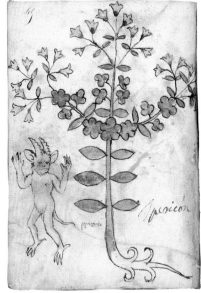

A page from a Hebrew Medical Herbal.

Manuscript, 15th century, Italy.

20 x 15 cm.

The illustration shows Hypericum perforatum, which was reputed to drive away the devil.

Bibliothèque Nationale de France, Paris, Ms. Hebr. 1199, folio 45r.

Maimonides.

Page from the Rothschild Miscellany. An illustrated interpretation of the Eight chapters of Maimonides who is seated in an environment of trees, symbolizing the study of Nature.

Ms., Ferrara(?), c.1470.

Israel Museum, Jerusalem.

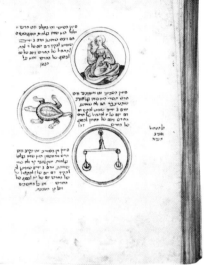

Astrology and Medicine.

Southern Germany, c.1480-1500.

23.5 x 18 cm.

A collection consisting mainly of medical treatises, written by Hippocrates, Galen, Maimonides and others. At the end of the volume (folios 135-146), there is an untitled treatise

discussing the relationship between astrology and medicine. This manuscript explains how the stars influence disease and how one can determine, according to the day of the month, whether it is a favorable time for bloodletting.

The instructions for phlebotomy in folios 143v-145, are illuminated with the signs of the zodiac, which illustrate the purpose of the anonymous author. The signs of the zodiac in medallion-shaped illustrations are painted in naive style. The zodiac iconography, characteristic of Ashkenazi manuscripts (Mahzorim) since the 13th century, is copied in this secular book.

Bibliothèque Nationale de France, Paris, Ms. heb. 1120.

Salerno.

Illustration of Roger of Salerno attending to a patient. The patient has a visible abscess from a diseased tooth and an eye complaint, for which the physician is administering a herbal remedy. Legend has it that the famous medical school in Salerno was founded by Elinus the Jew, Pontus the Greek, Adala the Arab and Salernus the Roman (Latin) and was free and open to men and women students of all religions. Hebrew, Latin and Arabic were the languages of instruction. The most famous woman physician of Solerno was Trotula, who wrote a book on gynecology. The most famous book written there was Regimen Sanitatis Salernitatus, later edited by Arnold of Villanova (1234-1311). There was constant contact with the Arab-speaking world through the Benedictine Monastery of Monte Cassino, where Arab medical works were translated.

Hulton Deutsch Collection, London.

Charles of Anjou, King of Naples and Sicily, presenting Arabic manuscript of Rhazes to Faraj ben Salim of Girgenti for translation.

Manuscript, 15th century, Italy.
Faraj ben Salim of Girgenti, who lived in the late 13th century, was court physician of Charles of Anjou, King of Naples and Sicily. He translated many important works from Arabic into Latin thus contributing to the development of Arabic medicine in southern Italy, notably Rhazes's great work, published in Brescia. This work was decorated by Friar Giovanni, the greatest illuminator of the day. Bibliothèque Nationale de France, Paris, Ms. Latin 6912.

Hebrew in the 13th century by two outstanding Hebrew translators, Moshe ibn Tibbon and Nathan ha-Meati, and became an integral part of medieval Hebrew medical literature. Nor was his influence confined to Jewish society. When scientific and philosphical literature was translated from Arabic to Latin in a major project launched at the end of the 12th century, his work made a strong impact in the Latin West as well.

From the end of the 11th century and, to an even greater extent, in the 12th and 13th, the hub of scientific activity, including medicine, shifted from the Muslim countries to Western Europe. At the same time that scientific research dwindled and rigid Muslim orthodoxy was in the ascent in both East and West, Christian-Latin culture became more receptive to philosophical and scientific study.

This process began with the translation of Greek philosophical literature, including the Arab commentaries, from Arabic to Latin. In medicine, the works of Hippocrates, Galen and other Greek physicians also became known to westerners through their Arabic translations. But no less significant was the translation into Latin of those encyclopedic Arab medical works of the authors mentioned above, such as the *Canon of Medicine* by Avicenna (one of the basic works in European medical schools until the beginning of the 16th century), *Kitab al-Hawi fi al-Tibb* (known by its Latin name of Continens), and *al-Kitab al-Mansuri fi al-Tibb* (known by its Latin name of *Liber almansorius*) by Rhazes, al-Majusi's work *Kamil al-Sinaia al-Tibbiya* (the Liber pentegni in Constantine Latin translation) and the great work on surgery by al-Zahrawi. Scientific knowledge was transmitted from Arabic culture to Latin culture by two main channels: first, from the end of the 11th century, by the Italian route, by the

Bernard of Gordon, professor at Montpellier from 1282 to 1318, shown before his class, evoking the spirits of Hippocrates, Galen and Avicenna.
Manuscript, mid-15th century.
Bibliothèque Nationale de France,
Paris, Ms. lat. 6966, folio 4v.

Benedictine monk Constantine the African; secondly, and this was the more fertile method, through Spain, where Jewish translators played a decisive role.

Concomittantly, a revolution was taking place in European Jewish society as well, particularly in Spain, France and Italy, as Hebrew began to replace Arabic as the main language of scientific discourse. This revolution may be regarded as the second renaissance of the Hebrew language, the first being the renaissance of Hebrew poetry in the 10th century. This process began with the migration of the Jews of Muslim Spain, in the mid-12th century, to Christian Spain and southern France, in the wake of the forced conversions of the Almohads, the fanatic dynasty which came to power in Al-Andalus and North Africa. Cut off from Arab culture, the Jews of Spain also abandoned the language of that culture and gradually created a scientific language common

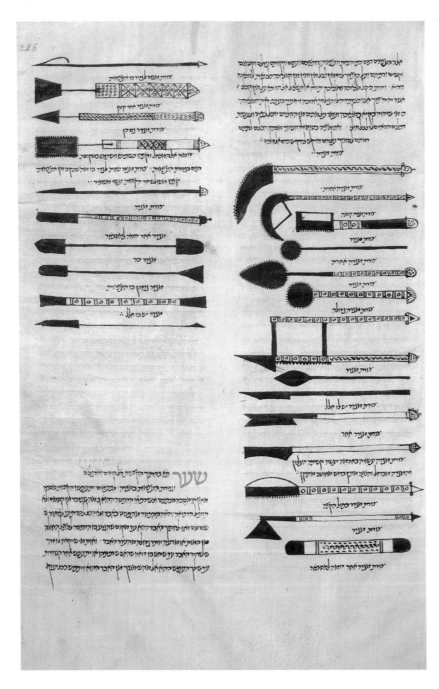

Al Tasrif, by Abulcasis (Abdul Qasim al-Zahrawi) (936-1013).

Spain or Provence, first half of the 15th century.

44. x 30.5 cm.

Abulcasis is the major Muslim writer on surgery and greatly influenced the Christian West.

Abulcasis's work was translated into Hebrew in 1258 by a Sephardi physician, Shemtov ben Isaac of Tortosa, who lived in Marseilles. The work is a medical encyclopedia of thirty treatises, deriving mainly from Greek sources, to which he added his own fifty-year long experience as a practitioner.

Obstetrics, pharmacology, dietetics, pediatrics, psychology and surgery are among the medical fields considered. The thirtieth and last book is devoted to surgical instruments. Al-Zahrawi describes the manufacture and use of scalpels, scissors, forceps and lancets. The manuscript contains accurate drawings of various kinds of scrapers and other instruments for surgical treatment, as well as small surgical procedures.

These drawings are typical of early Arabic manuscripts as well as of Latin and Hebrew manuscripts.

Bibliothèque Nationale de France, Paris, Ms. Heb.1163, folio 226.

to all the Jewish communities of Europe, namely Hebrew. Scientific and medical works were translated from Arabic and Latin into Hebrew, and original scientific works were composed in Hebrew. As we will see below, Arabic continued to play a vitally important role in the medical literature produced by the Jews of Christian Spain. However, it is an indisputable fact that Jewish physicians in Western Europe preferred to use Hebrew for scientific communication rather than either Latin, the accepted scientific language of the Catholic world, or the local dialects, in which scientific works were composed from the mid-13th century onward.

Jewish physicians in Christian Europe were usually denied the opportunity of studying and training in medical schools and universities. As a result they were dependent on medical literature for purposes of both study and keeping in touch with advances in the profession once they began practicing. Basic grounding in medicine for young Jews was acquired in a "closed system," passed on from father to son or received at the home of a distinguished physician. In those cases in which Jews were permitted to practice medicine in their communities and treat non-Jewish patients, they were required to sit for examinations set by the local authorities and the physicians' guilds. This meant that although they had received their medical training in Hebrew they were obliged to familiarize themselves with medical terminology in Latin or in the vernacular. This was true particularly in cases in which Jewish medical students completed their internship alongside Christian physicians, an accepted practice in Spain and southern France.

The first challenge which faced the translators and authors of Hebrew medical literature was the creation of a glossary of words, terms and expressions in the various spheres of medicine and pharmacology, which had not existed in Hebrew previously. The Hebrew translators borrowed terms from the Bible, the Mishna and Talmud, but were frequently forced to invent terms by translation or transliteration from Arabic or Latin. For example, of al-Majusi's important work, only one chapter was translated into Hebrew – the chapter on anatomy. It seems to me, after comparing the translation first with the original and then with later Hebrew medical literature, that the anonymous

Avicenna, the illustrious Persian physician, as represented in a Hebrew manuscript.
Spain (or Italy), early 15th century.
32.2 x 24.1 cm.
Biblioteca Universitaria di Bologna,
Ms. 2297, folio 4r.

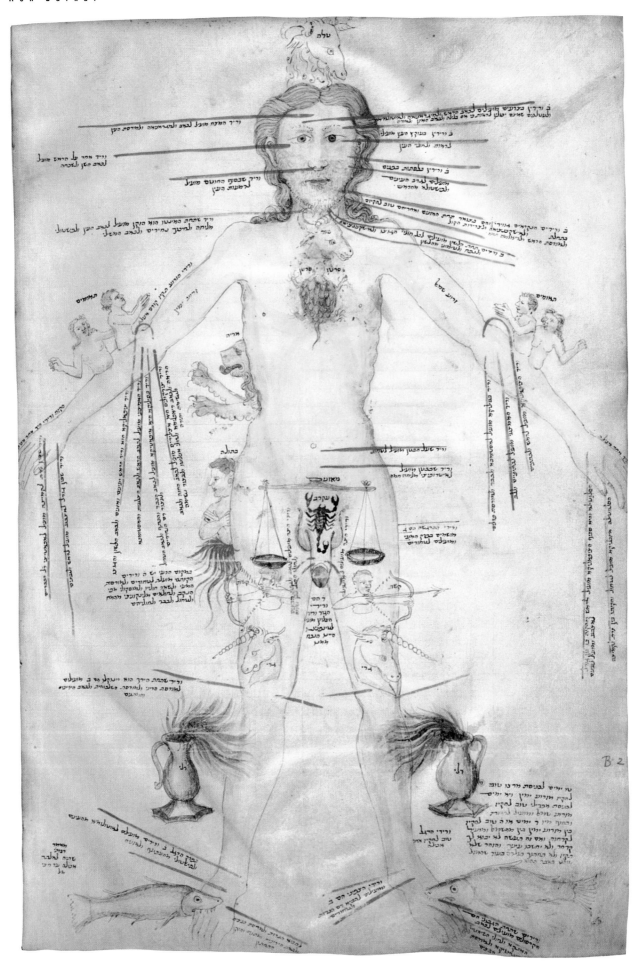

Bloodletting Man.

Manuscript from Provence, containing several medical texts, mostly translated fragments of the Medical Treatise of Jean of Damascus, c.1400.

36 x 24 cm.

The only known representation of the homo signarum combined with the homo venarum, where all the positions used for bloodletting are labeled in Hebrew. This illustrates the influence of astrology on the organs and on the choice of the place of bloodletting.

The signs of the zodiac are shown on the parts of the body and limbs they were thought to govern. The absence of any specifically Jewish features in the iconography of the signs of the zodiac indicates that this well-executed figure was copied from a non-Jewish model. Bibliothèque Nationale de France, Paris, Ms. hebr. 1181, folio 264v.

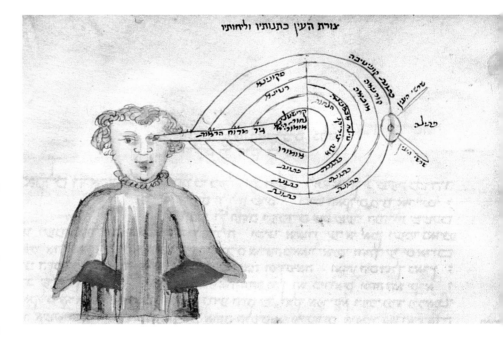

A cross-section of the eye, identifying the membranes with the four humors.

Manuscript from Provence, c.1400.

Bibliothèque Nationale de France, Paris, Ms. hebr. 1181, folio 265.

A doctor examining patients.

Illuminated manuscript of Avicenna's
Canon of Medicine.
Nathan ha-Meati's Hebrew translation.
Italy, c.1440.
43 x 49 cm.

The only manuscript among over 100
that contains the full translation.
Illustrated medical treatises were
widespread among the Jews of Europe
in the 14th and 15th centuries. Most of
these manuscripts were not illuminated,
however, and the illustrations that were
included were of a technical or
diagrammatic nature. Only during the
15th century did the illuminated
medical book come into fashion in Italy.
The Canon of Avicenna is one of the
most sumptuous examples of such a
work.

The first chapter of each book in the
Canon of Avicenna contains a page
with a decorative framed border
illustrating the contents of that
particular book. The style of the
illustrations and the decorations is
Ferrarese of the late 15th century,
characterized by the foliage scrolls
interspersed with flowers, animals,
birds, dragons, and grotesques. The
landscape and the figure style is also
Ferrarese in its depth and volume.

In 1587, the manuscript belonged to the
physician (Jehiel) da Pesaro who later
converted to Christianity as Vitale
Medici. Francesco Maria, Grand Duke
of Tuscany, offered him 200 ducats for
the manuscript, but Vitale would not
sell it. Vitale became a Dominican
Friar and the manuscript thus became
the property of the Dominican Convent
in Bologna. In 1796, the French
carried it off to Paris. In 1815, the
Pope retrieved the manuscript after the
fall of Napoleon. The manuscript
remained in the Medical Faculty of
Bologna until Pope Pius IX donated it
to the library of the university.
Biblioteca Universitaria di Bologna,
Ms. 2197, folio 7r.

Scene in an open-air pharmacy.

Illuminated manuscript of Avicenna's

Canon of Medicine.

Biblioteca Universitaria di Bologna,

Ms. 2197, folio 492r.

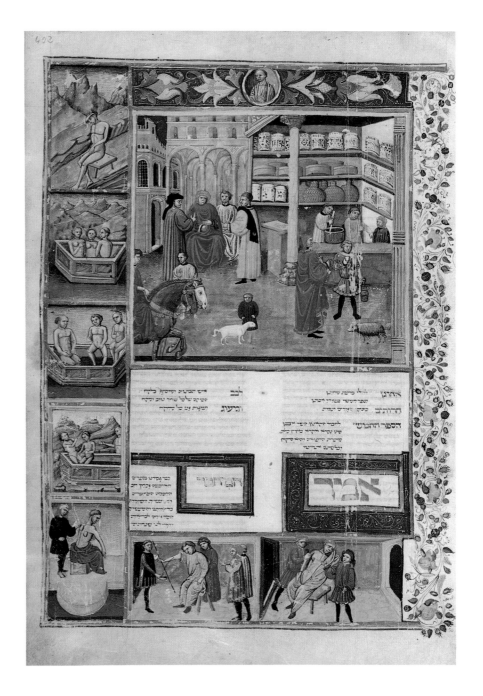

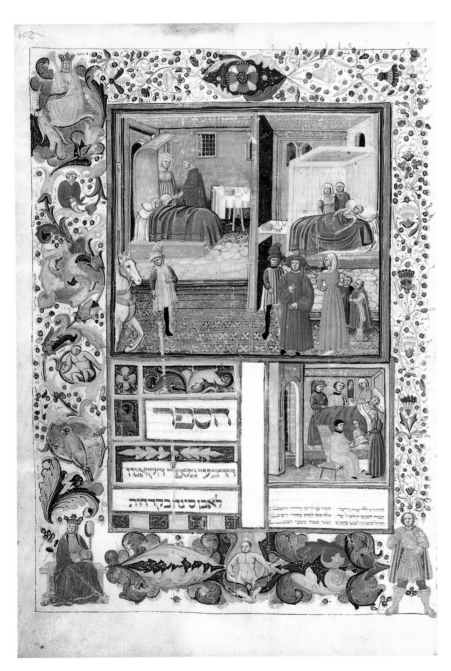

An Italian doctor visiting a patient.

Illuminated manuscript of Avicenna's

Canon of Medicine.

Biblioteca Universitaria di Bologna,

Ms. 2197, folio 402r.

translator simply wanted to provide Hebrew medical literature with an adequate anatomical terminology. His method was to use the Arabic forms in Hebrew translation. For example, arteries were called "pulsating" arteries to distinguish them from veins, which were called "non-pulsating" arteries. When the Hebrew terms were not sufficiently clear, the author appended terms in Latin, Arabic and the vernacular. In the section dealing with the foot, the author translated the Arabic term for the bone of the foot, *'adam al-safina* into the Hebrew term, *esem ha-sefina* (*safina* and *sefina* both mean boat), and added a comment in Castillian: "This is the *barqueta*, or small boat."[3]

In a manuscript in the Bibliothèque Nationale in Paris an anonymous translator, who apparently lived in Orange in the south of France, records the fact that between 1197-1199 he translated several theoretical treatises and seventeen practical works from Latin into Hebrew. An examination of the list of translations indicates, that he chose wisely and, that he was profoundly influenced by the Arabic-to-Latin translation project, which was completed by Constantine the African a century earlier. The most important contemporary works are included, such as the introduction to medical science by Hanain ibn Ishaq, based mainly on the writings of Galen; the medical aphorisms of Hippocrates; the *Prognostikon*, also attributed to Hippocrates; and the medical encyclopedia of Rhazes.[4] Of particular interest are the reasons which the translator gives for undertaking this task. It appears that his objective was to dissuade Jewish patients from consulting Christian physicians:

For I have seen the seed of the holy rising early to stand at the gates of the sages of other nations to consult them on their sicknesses and the sicknesses of their sons and daughters, and taking all that is given at their hand without understanding, for they distinguish not between what is unclean and what is pure, and they pour into their potions of wine all manner of resins and also add unclean meat and milk and blood, and none of them flee whether from prohibition or from disgust, and thus I have come to copy into the holy tongue all the works of the wise which I have obtained of medical wisdom and the best of the works of practice...[5].

Different methods of healing.

Illuminated manuscript of Avicenna's Canon of Medicine.

Biblioteca Universitaria di Bologna, Ms. 2197, folio 448v.

Mortar.

Italy, 1691 (?).

H14 D15 cm.

Bronze cast. Hebrew inscription:
"David Abohav [and Hebrew date]
(5)451(?)."

The mortar is in 16th century Italian
style.

Israel Museum, Jerusalem.

Introductions of this kind to translations and to original Hebrew-language medical treatises are unique to Jewish medicine and offer a variety of answers to the question of why they were written in Hebrew.

Hebrew, as has been noted, lacked the linguistic tools for precise scientific definition and medieval Hebrew medical literature never attained the level of sophistication and linguistic precision which characterized Arabic and Latin works. The introductions also reflect the various approaches prevalent in Jewish society towards the sciences, which were referred to as "alien" wisdom. The "apologetic" approach, for example, sought to prove that all the sciences, including medicine, were born out of Jewish culture, and tried to "Judaize" the translated works.

One example of this approach was *The Book of Procreation*, the most popular gynecological treatise in medieval Jewish society. *The Book of Procreation* was written in the 2nd century by the Greek physician Soranus. In the 6th century, the book was translated into Latin by Muscio, and the 13th-century Hebrew version was adapted from this version, apparently by the Granada-born Jewish physician, Shlomo ibn Ayub. He adapted it in the form of a dialogue between Dinah and her father, Jacob, inserting expressions and verses from the biblical and post-biblical literature. To these he added an introduction and an epilogue, which did not exist in the Greek and Latin versions and which serve to reinforce the impression that it is an original Hebrew work. The flavor of the language will be evident to the reader from several sentences from the introduction:

After God created man from the dust of the earth and breathed life into his nostrils, the sons of God saw the daughters of man who were comely. A voice was heard saying "Observe my laws." They looked to see who it was and behold it was Dinah. Dinah came before her father and fell at his feet and wept and beseeched him, saying: "My father, see my body, it is brought low and afflicted and wearied. Cold and moisture rule it and every breath of wind

ספר דינה לכל ענין הרחם וחלייה

The pathological positions of the foetus.

A collection consisting mainly of medical treatises, written by Hippocrates, Galen, Maimonides and others.

23.5 x 18 cm.

Bibliothèque Nationale de France, Paris, Ms. hebr. 1120, folio 70.

Sefer Dinah.

Gynecological tract including prescriptions for women's ailments. Written in Jewish-Arabic. The British Library, London, Ms.Or. 10539.

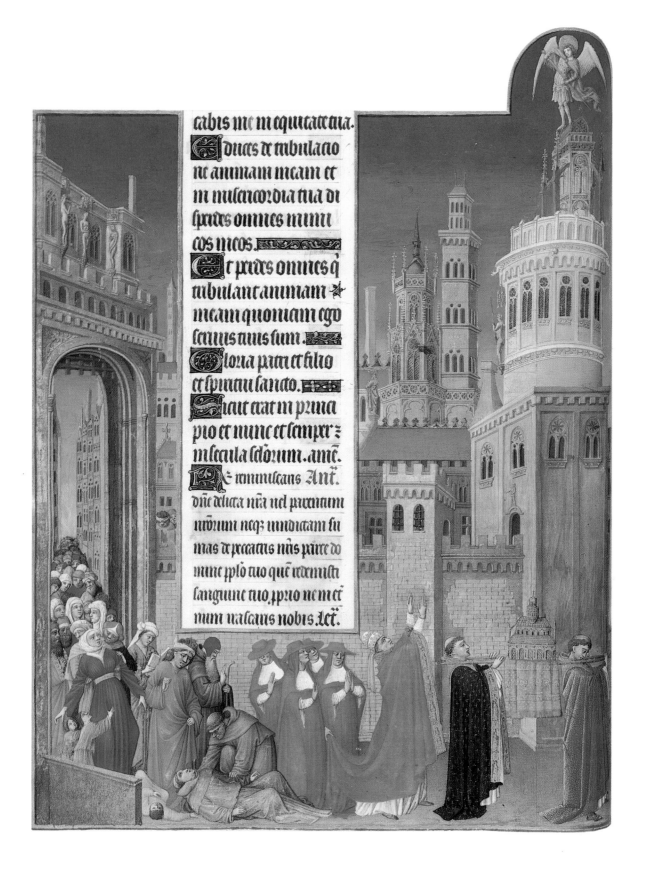

disturbs its activities. For sometimes great floods burst out and the gates of heaven open up, and sometimes they close and the waters of the sea are dammed and dwindle and the river dries up."

And then Jacob goes on to say:

Blessed art thou, my daughter, and blessed is your judgment, for your words are good and so is your question on this matter, and in truth the daughter's affliction has touched me and I have brought it to my heart and mind. And now, hearken, daughter, and see and lend me your ear and do not fear to ask.

After a description of all the tribulations of the female body and the appropriate treatment, the author concludes on an optimistic note, also taken from Jewish tradition:

And Dinah went out of her father's presence and Job her husband knew her and begot sons and daughters, and they were scattered over the earth, and the wise among them shone with the radiance of the heavens.[5]

In the introduction to the most ancient medical work written in Hebrew, Asaph the Physician (see above) endeavored to prove that medical science originated with the forefathers of the Jewish people. He quoted a tradition which relates that diseases were inflicted on mankind by evil spirits which rebelled against God in the days of Noah. In response to Noah's plea, God sent him the angel Raphael, who transmitted to him the secrets of medicine. Noah handed down this knowledge to his son, Shem, who recorded it in the first book of medicine. The book was disseminated throughout the world, and among those who copied it were the great figures in Greek medicine: Hippocrates, Galen and Dioscorides. In the same spirit, an anonymous medical manuscript, based on the writings of Galen, quotes the tradition that Titus, after conquering Jerusalem, was greatly impressed with the wisdom of the sages of Israel and asked them to compose a medical tract for him. The sages, led by Rabban Gamliel, wrote the book and called it the *Book of Galien*, after Gamliel.[6]

Many translators and authors of Hebrew medical literature explained that their activity was motivated by the contempt which the Gentiles displayed towards Jewish culture because it was believed to be impossible to compose

The Procession of Gregory the Great to end the plague in Rome represents an early papal reaction to the plague.
Clergy and laity fall dying even during the procession. Such scenes were repeated at Avignon and elsewhere during the Black Death.
From Pol de Limbourg et J. Colombe *Très Riches Heures du duc de Berry, France, 1585.*
Musée Condé, Chantilly.

scientific works, especially medical tracts, in the holy tongue. They wrote in Hebrew, they asserted, in order to restore the honor of the Jewish people and demonstrate to the nations among whom they lived that their language was in no way inferior to Arabic or Latin.[8]

Most of the translations and the original medical treatises in Hebrew were almost certainly written for the benefit of Jewish physicians who were not fluent in Arabic and Latin. Fascinating evidence to this effect can be found in the introduction which the translator Yosef, known as Vidal Ben ha-Sar Benvenisti Ben Lavi ha-Sephardi, wrote to *Gerem ha-Ma'alot*, a medical treatise written in Arabic by Yehoshua ha-Lorki. This work, written at the end of the 14th century, was indisputably one of the most important written by medieval Jewish physicians. Scholars ignored the book for many years, apparently because the author eventually converted to Christianity and conducted an acrimonious campaign against his former brethren. From statements by the author himself and the translator, we learn that the book was written for the benefit of Jewish physicians, at the request of the translator's father, R. Benvenisti, son of the distinguished philosopher R. Shlomo ben Lavi known as De la Cavalleria. But because ha-Lorki chose to write his book in Arabic, Yosef was required to translate it into Hebrew for those physicians who were not fluent in that language, as he pointed out in his introduction:

The great sage R. Yehoshua ben Bibash [ha-Lorki] resolved to compose a brief treatise to point the way for the community of physicians to investigate all the balms and drugs and to examine their composition so that there be no flaws to their handicraft Arabic language which was familiar to him, but since his words were to some like a sealed book since they were not familiar with that language, his wisdom dictated that he command me to copy the treatise in our holy tongue so that its general benefit could be brought into radiant light.[9]

Yet despite the dominant status of Hebrew, the great Jewish physicians in Christian Spain continued to compose their medical tracts in Arabic when they wanted to ensure accuracy. They also used Arabic medical manuscripts for study purposes. In recent years, research has shown that this phenomenon

Triumph of Death.

Oil painting by Bruegel (1556).
The Black Death of 1347-1348, which
killed perhaps one-quarter of Europe's
population, that is, about 25 million
people, was seen as a horrible loosening
of the forces of darkness on mankind.
The Prado, Madrid.

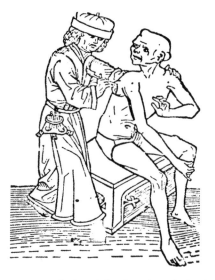

Surgeon lancing a bubo during the plague.

Woodcut by H. Flocz, 1482.

Buboes were quite painful, so surgeons often lanced them. During the plague mortality among surgeons was much higher than among physicians.

World Health Organization, Geneva.

Jews being burned alive after being accused of having started the plague.

Woodcut from Liber Chronicarum, H. Schedel, Nuremberg, 1493.

Jews were persecuted throughout Europe for allegedly having started the plague. The Wellcome Institute Library, London.

was widespread; all the medical manuscripts written in Arabic in Christian Spain were composed for the use of Jewish physicians. This is surprising in light of the fact that their Muslim colleagues in Christian Spain had almost no recourse to Arabic medical works.[10]

There is an unpublished Arabic manuscript in the National Library in Madrid, called *The Book of Royal Castillian Medicine*. It was written in the first third of the 14th century by a Jewish physician from Toledo, and has been studied in depth only in the past few years. Examination of the manuscript reveals that it is a highly sophisticated intellectual work, based on close acquaintance with the writings of Galen and the extensive literature of Arabic Galenism. It is the creation of a physician who, in addition to his clinical work, invested considerable thought in the theoretical aspects of his profession and took an active part in the scientific and medical polemics of his day. Scholars have now concluded that the manuscript "is unique in the framework of Latin, Arabic and Jewish late medieval medical literature."

Elias ha-Yehudi ben Abraham ha-Sephardi wrote a first-rate work in Arabic on the Black Death (bubonic plague), in which he compared the methods of treatment employed by Christian and Muslim physicians. This suggests that Jewish physicians, and particularly those practicing in Christian Spain and in southern France, although usually denied entry to universities, maintained the highest scientific standards, thanks to their direct and constant access to the classic medical literature in Greek, Arabic, Latin and, of course, Hebrew. Regrettably, the great majority of the medical works composed by these physicians (and many others, such as Gershom Ben Hizkiya of Provence, and Nathan Falaquera, author of the book *Zori ha-Guf* [Balm for the body], have not yet won the scholarly attention they deserve, and have not been published in critical editions. This omission prevents us from assessing to the full the importance of medieval Jewish medical literature, not only within the Jewish context but also, and perhaps more significantly, in the general context of medieval medical science.

Serta etas mundi

Anno mundi. 6691   Anno xpi. 1492.

Linea summor pontificu
Alexander sertus

Alexander sertus papa. natione hyspanus: ex valentia ciuitate rhodorie° boria antea vocatus. epus portuensis. Uacante sede post obitu Innocetij octaui. oim suffragijs hoc anno pontifex creatus. Et ad.s. ioanne laterane sem. xrvi. die augusti. corona papali decorat°. Uir magni animi. magneq; prudentie. Is in adolescentia bononie studijs litteraru operam dedit. gymnasiuq; illud scolasticu non paucis annis celebrauerit. Qui adeo virtutum gloria. z disciplinar laude. z adeo singular ac oim rer ornamento dotatus. vt Calixt° ter eius pontifex summus sedatis suo tempe ytalie rebus. cum nouem cardinales creasset. Et enea senensem in cardinalem assumpsisset. Buos quoq; ex sororib° eius nepotes. cardinales creauit. L. ioanne cognomento milanu ex sorore nepotem. z rhodoricu huc boriam. cuius vtutis z glorie liquidissimu documentum extitit. q̈ adhuc adolescens inter reuerendissimos z excellentissimos cardinales constitutus. Uel etiam q̈ no multo postvicecancellarij locum sortitus Hor oim scientia preditus z exprientia refertissimus. vere designadus z euocadus fuit. Qui fluctuante petri nauiculam gubernaret. Et si berilis z regia ipius faciei dignitas prese ferre videatur. Tamen in primis accedit nobilissima eius natio byspaniensis. Inter ceteras vniuerse terre prouincias aeris salubritate tempata. oimq; rer copia z bonitate precipua. viros pgeneras. q̈ z corpis agilitate. z ingenij acrimonia. z oim virtutum gloria summi clarissimiq; semp extitere. Uehinc eximia eius valentia ciuitas. que z sui antiquitate z situs pulcritudine z viror copia. Et oim mercamontor genere loge reliquas biberie ciuitates antecellit. Nec non z illustris boriaru familia. que cum peperit. Qui vere nationem patriamq; z familia illustrauit. Et recolende ac beatissime memorie auuculi eius Calixti semp emulator. litterali discipline. scientiaruq; peritia. z optima viuendi ratio. adest humanitas illa inclita cu auctoritatis ratione seruata. optimu z salubre consiliu. adest z pietatis cultus. z oim rer cognitio. que ta in inclite dignitati expedire aut vsui esse possint. Felix igitur tot virtutibus exornatus. In tam altissimi magistratus culmine collocatus. a deo optimo bene meritus. Speramus igitur cum vniuerso generi xpiano profuturum. Et per rabidos itinerum amfractus. perq; sublimes z periculosos scopulos transmigraturum. semitam tandem affectatam feliciter occupatur. Postremo ne longiori sue laudis comemorationi aliquos defatigari ptingat. Ceteri sequentes eius acta laude digna persoluant. Uic pontificatu suscepto maiestatem cum auctoritate augere conatus est. Et si in principio sui pontificat° aduersitates sentiat. Magna ti aio ccepit. Benignissim° de° sua gra donet. vt singla ad vtilitate ac comodu reipub. xpiane psequatur

Genus hominu calamitosur iudei. z si supioribus tepo ribus in plerisq; locis germanie ac alijs prouincijs. diuinissimu sacramentum. varijs temptatio nibus. molestijs. ac erroribus in dignissime tractarunt. precipue i Uratislauia patauia z ratispona te. nec impune hoc flagitiu inultum fuit. Nouissime anno salutis 1492. die. 22. mensis Octobris. in oppido Sternebarch sub dominio principur magnopolensiu auxilio petri sacerdotis. Eleazar iudeus et complices. sacramentu corporis christi. per hostiam maiorem et minore obtinentes. has perforarut. z cruor illico prosiljt quo lintheum precinctum rubo rem accepit. Quo miraculo territ ti ad Petrum deferut. Principes autem illustres balthasar z magnus fratres re comperta cum vestigia vulnerum (que remaserat) cerneret. iudeos cum maiestatem xpi contemserint ac religionem illuserint concremari fecerut. Recedat ergo omne infi delitatis ambiguu. Nec dubitet quisq; primarias creaturas. nutu diuine potetie. presentia summe maiestatis in dominici corporis transire posse naturas. Quid em ei possit esse difficile. Cui facile fuit hoiem (vt premissum est) de limi natura figurare. Imaginem etia sue diuinitatis induere. Cui promtur est eu rursimi reuocare de inferis. restituere de perditione. reparare de puluere. de terra in celum leuare. z figmentur suu in regni sui consortio sublimare. At qui corpus nostre fragilitatis assumpserat. nos in corpus sue imortalitatis assumat. Ad quam gloriosam resurrectionem pijs nos operibus prepare dignetur. Qui viuit z regnat in secula seculorum Amen.

Brunetta, a female Jewish physician, furnishing the needles used to draw the blood of the child Simon of Trent.

Toward the end of the 15th century, Bernardinus of Siena, engaged in a violent denunciation of the Jews, one of the tragic results of which was the martyrdom of the Jews of Trent. This has kept the name of the Jewish physician, Brunetta, alive. At the trial of the Jews for the alleged murder of Simon of Trent, Brunetta was charged with having furnished the needles used to draw the blood.

Woodcut from Liber Chronicarum, H. Schedel, Nuremberg, 1493.

The Wellcome Institute Library, London.

In addition to general medical treatises, Jewish physicians made outstanding contributions in gynecology and the treatment of the Black Death, which broke out in 1348 and killed at least one-third of the population of Europe. Important gynecological works were disseminated mainly in the Latin West. Up to the 12th century, the best-known was the work by the Greek physician, Soranus, which also appeared in a Latin version under the title *Gynaecia*. Subsequently, and until the end of the Middle Ages, the most important gynecological manual in Europe was *Trotula*, named after a woman physician from Salerno, to whom the book was attributed. After many years of debate, it has been established with certainty that Trotula did in fact compose a work on gynecology, but not the book which bears her name.[11] Other works were also distributed in western Europe, on a more limited scale.[12] In the Muslim world, on the other hand, there were only two known gynecological treatises, devoted mostly to problems of obstetrics. The more important was indubitably *Embryology and the Care of Mothers and Infants*, written by the Cordovian scholar, Arib ibn Sa'id. It should be noted that these two books enjoyed only limited circulation.

On the other hand, an examination of Jewish gynecological literature yields surprising results: In medieval Jewish society there were at least fifteen such treatises, of which twenty-four different manuscripts are known to us today. This was certainly a large number, when compared to figures for Christian and Muslim medicine. One of these works, *The Book of Dinah*, which gave details of cures for various womens' diseases, was written in Judeo-Arabic, the rest in Hebrew. Seven of these works are translations from Arabic and Latin (including translations of the works mentioned above), while the remaining

Patients in 13th century Europe queue up to describe their ills and receive medicine from an itinerant physician.

Urine inspection was a common method of diagnosis, with twenty-nine variations, and the urine flask became the symbol of the doctor.

Hulton Deutsch Collection, London.

eight are original Hebrew treatises. No less prolific and of equally high quality was the branch of Jewish medical literature devoted to the Black Death. This epidemic was usually referred to in Hebrew medical literature as "plague-like fever," to distinguish it from other types of fever. Here, too, an important part was played by translations into Hebrew of Latin works by distinguished Christian physicians, written in the second half of the 14th and the 15th

centuries. Shlomo ha-Rofe ben Moshe Shalom ha-Sepharadi explains his Hebrew translation of a work by Antonio Guinerium of Pavia as follows:

This is a book composed by a wise man named Antonio of Pavia, renowned for his wisdom in the knowledge and practice of medicine. And when it came into my hands, I read it twice and thrice and perceived its great qualities. And I saw also many of the sages of the Christians boasting and taking pride in it and speaking against us, saying that we are unable to cure the fevers altogether ... Then I was greatly troubled and my envy consumed me and I resolved to copy it to the best of my ability into our holy tongue.[13]

The most important of the original Jewish works in this field was that of Abraham ben David Kashlari, who wrote while the Black Death was raging, and began his book as follows:

My heart was disposed to compose this treatise by the fevers which occurred in the summer and the end of spring throughout Provence and Catalonia and Aragon, for no town escaped the fevers...and these fevers were mortal diseases; not eleven days passed and many died of them, and the fevers were never-ending, and there was great fainting and distress.[14]

Also deserving of mention are Abraham ben Shlomo Hen and Ilias ben Abraham ha-Sephardi who, in contrast to both Muslim and Christian

Roderigo Lopez plotting to poison the queen.

Engraving by F. Hulsius, 1624.
Roderigo Lopez (1525-1594) was a
Portuguese Marrano physician who,
after graduating at Salamanca, settled
in London early in the reign of Queen
Elizabeth. He became a member of the
College of Physicians and was the first
house physician at St. Bartholomew's
Hospital.
Early in 1594 he was arrested and
accused of plotting to poison Elizabeth,
was found guilty and executed at
Tyburn (June 7, 1594). There is little
doubt that he was innocent, though his
aims and methods were not above
suspicion. The case attracted much
attention, and it is generally believed
that Lopez was the prototype of Shylock
in Shakespeare's Merchant of
Venice.
Alfred Rubens Collection, London.

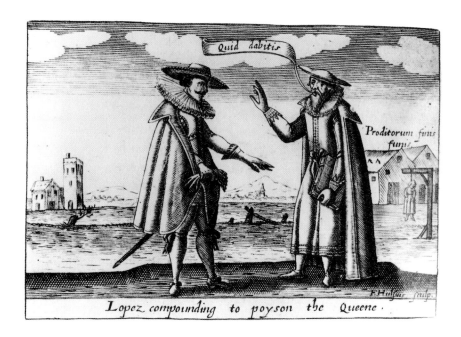

Lopez compounding to poyson the Queene.

Opposite:

Spanish physician's mortar.

North Africa, second half of the 16th
century.
Bronze cast.
H 13 D 12 cm.
Hebrew inscription reads: "I am Yosef,
son of Dan, son of the greatest physician
among the exiles from Spain, Azaria,
son of the Holy Hushiel, physician."
Collection of the Israel Museum,
Jerusalem, purchased through the
Feuchtwanger Memorial Fund with the
help of P. Mayer, New York.

Ron Barkai

Portrait of Moses Hamon, physician to Suleiman the Magnificent.

Colored woodcut from Nicolas de Nicolai's Les quatre premiers livres de Navigations et peregrinations orientales (Lyon 1568), later edition.

Moses Hamon was born into a distinguished Spanish family of physicians. Following expulsion from Spain, Moses' father, Joseph accepted the invitation of Sultan Byezid II (1481-1512) to settle in Turkey and became a doctor at court. Moses in turn became physician to Sultan Suleiman. Hamon used his influence with the sultan to intercede on behalf of fellow Jews. Thanks to Hamon's influence, the sultan also intervened on behalf of Dona Gracia Mendes in her struggle to force the Venetian government to allow her to emigrate to Turkey with her considerable wealth intact.

Yitzhak Einhorn Collection, Tel Aviv.

physicians, consulted both Arabic and Latin medical literature and, when these two sources were in dispute, drew their own independent conclusions.

No comprehensive sociological study has yet been conducted on the role of Jewish physicians in medieval society, but it is an incontrovertible fact that the number of Jewish physicians was proportionally much greater than the number of Jews in the population, despite restrictive legislation and anti-Jewish prejudice. The population of Marseilles in the 14th century, for example, was 20,000, of whom less than 5 percent were Jews. Archival sources reveal that between 1300-1349 there were twenty-three physicians in the city, ten of whom were Jews. The proportion is even more striking in the period following the Black Death: Of thirty-five physicians in the city, nineteen were Jews. In Christian Spain, throughout the High and Late Middle Ages, medical care of church dignitaries and royalty was frequently entrusted to renowned Jewish physicians, despite the fact that church synods repeatedly banned Jewish doctors from treating Christian patients. Even at the court of the "Catholic monarchs," Ferdinand and Isabella, who were responsible for the expulsion of the Jews of Spain, there were physicians among the other Jewish courtiers. This phenomenon continued even after the expulsion of the Jews from Spain in 1492.

Many Jewish physicians left Spain and found refuge in places such as Portugal, the Ottoman Empire, North Africa and the Netherlands, where they continued to practice medicine and win public esteem. But even those who converted to Christianity and remained in Spain continued to play a leading role in medicine, despite the suspicion and persecution which were their lot for generations to come. Particularly prominent among them were the Castro family of Toledo, which produced three consecutive generations of physicians who wrote important medical works in Latin. The standing of the conversos physicians was in sharp constrast to that of the *Morisco* (i.e., Muslim) physicians, who were forced to convert to Christianity at the beginning of the 16th century, and were, for the most, relegated to the margins of Spanish society.

El Olam Shimush Tehilim [The use of
Psalms] *c. 16th century.*

18.5 x 14 cm.

*One of the most important medieval
Jewish texts on magic in which complex
rituals are based on the Psalms and the
secret names of God, concealed in each
one of them. Although healing was not
the main objective of these magic texts,
Psalm 107 was considered effective in
curing a five-day fever.*

*The Wellcome Institute Library,
London, Heb. Ms. 34.*

In summing up this aspect, it appears to me, that two major factors explain why the medical profession was considered so prestigious in medieval Jewish society, and impelled Jewish writers and translators to engage intensively in literary medical activity. First of all, practicing medicine was one of the most important means for medieval Jews of achieving social mobility and integrating into Christian society. Study itself was relatively costly, but specialization in medicine did not require as great an initial capital investment as did commerce and money-lending. In a society in which both law and cultural tradition set obstacles in the path of advancement for Jews, private education was one of the more effective means of breaking down social barriers. One can, thus, easily understand the relatively large number of Jews who became translators of scientific literature, interpreters, writers of various kinds of scientific literature or physicians. Their command of several languages (Arabic, Latin, the vernacular and, of course, Hebrew) was a valuable tool, enabling them to specialize in their profession and to mediate effectively between scientific knowledge from foreign sources and the local educated classes.

Secondly, it should be recalled that in Jewish society there was also a bitter struggle between "conservative" traditional circles, opposed to dabbling in science or "alien" wisdom, and the educated classes, who saw no contradiction between science and faith. But even those who were vehemently opposed to scientific practice exempted medicine from their prohibitions. This was because the Torah and Halakha regarded saving life and curing the ill as supreme religious injunctions. Thus, for example, one of the most famous bans on the study of "alien" sciences, issued in 1305 by the rabbis of Barcelona, headed by Shlomo ben Avraham Aderet, stated:

And we have decreed it and accepted it for ourselves and our seed and all those accompanying us. By force of this prohibition, let no member of this community study the books of the Greeks which they composed on the wisdom of nature and divine wisdom, whether these were composed in their language or copied from another tongue, from this day forth for fifty years hence until he is twenty-five years of age.[15]

However, a qualification was appended to the ban: "But we have excluded from this decree the study of medicine although it is taken from science, because the Torah has granted permission to heal."[16] Those who studied medicine, therefore, were not at risk of clashing with the religious and social leadership of the community. This was so despite the fact that medical studies entailed the study of other, unquestionably "alien" subjects such as logic and astrology, considered necessary to round off the physician's education.

"Learned" or "rational" medicine was not the sole method of treating patients in the Middle Ages. At odds with it, but often existing alongside it, were two alternative methods: one grounded in accumulated experience, the other in magic. This is, of course, a generalization and the dividing lines between the methods were not clearcut. In many cases "learned" medical tracts recommended use of therapeutic measures based on experience or magic.

This type of medical literature was particularly extensive and I would like to quote three texts which illustrate its sources and character. The first, *The Book of Experiences*, attributed to Abraham ibn Ezra, was adapted from an Arabic work by Abd el-Rahman ibn al-Haitham, a Muslim scholar who lived

Liquttei ha-Refu'ot.

Yiddish and Hebrew prescriptions from the 16th century. Prominently displayed is the word Abracatabra (sic!), in a decreasing pattern, which, if uttered properly, caused the illness i.e., the demon, to vanish.

15.5 x 9.5 cm.

The Wellcome Institute Library, London, Heb. ms. A19.

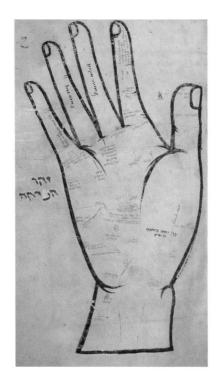

Palmist's drawing of the right hand.

Miscellany manuscript.

Northern France, end of 13th century.

16.1 x 12.2 cm.

*The right hand of a man is shown,
from which his character and fate can
be read; a woman's fortune was read
from her left hand. The significance
read into the lines and marks on the
hand reveals familiar preoccupations:
length of life, happiness, health, as well
as peculiarly medieval obsessions such as
fear of leprosy, desire for male offspring,
or the outcome of a sea crossing -
probably signifying a pilgrimage to
Jerusalem or exile to a remote country.
The British Library, London, Ms. Add.
11639, folio 115 r.*

in Cordova in the first half of the
10th century. The Arabic work was
lost and only a Hebrew translation
has survived under the name of *The
Book of Remedies.*[17]

The author of *The Book of Experiences* used the Arabic text (or
its Hebrew translation) as the basis,
and added a long list of medical
treatments from various sources. Despite the fact that they proclaimed their
work to be based on experience, the authors frequently "quoted" renowned
medical authorities like Galen, Dioscorides, Rhazes and others. Thus, for
example, in the chapter dealing with complications during childbirth, the
Hebrew author lists various "experimental" and magical methods of
alleviating the mother's suffering:

*Galen said that if saffron alum is applied to the hip of a woman, this will
quicken the birth. He said: Take a new potsherd, which has not been touched by
water from the day it was made, and draw on it the following pattern, and write
on it the calculation which adds up to fifteen, no matter how you write down the
numbers, horizontally or vertically, from an angle or diagonally. Then put the
potsherd under the soles of her feet and she will immediately give birth.*[18]

He further advises drawing a "magic square" and specifies the numerical
values to be written there in Hebrew letters.

The second example is taken from *The Properties of Animals*, a work
which was quite popular in the Middle Ages in its Arabic, Hebrew and Latin
versions, and was attributed to various authors, among them Aristotle. It
describes the attributes of various animals, their character, nature and the
curative powers of their different organs. What is of interest in the Hebrew
version is the author's effort, albeit far fetched, to link the text to Jewish
tradition. Of the stork he wrote:

*Our sages of blessed memory said: Why was it called stork [the Hebrew, hassida,
also means "pious one"]? Because she sacrifices her sons...and many sages say that*

the female stork immerses herself in a ritual bath before having intercourse with the male and many sages did not believe this...and her flesh has healing properties and cures epilepsy... and is beneficial for lepers and for boils.[19]

The third example is *The Use of Psalms*, the most important medieval Jewish text on magic, in which complex rituals are based on the psalms and the secret names of God concealed in each. Although healing was not the main objective of these magic texts, Psalm 107 was considered effective in curing a five-day fever:

The psalm of David ... is beneficial for a five-day fever. It must be written first in the proper order and then in reverse order, with his name and reference to El Shadai with the names therein: "Argi Sargi Argi Sargi, save this man from this sickness and help him and support him speedily and in our time, Amen Sela, and suspend it from the neck of the sufferer."[20]

As noted, the various medical methods were not mutually exclusive, and when one failed another could be tried. But in most cases, all these methods were of limited efficacy. This would appear to be one of the reasons for the flourishing of satirical literature which mocked physicians for their inability to cure their patients and for their greed. It is fitting, perhaps, to conclude with a quotation from a satirical poem written by an anonymous Hebrew poet in the 13th century and preserved in Ibn Zabara's *Book of Entertainments*:

> *Quoth Fate unto the Fool: A doctor be,*
> *Who, killing folks off, netteth income large;*
> *So hast thou vantage o'er Death's Angel;*
> *He must take the lives of people free of charge.*[21]

~

NOTES

1. Rabbenu Moshe ben Maimon (Maimonides), *Sefer ha-Kaseret* [On asthma] (Hebrew), in *Ketavim Refuiim*, ed., S. Muntner, Jerusalem, vol. 4, 1965, pp. 112-113.

2. M. Ulmann, *Die Medizin im Islam*, Leiden, 1970, p. 99.

3. For a detailed description of this technique, see my article "The Hebrew and Judeo-Arabic Versions of al-Majusi," in *Constantine the African and Ali al-Abbas al-Majusi, The Pantegni and Related Texts*, edited by C. Burnett and D. Jacquart, The Warburg Institute of London, C.N.R.S. Paris, Brill, Leiden.

4. The full list and identification of the works mentioned therein appear in my book, *A History of Jewish Gynecological Literature in the Middle Ages*, forthcoming.

5. Bibliothèque Nationale (B.N.), Paris, ms. heb. 1190, ff. 44r - 45v.

6. The entire text with a French translation was published in the second part of my book: *Les Infortunes de Dinah, ou la gynécology juive au Moyen Age*, Paris, 1991.

7. Oxford. Bod. Heb (opp.180 or.1138), f. 159V.

8. For an excellent analysis of this type of foreword, see J.P. Rothschild, "Motivations et méthodes des traductions en hébreu du milieu du XIIe a la fin du XVe siecle," in *Traduction et traducteurs au Moyen Age*, Textes réunis par G. Contamine, Paris, 1989, pp. 279-302.

9. B.N. Paris, ms. héb.1143. f. 86r.

10. This emerges from a thorough examination of all the Arabic manuscripts written and disseminated in Christian Spain. See P.Sj. van Konigsveld, 'Andalusian - Arabic Manuscripts from Christian Spain: A Comparative Intercultural Approach," in *Israel Oriental Studies*, 12 (1992), pp. 75 - 110.

11. See J. F. Benton, "Trotula, Women's Problems and the Professionalization of Medicine in the Middle Ages," in *Bulletin of the History of Medicine*, 59 (1985), pp. 30-53.

12. See M. H. Green, 'The Transmission of Ancient Theories of Female Physiology and Disease Through the Early Middle Ages," Ph.D. dissertation, Princeton University, 1985.

13. Pavia, ms. heb 1365, f. 23r.

14. B. N. Paris, ms. heb. 1191, f. 135v.46. On these and similar data in southern France, see: Schatzmiller, *Medecin et Justice*, pp. 5-34.

15. Shlomo ben Abraham Adret, *She'elot u-teshuvot* (Hebrew) [Questions and answers] Ramat Gan, 1958.

16. Ibid.

17. For a description of these two treatises, see *The Book of Experiences. attributed to Abraham ibn Ezra*, edited, translated and commented upon by J.O. Leibowitz and S. Marcus, Jerusalem, 1984, pp. 7-110.

18. Ibid, p. 238.

19. Oxford, Bodleian Library, ms. opp. 181. f. 77v.

20. London, Wellcome Institute, ms. Heb. 34, f. 31v-32r

21. Yosef ben Meir ibn Zabarra, *Sefer ha-Sha'ashu'im* [The Book of entertainments] (Hebrew), edited by Y. Davidson, Berlin, 1925, p.123.

BIBLIOGRAPHY

ALTMAN, A. AND S.M. STERN, *Isaac Israeli. A Neoplatonic Philosopher of the Early Tenth Century. His works, translated with comments and an outline of his philosophy.*

BARKAI, R., *Les Infortunes de Dinah, ou la gynécologie juive au Moyen-Age*, Paris, 1991.

BAR-SELA, A. AND H.E. HOFF, "Isaac Israeli's fifty Admonitions to the Physicians," *Journal of the History of Medicine and Allied Sciences*, 17 (1962), pp. 245-257. This is an English translation of the work by D. Kaufman which appeared in *Magazin fur die Wissenschaft des Judenthums* in 1884.

EBIED, R.Y., *Bibliography of Medieval Arabic and Jewish Medicine and Allied Sciences*, London, 1971, pp. 110-116. An extensive bibliography of Maimonides's medical writings.

LATHAM, J.D., "Isaac Israeli's Kittab al Hummayat and the Latin and Castilian texts," *Journal of Semitic Studies*, 14 (1969), pp. 80-95.

MACKINNEY, L.C., *Early Medieval Medicine with Special Reference to France and Chatres*, Baltimore, 1937.

NEUMAN, A.A., *The Jews in Spain: Their Social, Political, Cultural Life during the Middle Ages*, Philadelphia, 1942, Vol. II.

ROTH, N., "Jewish collaborators in Alfonso's Scientific Work," in R. Burns, ed., *Emperor of Culture, Alfonso X the Learned of Castille and his Thirteenth Century Renaissance*, Philadelphia, 1990, pp. 59-71

SIRAISI, N., *Avicenna in Renaissance Italy. The Canon Medical Teaching in Italian Universities after 1500*, Princeton, 1978.

AARON J. FEINGOLD

THE MARRIAGE OF SCIENCE AND ETHICS: THREE JEWISH PHYSICIANS OF THE RENAISSANCE

The life, works and ethics of the three physicians chosen for this essay were characterized by their deep commitment to the development of medical knowledge, but only insofar as it accorded with the dictates of ethical introspection. Amatus Lusitanus, Jacob Zahalon and Abraham Zacuto all lived lives which were complicated by persecution directly related to their Judaism. Judaism set them apart and reinforced their belief in medicine as a profession in which ethics and medical science were fundamentally interwoven. As will be shown, their concerns, rooted in the past, can help all of us face the future.

Jewish physician taking the oath on graduation.

Watercolor illustration from the Gradenigo Dolfin manuscript, Venice, c. 1750.

Museo Correr, Venice.

Amatus Lusitanus

The life, works and ethics of Amatus Lusitanus, according to the historian Solomon Grayzel, illustrate "the fate of the Jews and the part they continue to play in the diffusion of human knowledge." Cecil Roth, another historian, describes him as "the most distinguished physician of his age." Joao Rodrigues de Castelo Branco, who was later to be known as Amatus Lusitanus, was born in 1511 to Marrano parents in Portugal. He studied medicine in Spain at the University of Salamanca, receiving his degree in 1530. For a short period of time he practiced medicine in Lisbon and in 1533, when hostility towards Marrano physicians in Portugal significantly increased, he moved to Antwerp, in the religiously tolerant Netherlands, where he remained for seven years. There he established his reputation by treating many prominent citizens, including members of the family of the noted Marrano statesman, Joseph Nasi, and by publishing his first book, *Index*

Amatus Lusitanus (Joao Rodrigues de Castelo Branco), 1511-1568.

Anonymous woodcut, 1580.
Physician, one of the greatest Jewish figures in medical literature in the first half of the 16th century.
The Jewish National and University Library, Jerusalem.

Dioscorides (1536), on medicinal botany. His fame spread as a scientist, and in 1540 the Duke of Ferrara, Ercole II d'Este, who supported and encouraged scientific research, appointed him lecturer in medicine at the University of Ferrara. In Ferrara, Amatus taught and worked with the famous anatomist Canano, dissecting corpses. In 1547 Amatus left Ferrara and moved to Ancona where he openly professed his Judaism and, in 1549, published his first *centuria*, a collection of 100 medical case histories, their treatment and results. In 1553 Amatus published *In Dioscoridis enarrationes*, a commentary on Dioscorides's work, in which he notes several mistakes in Matthioli's commentary on Dioscorides. Matthioli was a famous botanist and the influential court physician in Vienna. In 1555 when Pope Paul IV was elected, new decrees against Marranos were published in the Papal Provinces and Marrano physicians were forbidden to treat Christian patients. Amatus's home was looted together with his library and manuscripts. It is believed that Matthioli was largely responsible for this, judging from what he wrote in his *Apologia*, in response to Amatus's criticism:

Salamanca University School of Medicine, Spain.

Alfonso X (1252-1284) founded academies and schools of philosophy and literature which attracted and employed Muslims and Jews. At this time the first universities were founded, but there are no Jewish names among the founders. Salamanca appears to have been the favorite university of the Spanish and Portuguese conversos. The following note contained in Regimento dos Medicos Baticarios Christaos Velhos published at Lisbon in 1604 is significant for the period. "All members of the Jewish race, New Christians (Jews who had been converted and their descendants) and Moors should be excluded from studying or practicing medicine..."

National Library of Medicine, Bethesda.

Holy Saints Hospital, Lisbon, 16th

century.

Panel of blue tiles, early 18th century.

Municipal Museum, Lisbon.

Title page of *Index Dioscorides* by

Amatus Lusitanus, Venice, 1553.

The Jewish National and University

Library, Jerusalem.

For as you now pretend to adhere to our faith (so I learn), and then give yourself over to Jewish laws and superstitions and thus insult not only your fellow beings, but also God, the Almighty, it is not to be wondered at that you are false even to yourself and are losing your mind. Just as there is no faith and no religion within you, so in truth you are completely blind as to medical art which you unworthily profess. That explains to my view that you are not only a burden and an object of disgust to yourself alone but to others; and that driven by wild furies you have brought it about that you neither enlighten others nor yourself in medical science, just as you are blind in your heresy to divine truth.

Thus, according to one of the most prominent physicians of the time, Amatus was unable to see truth in medical science because he was a Jew.

Forced to flee Ancona, Amatus reached Pesaro, and in 1556 when the Inquisition reached that city he fled to Ragusa. There he lived for three years completing his *Centuria VI*. In 1558 Amatus moved to Salonica where many Jews and Marranos lived openly under the protection of the Sultan, and in 1559 he completed his seventh and last *centuria*. In the seven *centuriae* composed between 1549 and 1559, one of which was dedicated to Joseph Nasi and others to high church officials, Amatus discoursed on 700 medical cases and, inter alia, on anatomy, internal medicine, dermatology and mental illness.

Amatus was a learned physician, a brilliant clinician and an independent investigator. He did pioneer work in pathological anatomy and medical botany. From the point of view of Jewish history Amatus's life exemplifies the internal struggle and emotional burden to which Marranos were subjected. Despite the necessity of concealing his origins, he emphasized in his books, long before his open return to Judaism, his attachment to Jewish values. In one of his *centuriae*, he quotes the opinions of Maimonides, with no

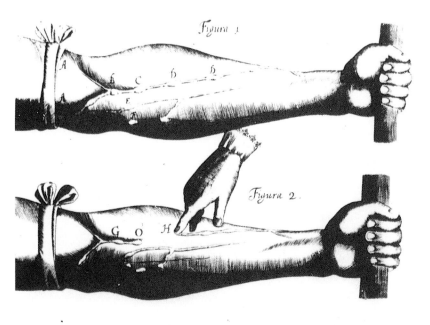

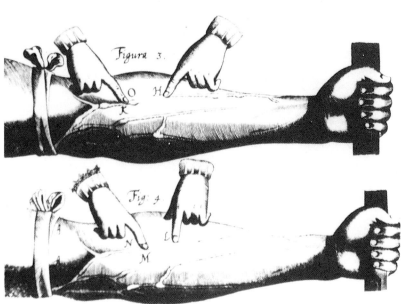

Woodcut from William Harvey's treatise.

London, 1628.

In 1603 William Harvey wrote: "The movement of the blood occurs constantly in a circular manner and is the result of the beating of the heart." However, this momentous insight which overthrew Galen's theory did not reach the outside world until 1628, when Harvey published his masterpiece Anatomical Treatise on the Movement of the Heart and Blood.

World Health Organization, Geneva.

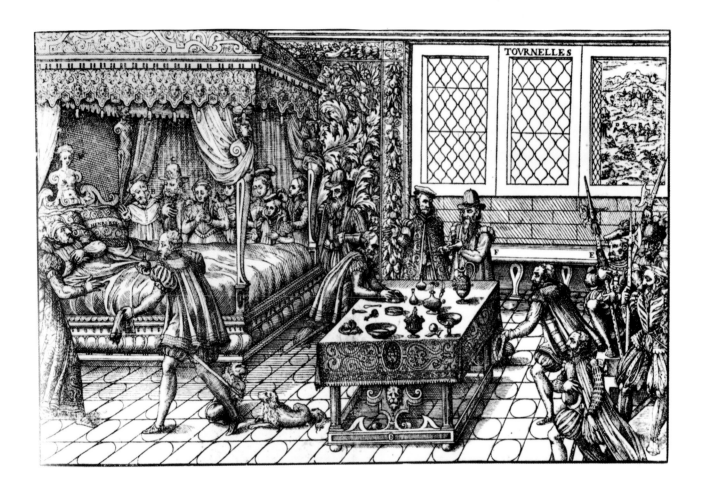

Andreas Vesalius and Ambroise Paré in attendance at the deathbed of Henri II.

Woodcut, c.1560.

Henry II named Paré a master surgeon on his merits despite a lack of academic credentials.

National Library of Medicine, Bethesda.

particular relevance to the context. In his description of the treatment of Azaria de Rossi, who was apparently suffering from a gastric ulcer, Amatus described the customs and eating habits of the Jews.

Amatus expresses the traditional concern of medieval Jewish physicians with medical ethics in the oath printed at the end of his sixth and seventh *centuriae*, which follows in abbreviated form:

I swear by God the Almighty and Eternal [and by his most holy Ten Commandments given on Mount Sinai by Moses the lawgiver after the people of Israel had been freed from the bondage of Egypt], that I have never in my medical practice departed from what has been handed down in good faith to us and posterity; that I have never practiced deception, I have never overstated or made changes for the sake of financial gain; I have not been desireful for the remuneration for medical services and have treated many without accepting any fee, but nonetheless with care. I have often unselfishly and firmly refused remuneration that was offered, preferring through diligent care to restore the patient to health, to being enriched by his generosity. [I have given my services in equal manner to all, to Hebrews, Christians and Muslims.] Loftiness of station has never influenced me and I have accorded the same care to the poor as to those of exalted rank. I have never produced disease. In stating my opinion, I have always told what I believed to be true. I have favored no druggist unless he excelled others in skill in his art and in character. In prescribing drugs I have exercised moderation guided by the physical condition of the invalid. I have never revealed a secret entrusted to me. I have never given a fatal draught. No woman has ever brought about an abortion with my aid. In short, I have done nothing which might be considered unbecoming an honorable and distinguished physician. I have been diligent and have allowed nothing to divert me from the study of good authors. The many students who have come to me have all been regarded as though they were my sons; I have used my best efforts to instruct them and to urge them to good conduct. I have published my medical works not to satisfy ambition, but that I might, in some measure, contribute to the furtherance of the health of mankind; I leave to others the judgment of whether I have succeeded; such at least has always been my aim and ever had the foremost place in my prayers.

The oath, written after his return to Judaism, is one of the most exalted literary documents in medical ethics. In the first part, Amatus strongly reaffirms his Jewish faith, dealing both with the ethical aspects and with the duties of the physician towards his patient. Amatus emphasizes the philanthropic aspect of the art of healing, differing in this from the professional materialism of the Hippocratic oath. The second part of the oath reaffirms the principles of the Hippocratic oath, that is, trying to be an excellent physician by giving the right treatment, and by being a diligent student and a good teacher. The oath ends by emphasizing the importance of medical research. It is believed that Amatus died in 1568 fighting the plague in Salonica.

A physician holding a clyster.

Painting.

Spain, 17th century.

The Louvre, Paris.

A page with Hebrew names for anatomical structures.

From De Humani Corporis Fabrica by Andreas Vesalius. Basel, 1543.

Vesalius gave Hebrew names together with Greek and Latin equivalents for the anatomical structures, thus emphasizing the importance of medieval Hebrew medical literature. Vesalius did not know Hebrew, but the information was furnished to him by a learned Jewish scholar, Lazaro de Frigeis (1514-1564). The Hebrew anatomical terms used are for the most part taken from the Hebrew translation of the Canon of Avicenna and in some cases directly from the Talmud.

Jewish National and University Library, Jerusalem.

Opposite:

Illustration from *De Humani Corporis Fabrica* by Andreas Vesalius.

Basel, 1543. Woodcut, anonymous, possibly Jan van Calcar (Flemish, c.1499-c.1550).

He was a pupil of Titian and did the illustrations for the anatomy books of Vesalius.

Jewish National and University Library, Jerusalem.

PRIMA
MVSCVLO,
RVM TA-
BVLA.

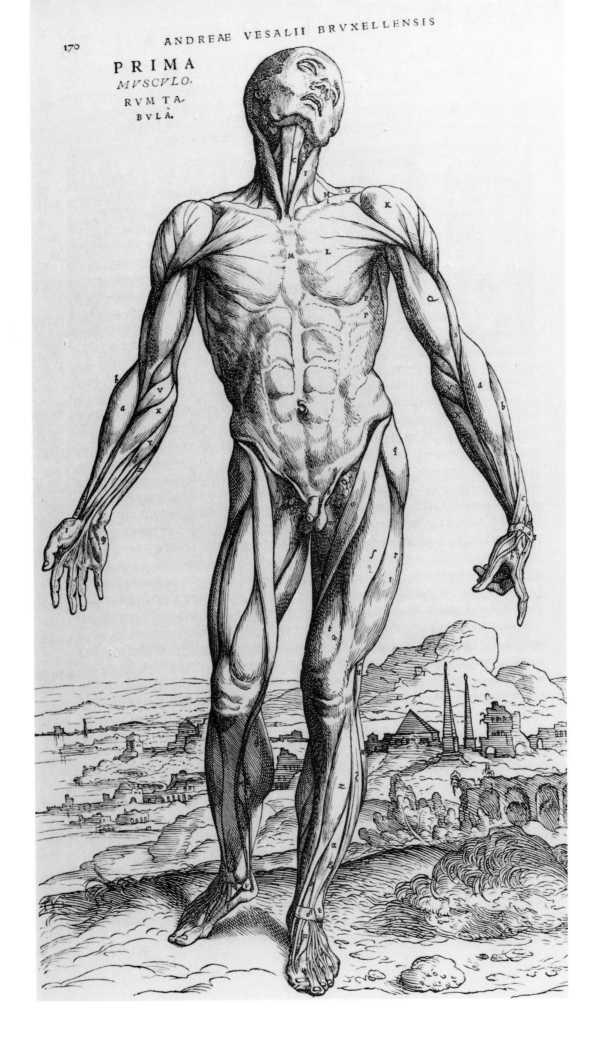

Jacob Ben Isaac Zahalon

Jacob ben Isaac Zahalon was born in Rome in 1630 to a family of distinguished rabbis and scholars, which settled in Italy after their expulsion from Spain. Jacob received a traditional education in Hebrew literature and a medical education at the University of Rome. He soon acquired a fine reputation both as physician and Talmudist in Ferrara, continuing the tradition of rabbi-physician. Zahalon was a prolific writer, best known for his *Otzar ha-chayyim* [The treasure of life], published in Venice in 1683 as the third part of a larger work, *Otzar ha-chochmot* [The treasure of wisdom]. The book is encyclopedic in character, including the accepted cures of the day, and Zahalon felt that it could serve as a manual:

In some towns there are no physicians, but there is a scholar who is able to understand and to study closely and to seek cures for the sick in this book.... I have only given the most proper, accepted and well tried method of cure.

The book is divided into thirteen parts beginning with general hygiene and ending with mental disease, covering practically every branch of medicine. A recent publication describes Zahalon's recognition of ailments with other than somatic origins:

His discussion of the treatment of "love-sickness" sounds like modern psychoanalytic literature: "This disease is recognized by the sinking of the eyes, and weeping-like voice without tears. The patient's lids droop and are shaky, and his pulse is rapid, like one who is troubled a great deal. His mental state is changed, although he appears well otherwise." As for treatment, it varies as follows: (1) to obtain the desired object; (2) to let him think of some fault of his sweetheart; (3) let him indulge in other, higher interests; (4) let him change his place of residence and go to a large city where they will not meet; (5) bloodletting as a last resort.

His first suggestion is obvious; his second we now call rationalization; and his third sublimation.

His description of the plague is of particular interest.

In 5416 (1656), a disease called morbilli [measles, ed.] broke out among the children; most of them died. Afterwards adults became ill with blotches called petechiae, and in three days they were dead. It appeared three months earlier

Cavalry following Lorenzo the Magnificent down the Hill at Fiesole. Among the riders is Elijah Delmedigo (first row, third on the left). Painting by B. Gozzoli.

Elijah Delmedigo (1460-1497), the great Jewish philosopher and physician, lectured on philosophy, teaching successively (but not in official positions) at Padua, Florence, Venice and Perugia. Among his students was the eminent scholar Pico della Mirandola, who became his friend and protector. Palazzo Medici Riccardi, Florence.

ISOLA DI S·BARTOLOMEO   LA

Città. 3. S. Bartol.º 4. Lazzar. p l'huomini. 5. Lazzar.º delle Donne. 6. Lazzar.º de Nobili. 7. Conuento de Zoccolan
brutta cõ li morti. 12. Barca netta. 13. Barca cõ li morti de Giudei. 14. barca netta de Giudei. 15. Carrozze, Carre.

among the Gentiles than among the Jews. It also came to an end earlier among the Gentiles. The Jews were forbidden to leave the Ghetto and enter the city, as was their custom. Two officers were sent to the Ghetto to prepare a suitable "Lazaretto," where the sick could be placed so that they were separated from the healthy and thus prevent the spread of the epidemic.

This was the procedure. The Jewish physician visited the sick and if he saw any sign of the disease, a black "carbuncle" or a bubo in the groin with fever or other serious symptoms, especially if the tongue was white as snow, he would call the Gentile physician to examine the patient, the latter would order that they take the patient and his bed to the Lazaretto to Samuel Gabbai [a physician, ed.], or the patient might remain home and be treated there.

When the physician visited the sick it was customary that he take in his hand a large torch of tar, burning it night and day to purify the air for his protection [it acted as an insect repellent, ed.], and in his mouth he had theriac [an antidote to poison, ed.]. In the nine months during which this epidemic lasted, there died, both young and old, about 800; among them a young scholar, expert in the science of surgery, Isaac Zahalon, my father's brother's son of blessed memory. They brought the dead to the river in small boats and carried the bodies to the cemetery outside the city to a place called Piano dei Devisori. Since the people were not able to go to synagogue, on Sabbath Toledoth (Kislev 2, 5417), I, Jacob Zahalon, preached in Catalen Street, from the window in the corner house of David Catigno, to the people (may God preserve them!), standing in the street. At another time I preached in Toscana Street, from the window of the house of Judah Catigno (of blessed memory), to the people standing in the street to listen to the sermon. In other streets scholars would preach from the windows of their houses.

After nine months, the Holy One (blessed be He) remembered His people because of the merit of their forefathers, and the diseases came to an end.

In the introduction to his book Zahalon stresses the ethical side of medical practice, giving practical advice to physicians by enumerating the seventy-seven aphorisms of medical conduct published by Zacutus Lusitanus (Abraham Zacuto, see below). His main ethical work, however, the "Physician's Prayer" is contained in *Sefer Margaliyyot Tovot*, printed in Venice in 1665. From the prayer, it is clear that Zahalon looked upon medicine as a sacred calling. The physician is merely God's servant on earth, put there to help his fellowmen. Zahalon's prayer attempts to show God's presence in all medical therapy and research. The physician merely treats and God cures. Thus he prays to God to enable him to know the peculiar curative powers that he placed in "herbs and minerals, in seeds and flowers, in living organisms." While Zahalon's prayer also deals with the humanistic ethical issues his anxieties and concerns are as relevant today as they were in his day. He prays for "knowledge and insight" and for the "family not to accuse and suspect me of being the cause of death."

Physician during the plague.

Colored engraving, 1725.

A distinctive outfit with sweet smelling substances carried in the "beak" to combat contagion developed to protect against the plague during the Middle Ages.

The Wellcome Institute Library, London.

Abraham Zacuto

Abraham Zacuto was the central figure among Jewish doctors in the 17th century just as Amatus was in the 16th century. His life story, like that of Amatus Lusitanus or Judah Abravanel, is another example of a brilliant ethical thinker, working and writing against a background of exile and despair. Abraham Zacuto, who was born in 1576 to a Marrano family in Lisbon, was the great-grandson of Abraham Zacuto, the renowned astronomer and physician, inventor of the astrolabe and the inspiration for Vasco da Gama and, perhaps, for Columbus. He studied medicine in Salamanca and Coimbra, returned to Lisbon and practiced medicine there for thirty years. In 1624 Zacuto fled to Amsterdam and joined the Jewish community. While in Lisbon he did not publish a single book, whereas in Amsterdam he became an

Zacutus Lusitanus (Abraham Zacuto, 1575-1642).

Engraving by S. Saveri, 1634.
A leading figure among the Jewish doctors of the 17th century.
Jewish National and University Library, Jerusalem.

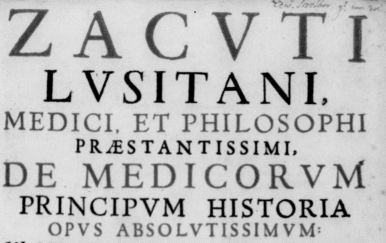

Opera omnia by Zacutus Lusitanus, 1642.

Jewish National and University

Library, Jerusalem.

Dr. Ephraim Bueno.

Rembrandt, c.1647.

Oil on wood, 19 x 15 cm.

Ephraim Bueno was born in Portugal. Like his father, he was qualified as a doctor of medicine at the University of Bordeaux. In 1624 Ephraim came to Amsterdam, where he practiced medicine, and was also involved in poetic work. In 1636 he wrote a sonnet, praising Menasseh ben Israel. In 1656 Bueno founded together with Abraham Pereira a scientific society Or Tora. Bueno died in 1665 in Amsterdam, and was buried at the Jewish cemetery Ouderkerk.

Rijksmuseum, Amsterdam.

extremely prolific writer. Zacuto was the author of the extremely popular *De Medicorum Principum Historia* (twelve volumes). His other publications were also of significance and popular in his time. His most important essays were collected in *Opera Omnia* (two volumes) and published after his death (in the 1640s) at Lyon. This remarkable work went through five editions and was extensively quoted by medical authors for many years. Although the work was written in Latin and addressed to a Christian audience, in the introduction he emphasizes his Jewish origin:

If my style will seem to you unpolished, do not be astonished for I am a Jew and a stranger who fled from Portugal and my beloved and most lovely birthplace, Lisbon, tossed about hither and thither by severe misfortune and the storms of a long life. I have allowed no day to pass without writing a line in which I showed my love for the Republic of Medicine.

Zacuto was true to the spirit of the Renaissance. He was a good physician and

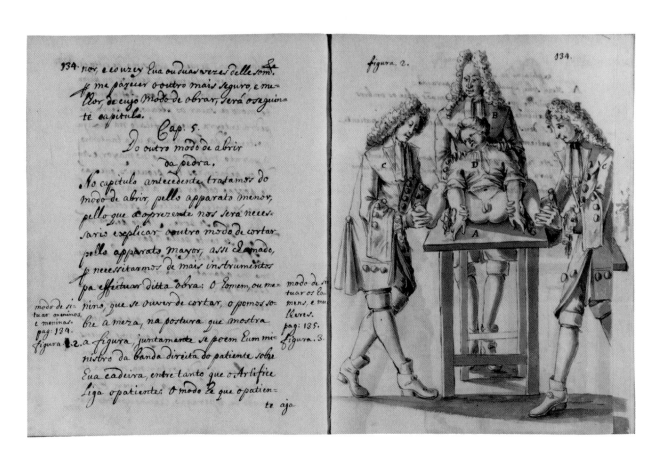

Libello aurio da difficulta de ourinar, by

Samuel de Lion Benavente.

Amsterdam, 1699.

Autographed manuscript.

Benavente (1643-1722) was a

distinguished surgeon from Amsterdam,

who called himself "stone-cutter." He

considered his own method for the

removal of kidney stones successful

enough to publish it. The illustrations

were done by the author himself.

Jewish National and University

Library, Jerusalem.

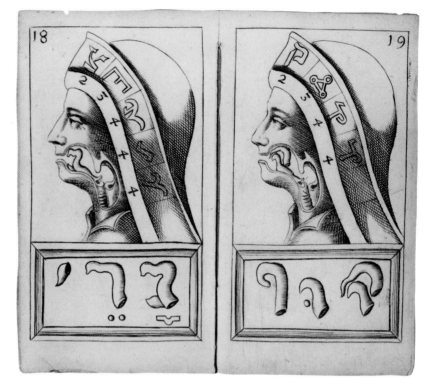

Alphabeti vere naturalis hebraici brevissima delineation.

Phonological treatise by Franciscus Mercurius van Helmont, 1667. With instructive copper engravings by F. Franck Sulzbach.

The itinerant Dutch physician and philosopher, Mercurius Van Helmont, adhered to the idea that Hebrew was the natural language of mankind. This treatise contains the theory underlying his logotherapeutical work for the deaf and dumb. The plates show the labial, guttural and laryngeal positions of the Hebrew "letters." His monad theory shows a remarkable resemblance to that of the contemporary German philosopher Leibniz.

Jewish National and University Library, Jerusalem.

humanist. In his *De Medicorum Principum Historia*, he outlined eighty aphorisms of medical conduct and his code of medical ethics is still valuable today. To give just a few examples:

He shall not be envious.

He shall possess few and good medical reference books.

He shall cultivate the habit of discussing and consulting about his patients with other physicians.

He shall not take upon himself to cure those who are beyond his skill.

In dispensing medication let him start with milder ones.

Let him always help nature, for that is the primary factor in health.

The life, work and ethics of the three physicians chosen for this essay express certain universal and inspirational truths for physicians for all times. Their experiences, travels and moral commitments transcend and epitomize the Jewish Diaspora experience. Even when faced with persecution, adversity and oppression, as demonstrated by these three figures, we see that Jewish physicians were able to elevate mankind and the Jewish people to superior levels of moral and ethical scientific thinking.

~

BIBLIOGRAPHY

Encyclopedia Judaica, Jerusalem, Keter Publishing House, 1972, vol. 1, p. 797; vol. 16, p. 919.

FRIEDENWALD, HARRY, M.D., *The Jews and Medicine*, Essays, Baltimore, Johns Hopkins University Press, 1944, p. 340.

GRAYZEL SOLOMON, *A History of the Jews*, Philadelphia, Jewish Publication Society of America, 1969.

LEVINSON, ABRAHAM, M.D., "Jewish Physicians of the Middle Ages," *Medical Leaves*, 1937, pp. 101-113.

ROTH, CECIL, *Dona Gracia of the House of Nasi*, Philadelphia, Jewish Publication Society of America, 1977.

SACHAR, HOWARD M., *Farewell Espana, The World of Sephardim Remembered*, New York, Alfred A. Knopf, 1994.

SAVITZ, HARRY A. M.D., *Profiles of Erudite Jewish Physicians and Scholars*, Chicago, Spertus College of Judaica Press, 1973.

LUSITANUS, AMATUS, *Centuria VI*, Venice, Valgrisius, 1560; translation in Friedenwald, *The Jews and Medicine*.

MATTHIOLI, *Apologia*, 1558, translation in Friedenwald, *The Jews and Medicine*.

ZACUTUS, ABRAHAM, *Opera Omnia*, 1642, translated in Friedenwald, *The Jews and Medicine*.

ZAHALON, JACOB, *Otzar ha-chayyim*, Venice, 1683, translations in Friedenwald, *The Jews and Medicine*, and Savitz, *Profiles*.

ZAHALON, JACOB, *Sepher Margaliyyot Tobot*, Venice, 1665; translation in Savitz, *Profiles*.

JEWISH FOLK MEDICINE IN THE 19TH AND 20TH CENTURIES

Amulet.

Micrography.

Germany, 1863.

Printed on paper, 27 x 21.5 cm.

William Gross Family Collection,

Tel Aviv.

Folk medicine as a system for the preservation of health has existed all over the world from time immemorial. Its methods of healing and treatment and the ways in which it uses the materials at its disposal change with changes in living conditions. At the same time it has always maintained reciprocal relations with other health systems.[1] Folk medicine is holistic in its approach, concerned not only with the physical and mental health of the people, but with their general well-being: home and family, the state of their property, livelihood and security, and their relations with their immediate environment.

Folk medicine is generally considered to have two essential components: the natural-rational, in that it uses remedies derived from natural substances; and the religious-magical, in that it believes in the existence of good and evil forces between which a balance must be kept. To this end it employs incantations, prayers, amulets, etc., often in conjunction with natural remedies, in order to strengthen their effectiveness.

The approach of folk medicine is both direct and indirect. Direct treatment is designed to cure the symptoms of disease and distress, while indirect treatment is designed to protect the patient and his environment and ward off bad luck. Home healing has traditionally been transmitted as the legacy of the community as a whole. While its main practitioners are women, the magic ceremonials are carried out by trained men, who act as mediators between human and supernatural forces. Folk medicine continues to exist because of the effectiveness of ancient techniques and the knowledge imparted by them of the use of simple and natural remedies.

Foundations of Research

The foundations for research into folk medicine were laid in the middle of the 19th century as part of the research on the development of society and folk culture. After observing the customs of healing among the peasant cultures of Europe and among remote tribal communities, and studying texts, such as the Bible and ancient mythologies, scholars were able to distinguish the components of the healing system within religion, magic and science. W.H. Rivers (1864-1922) proposed that a distinction be made between magical, religious and medical acts: at the center of religious acts was the belief in the

Amulet for a child's bed.

Persia, 18th-19th century.

Silver, engraved, 8 x 7.5 cm.

Yitzhak Einhorn Collection, Tel Aviv.

existence of a great and powerful outside force; magical acts depended on utilizing the powers inherent in man; while in medicine man based his acts on accepted social practices.[2]

Since the 1950s research has expanded to the western countries and the cardinal importance of the cultural component has resulted in developing areas of study in which the ethnic element is common to them all: ethnobotany, ethnopharmacology, ethnopsychiatry, and others.

Research into Jewish Folk Medicine

Research into Jewish folk medicine runs parallel to the general research on the subject. Two main trends are evident in studies written between the end of the

Amulet.

Gibraltar, 19th century.

Silver, cast and engraved, 7.1 x 4.6 cm.

In the center a large letter ה and the

word שדי above (the names of God).

William Gross Family Collection,

Tel Aviv.

19th century and the middle of the 20th century: members of the medical and rabbinical establishments saw folk medicine as part of ancient culture; scholars of folk culture and philologists considered traditional Jewish folk customs and beliefs the residue of a culture passed down from ancient times through language and from remote places through immigration.

The physical dispersion of the People of Israel precluded any comprehensive conclusions in these studies. The most common approach was the view of folk medicine as "idol worship" or "foreign" superstition, a result of the fact that as a national minority, the Jews were influenced by the customs of the countries in which they lived.

These trends persisted into the 1950s and 1960s as well. Groups of immigrants reaching Israel from the far ends of the earth were observed and the ways in which they dealt with problems of sickness and health were assessed according to the standards of conventional medicine. On the one hand, their folk customs and beliefs were considered "exotic," compared to general Jewish historical and cultural sources.[3] On the other, their system of traditional medicine was considered by members of the medical and Halakhic establishments as "irrational", "primitive", and "oriental", something to be done away with.[4]

This meeting of cultures, however, awakened the curiosity of scholars as to the historical sources of the esoteric facet of folk medicine in Judaism. Scholars like Trachtenberg, Schrire, Bergman and Zimmels, who made in-depth studies of magical systems and the belief in amulets and incantations, also saw them as remnants of ancient times.[5]

In field studies undertaken during this period (by the School of Pharmacology of the Hebrew University, among others) in order to study the uses of natural

---

Amulet inscribed with the name Sarah Varda daughter of ha-Meyl, including the names of God and inscribed invocations of Tetragrammaton and angels.

Jerusalem c.1900.

Silver, engraved, 9.2 x 9.2 cm.

William Gross Family Collection, Tel Aviv

remedies among Israel's various ethnic communities, an apologetic tone prevails throughout regarding the use of substances which were considered "shameful," "born out of ignorance," and incompatible with the laws of purity and observation of the *mitzvot.*

Scientific interest in folk culture and, particularly, folk medicine, began in Israel, as in the rest of the world, in the 1970s. Studies touched on a variety of subjects: the natural components of medicinal plants used in folk remedies, the artistic impulse given expression in various customs (amulets, magical ceremonies, etc.); the world of beliefs and subliminal fears; the struggle against agents of distress (the evil eye and demons); folk healers' methods of treatment, and the relations between folk healers and their patients.[6]

During this period there were two major directions in Israeli research: understanding the components of the various folk cultures in order to facilitate the cultural integration of the ethnic communities; and collecting and preserving as much information as possible about them before they disappeared. An analysis of the data pointed to a strong resemblance in the healing materials and methods used by Jewish communities from different parts of the world, even though there had been no contact between them. It was discovered that beliefs and practices which had originally been defined as "oriental" were prevalent in "Western" systems of folk medicine as well: They were common attempts to deal with day-to-day stress and the afflictions of ordinary life.

Since the 1980s, in the wake of the shakeup in Israeli politics and the ascent to power of social groups which had previously been marginal, society became more open to diversity, and studies into folk culture acquired greater legitimation. Both biomedical and ethnomedical research point to the advantages of integrating the methods and the materials of conventional and folk medicine in treating patients, as well as the importance of folk heritage, Western and oriental, in rehabilitation therapy.[7]

Historical research which combines new interdisciplinary knowledge with the decipherment of old documents has revealed the presence of folk healing methods such as amulets, incantations and alchemy among the Jews of former

Amulet for guarding against all forms of the evil eye, including Lilith and all other demons.

Persia, 19th century.

Paper, pen and ink, watercolor on paper. 35 x 22 cm.

Yitzhak Einhorn Collection,

Tel Aviv.

times. Moreover, it has underscored the fact that Jews were considered the bearers and disseminators of this tradition down through the ages.[8]

It would appear that the world of folk medicine among Jews at all times, and in Israel today, bears a strong resemblance in all its aspects to folk medicine in other parts of the world. It is only natural that it should contain elements which are both universal and particular, and theories both old and relatively new. The complexity of the elements employed in daily practice was amassed from the experience of ancient cultures which left their mark on life in this country and on the traditions of the ethnic communities which settled here after the establishment of the State of Israel.

What is Jewish Folk Medicine?*

Jewish folk medicine is distinguished by the cultural distinctiveness which characterizes the complex of beliefs and customs traditionally practiced by the Jews in this area. This distinctiveness is rooted in the Hebrew language, in Written and Oral Law, and in Jewish symbolism.

The Hebrew language has been the most important bridge between the Jew and his cultural heritage throughout the ages. In folk medicine this link acquires a significant historical and cosmological dimension: the letters of the alphabet connect the Creation to the names of God. They possess an arcane magical force and are often written on amulets as well as on bowls or on pieces of paper: when the latter are submerged in water and the letters washed away, the water becomes a potent healing potion. The letters of a person's name play a role in deciding his fate: his name is given to him when he enters the Jewish world and remains with him all his life, serving as a social and cosmological

---

This information is based on ethnographic data from articles on the subject which have appeared since the 1950s, and on my own and others' field work and research since the 1970s within the framework of the Center for Folklore Studies and the Unit for Folklore Studies at the Hebrew University of Jerusalem. I have also used relevant newspaper articles and items.

Child's Amulet.

Pendant inscribed with two large letters
א ה (the names of God).
Galicia, 18th–19th centuries.
Silver, engraved, 4.2 x 3.6 cm.
William Gross Family Collection,
Tel Aviv.

identity card. During therapy, the healer-diagnostician calls out his name and the name of his mother; then through numerological calculations and the addition of his birth date, he assembles the suitable remedy. The number of letters in his name determines the amount of charity that the patient has to donate in order to assure recuperation. Sometimes, in order to stave off bad luck, it is necessary to change the patient's name – to Chaim (life) or Yechye (he will live), especially if his disease is fatal. The name "Alter," which means old man, may be added to the name of a child in order to confuse the Angel of Death. Because of the sacredness of the letters, their numerical equivalents are used as in magic squares or for the names of God which it is forbidden to pronounce.

Double entendre is also employed in folk medicine. For example, the biblical verse [Genesis 49:22], "Joseph is a fruitful bough, a fruitful bough by a spring," protects a child from the evil eye because the word for "spring" also means "eye". For this reason it is inscribed on amulets. The root of the Hebrew word for medicine, *r-f-a*, is linked to *refael* and also to *refaim*, the world of spirits, indicating the duality of medicine, which is derived from and unites the world of nature with the "other world".

Prayers for the wellbeing of the patient, verses which have the power to placate evil spirits and subdue enemies, or relieve stress, have been chosen from a large corpus: the Bible, the Midrash, the Zohar and the Prayerbook. Other methods used to help the patient, in addition to conventional remedies include: recalling specific events and chanting verses associated with them, appealing for help to characters who have been miraculously saved, or who are especially beloved of God, or making a pilgrimage to the traditional graves of ancient heroes.

According to folk tradition, there are passages in the Torah which, in certain combinations, can ward off disease and danger, save life and cure the sick. The combinations are derived from the first or last letters of the words of a verse or the entire verse read either in its proper order, or by interchanging the order of the letters. For example, the Hebrew letters beginning each word of the fifth verse of Psalm 91 ("You will not fear the terror of the night"), *lamed,*

Incantation bowl.

Terra Cotta.

Babylonia c.7th century,

H 7.3, D 1.7 cm.

This is the figure of the demon who

appears in dreams and in images.

The text is in Aramaic and Hebrew

and is for the guarding of households

and for healing from heaven.

William Gross Family Collection,

Tel Aviv.

taf, *mem*, *lamed* were inscribed on amulets and chanted to ward off nocturnal emission. The first letters of other verses were similarly used against miscarriage and for the protection of children. The last letters of the first five verses of Genesis or the first letters of "I am who I am" (Exodus 3:14) were inscribed by healers as substitutes for the name of God for use in relation to "supernatural worlds".[9]

The Book of Psalms provided talismans for certain contingencies. The most famous are Psalm 67, written in the form of a seven-branched candelabra, and Psalm 91, using either the first or last letters, both for general protection; Psalm 121 is used especially for the protection of women after childbirth. In general the Book of Psalms as a whole was considered especially powerful

against danger and was carried around in a pocket or placed under the pillow or mattress. According to a well known tradition from the Middle Ages every chapter contains a secret message for practical ends.[10]

Time, place and Jewish symbols fulfilled an important role in the success of the healing process. The very connection of various materials to the cycles of life and the Jewish year endowed them with sacredness and, by their very nature, utility for health purposes. A special potion for the entire year was prepared in the Old City of Jerusalem on the eve of Tisha b'Av. Brought from Egypt and known as "the dream potion," it was made from a blue stone and small cucumbers and used for salves and elixirs. Just before Passover, bleeding was practiced in order to welcome the Spring with clean blood and a pure body.

Amulet for general protection against Lilith including texts from Psalms, with names of God and his angels. There is a separate amulet for males and females.

Printed on paper, 22 x 36 cm.

Germany, 18th century.

William Gross Family Collection,

Tel Aviv

This page and opposite:

Child's Amulet.

Central Europe, 18th century.

Lead, cast, D 37.5 cm.

Round medallion with beaded border.

In center, larger letter ה (the name of

God), floral motif within.

William Gross Family Collection,

Tel Aviv.

A piece of the *afikoman* was considered a charm against trouble in general and long-distance traveling in particular, with special reference to seasickness and stormy seas. The salt used in counting the days between Passover and Pentecost was also a charm for a good journey. Herbs used at the conclusion of the Sabbath (*Havdalah*) service could be used as inhalation against colds, a brew against diarrhea, high blood pressure, balding, thieving and pestilence during the week. If one drank water from a glass which had been placed under Elijah's chair during the circumcision ceremony, one was assured of pregnancy and the birth of a son. Eating the foreskin of an infant after circumcision or an egg from a wedding feast produced the same result. Longevity could be assured by lighting an oil lamp made from new oil at the grave of King David on Mount Zion, praying and whispering the name of the petitioner. In order to turn a nightmare into a pleasant dream one had to go up to a mezuzah and ask for salvation in the name of Joseph the *Zaddik*.

The Jewish Folk Healer

The necessary traits of a folk healer in Judaism are three: he must be learned in the Torah, possess knowledge of arcane matters, and have ancestral merits. According to tradition, a person dealing with holy names or using books to discover the fate of a patient, or praying for his life and placating evil spirits, must be at least forty years old, must observe fasts and the laws of purity, refrain from sexual intercourse, and wear white while performing his duties. They are also supposed to be Scripture copyists. Many of them, even though they are aware of these traditional injunctions, acknowledge that they do not conduct themselves according to them.

In addition to being learned in the Torah, a dignitary and preacher, Jewish healers have always been famous for their expertise in medicinal plants, fractures and sprains, cupping, exorcizing the evil eye, curing throat infections and dealing with problems of childbirth. Other members of the community also contributed their skills. The barber was expected to bleed with leeches which he bred in a glass jar on the window sill of his shop. The shepherd who tended his sheep and was familiar with everything that grew in the meadow was expected to be versed in the healing of human bone fractures. The midwife was called in for problems resulting from miscarriage, inability to conceive, sexual dysfunction, hemorrhage and, of course, infant care.

In matters requiring first aid or a common ailment, it was customary to call upon neighbors or community elders before going to a doctor and it wasn't important if they were Jewish or not. Conversely, the Yemenite *mori* (healer and scholar), the East European *feldscher* (medic), the Iraqi chacham (sage), etc., also treated non-Jewish patients.

Folk Healers in Israel

Many folk healers reached Israel during the 1950s. Some of them continued their traditional practice, others abandoned it for personal or social reasons because they were not familiar with the local materials. Folk healers are accepted practitioners in Israel even today. Most of them "emerged" in small, outlying places, remote from the center of the country. They work, for the most, in their own villages or townships although there are some who come to larger towns, where they maintain regular office hours for the large clientele that await them. Notable among them are the "Baigelmacher," who treats backaches and stiff necks, and the recently deceased "fingernail Zvi," who made his diagnosis by examining a person's fingernails.

The need for physical contact with the healer and/or anything associated with him or his name for purposes of encouragement or the solution of a medical problem led to the manufacture of holy relics. The possessions of the healer may be passed from hand to hand and worn, as in the case of the robe of the sainted Baba Sali, pictures of whom are sold in shops all over Israel. Such contact may be achieved through his disciples, or by seeing him in a dream.

People who turn to folk healers in Israel today come from all walks of life, regardless of age, class and ethnic origin. Most have been disappointed with conventional medicine, and even if the folk healer is unable to cure them completely, they usually find the experience satisfying. The folk healer serves them, as a mediator with the supernatural world. Because of his innate or acquired talents, he is acquainted with the existence of other "worlds" whose influences can be tamed by his powerful intuition and the use of age-old instruments.

Books of charms and remedies are considered by some healers to be among the most important of their traditional instruments. These books, which are still being published in new editions today, have been known in Hebrew publishing from the beginning of the 18th century. They were most widely disseminated in the 19th century in Europe. They contain advice about life in general and individual health in particular. They are full of incantations, oaths and prayers, combinations of biblical verses, stories of miracles – together with quotations from books of ancient medical lore and magic formulae. On the one hand, they are quite similar to books in this tradition belonging to other European cultures. On the other, their distinctive Jewish elements are evident. The printed formulae for remedies are given in great detail with regard to preparation, quantities, the utensils to be used, the time, place, etc.

Amulet for general protection against the evil eye. Promoting success, a good livelihood, and good health. Inscribed with the names of God and the Cohen blessing and with the photographs of the Rabbi of Lubawitz and Baba Sali.
Printed in Bnei Beraq, 1985.
Paper, 10 x 14 cm.
Hagit Matras, Jerusalem.

The titles of some of the books are the names of angels or of lost texts. Handwritten books reached Israel together with healers from various countries, written in the language of the country and in Hebrew. They were copied from known works in the field, both printed and handwritten, and every healer added his own experience to the manual in his possession. Most healers used more than one book and the most widely used today are: *Health and Life*, *The Sight of Children*, and *The Book of Charms of Israel*. Both healers and patients consider these books holy texts which confer status on their owners. In recent years the number of such books being published has grown. Changes in the format or additions to the contents point to a change in the target clientele and their standard of living.[11] Some of

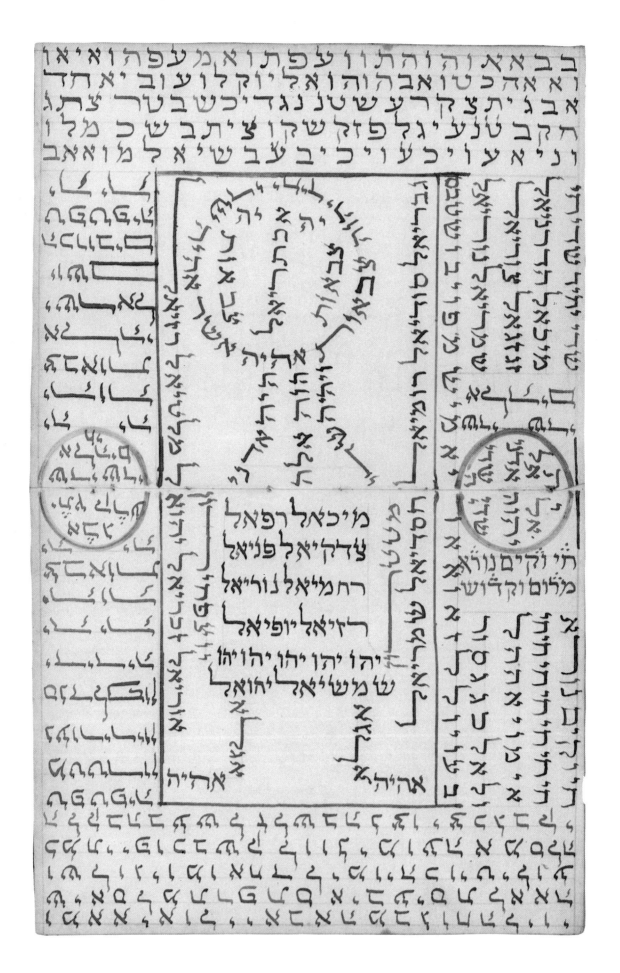

the books are more elegantly printed, with hard covers and numerous illustrations. Others are printed in pocket-sized editions and used as amulets.

"Jewish" Illnesses

In the folk jargon of community elders living in Israel today the names of certain diseases are preserved in their original languages. A few examples will suffice. Among the Iraqi Jews is the "monthly disease", a fever and malaise which attacks every month or so and is treated by letting blood from behind the ears or from the back. Among the Jews of Morocco the "*takaf*" leads to sterility in men and women and is assumed to be caused by witchcraft. Among the Jews of Eastern Europe, and not only there, there is the fear of the "changing of children", an infant's disease characterized by unexplained crying and caused by the substitution of a demon child for the original. The Persian Jews distinguish between "hot and cold diseases", assumed to have been derived from the ancient physiological concept of the four bodily humors.[12]

These names, however, are only "local" appellations for universal illnesses. The "binding of the bride or groom" – a name for problems of sexual behavior at the beginning of marriage – is known in every culture, as are physical and mental symptoms considered to be caused by demons or "the spirit of a dead man in the body of the living". In general, symptoms such as fever or change in color or moodiness are linked to the religious concepts of reward and punishment or to transgressions against the laws of purity. Road accidents, a bad fall, theft, a hemorrhage, stomach aches, hypertension and even headaches are assumed to be symptoms of bad luck, anger or revenge by human or supernatural forces. Certain acts are believed to be downright dangerous, among them, dumping unclean water, body waste or leftover foods outside the house, cursing or libeling people, thinking jealous or revengeful thoughts or, on the other hand, extolling and praising people. According to this way of thinking, bringing a menstruating woman into a house where there is an infant may cause German measles, panic which can

Pages from a practical Kabbalah of charms and remedies.
Holland(?), 18th-19th century.
Paper, 23.2 x 18.2 cm.
William Gross Family Collection,
Tel Aviv.

Amulet guarding against the evil eye, with names of angels, Magen David and text.

Italy, c.1800.

Pen and ink, watercolor on paper, 26 x 1.5 cm.

Yitzhak Einhorn Collection, Tel Aviv.

result in jaundice, or cancer which comes from "nerves". Headache, hiccoughs, fever, fainting, and inability to concentrate all come from the evil eye. In Jewish sources (Midrash, Vayikra Raba 8-15) the evil eye is responsible for 99 out of the 100 diseases on earth. Whether the evil eye is the disease itself or its cause, it is considered the most difficult to treat and can cause death.

The folk view that "he who doesn't believe in the evil eye doesn't believe in God" and the folk saying "he/she has the evil eye" (about someone who has been injured in some way or suffered some kind of setback), make it obligatory that steps be taken to ward it off. The evil eye is sometimes used to denote all sorts of hidden dangers. But it is used in particular to refer to the cause of someone's inability to fulfil the injunction "be fruitful and multiply". Sterility, the death of a child, the inability to remember what one has learned, various diseases and states of distress all may affect, directly or indirectly, the ability to fulfil this fundamental *mitzvah*. Jewish folk medicine proposes a number of options for overcoming these problems.

Jewish Folk Remedies

One may eat the foreskin of an infant after circumcision or the top of an etrog in order to assure the birth of a son.[13] Sitting on the point of a rock in the sea will assure pregnancy as will swallowing a live fish which has been found in the intestine of another fish, or warming the womb by inserting the womb of a rabbit wrapped in wool. To protect oneself from miscarriage one should tie a red string (from Rachel's tomb) around one's waist. These options are in keeping with Frazer's main laws of magic, similarity and contagion. Performing the act three times, counting to seven or one of its multiples, adding an incantation of prayer will all improve the efficacy of any of these remedies.[14]

Certain customs that were prevalant in Eastern Europe in the last century – such as curing jaundice by placing pigeons on the navel of the patient – have become common practice today in Israel among all sectors of the population.[15] Flocking to the graves of *zaddikim* and miracle workers – a custom which was practiced in North Africa and Iraq – has also become a common practice in Israel today, regardless of the ethnic origin of the person doing it. During the 1950s, representatives of the Israeli establishment forcibly removed amulets which new immigrants wore around their necks or carried in their pockets. Today they are in great demand. Many shops carry them not only as ornaments but also as charms to ensure a good livelihood. They can be found in maternity wards to prevent complications from childbirth and under the hospital mattresses of about one-half of all newborn infants - to ward off the evil eye. Many young people consider amulets part of their necessary personal gear when they join the army. The use of cupping glasses, the breeding of leeches, the sale of mumia (a kind of red substance) as a panacea against broken limbs and for general good health, and chewing or smoking the leaves of the *Gat* plant, have become accepted and legitimate practices as part of the modern healing world, although most of them were considered insufferable if not downright illegal until recent years.

Frequently the materials used in folk remedies do not conform to the laws of purity and the spirit of the Halakhah. Nevertheless, representatives of the rabbinical establishment, many of whom were themselves healers, dispensers of potions and composers of amulets, have always known how to resolve the

Amulet for the protection of mother and
baby. Inscribed with the blessings for
the circumcision and pidyon ha-ben
ceremonies. The spell against the evil
eye was written by Rabbi Hida.

Djerba, c.1925.

Printed on paper, 28.2 x 41.8 cm.

William Gross Family Collection,

Tel Aviv.

contradiction by alluding to *pikuach nefesh*, the saving of life. Since time immemorial Judaism has also accepted the idea of applying to non-Jewish healers for help, an idea which is not considered contrary to Jewish law.

Public Places

Public gathering places have always played a role in folk medicine. Prayers, donations to charity, appeals for help and contributions of food for the poor were acts associated in the distant past with the Holy of Holies. In Israel the Wailing Wall, synagogues and the tombs of the patriarchs and prophets were always centers for these practices, although only in recent years have they been used by a significant number of people. In countries where there were no historical gathering places, their places were taken by the graves of *zaddikim* or local heroes, some of whose bodies have been transported to Israel by their flocks. Others, long forgotten, have been "brought back to life". Some of these sainted rabbis were practitioners of folk medicine during their lives. Others have become effective healers only after their deaths.

Reasons for the Growth of Interest in Folk Medicine in Israel

It would seem that interest in this tradition today stems from its ability to serve as an alternative solution to individual problems. In Israel today people face considerable existential problems related to housing, livelihood, security, etc., deriving from the fact that Israel is an immigrant society. Its geographical location and political reality add to this. Furthermore, social and cultural difficulties increase personal insecurity, intensifying daily stress. Various activities help people relieve their anxiety over, for example, the fate of their sons or husbands serving in the army: taking vows, giving or attending charity benefits, wearing amulets, helping the poor, making pilgrimages to the graves of *zaddikim*, etc. Their anxieties are also lightened by receiving spiritual support in the form of talismans, an elixir or a tranquilizing potion from a rabbi who is considered a *zaddik*, or from a sage noted for his miracles, or merely by having conversations with them.

The dissemination of folk medicine in Israel is also connected with the rise of

Raziel ha-Malach.

Miniature book with picture of
Zaddik (righteous) on the cover.
Jerusalem, 1990.
7.5 x 5 cm.
Hagit Matras, Jerusalem.

certain charismatic religious figures who have had a strong social-political influence on the Israeli public. During the elections in 1977 (and again in 1981), Rabbi Israel Abu-Hatzera and Rabbi Schneurson (the Lubavitsher) appeared as figures of great authority, and people flocked to them for words of wisdom and for help in matters of health and illness. After their deaths, their graves became places for holy pilgrimages. In Netivot (where Abu-Hatzera lived), Brooklyn (where Schneurson lived), and Kfar Habad (where his Israeli followers reside) the common belief is that a cup of water blessed by the rabbi can restore family harmony, that almonds on which are inscribed verses from the Bible can cure depression if they are eaten on an empty stomach, and that a charity meal on the grave of the *zaddikim* can restore the sight of a blind man.

The commercialization of materials employed by folk medicine is another reason for its increased dissemination. They are displayed in shops all over the country and compete for the attention of the buyer, offering a number of solutions to distress and disease. The willingness of the public to pay for folk remedies serves as a strong incentive for the various manufacturers to increase production and vary their products. Pharmacies and credit card companies advertise a variety of folk cures for problems of aging, memory loss, sexual performance, arthritis and others.

But the most influential role in bringing folk medicine to the public has been played by the media which feature sensational items in the newspapers, on TV and radio. Notable among them was the story of the man who ate the seeds of certain grapes and saved himself from having to undergo open-heart surgery; another was about a man who changed the mezuzah in his house and brought about an improvement in his son's eyesight. Stories of children who were bewitched or houses that were cursed or evil spirits that were exorcised or *zaddikim* who appeared in dreams are just a few of the items that fill the weekend supplements and the TV talk shows.

The fact that the courts investigate cases of alleged witchcraft or that public figures meet with folk healers catches the imagination of the public and convinces them that these matters are in the natural order of things. The papers are full of articles about "amazing" events: the late Rabbi Goren was saved from imprisonment during a visit to the Soviet Union because he was carrying a religious amulet with him; the ex-Deputy Prime Minister David Levi emerged unscathed from a road accident because there was a holy book in the car with a picture of the Baba Sali in it; the late Ofira Navon, wife of former president Yitzhak Navon, presented Mme. Jihan Sadat with a gift in which a blue stone was embedded for protection against the evil eye; U.S. First Lady Hillary Clinton put a note in the Wailing Wall on a visit to Israel. Still none of these stories can compare in influence to that generated by the deaths of Rabbi Abu-Hatzera in 1984 and Rabbi Schneurson in 1994.

In Conclusion

In conclusion, it can be averred that the influence of folk medicine throughout the modern world has increased considerably in the last years. There are numerous reasons for this. Disappointment with conventional medicine in certain areas is one, and the rapidity with which knowledge is now transmitted from one part of the world to others is another. Patients have become more open minded with regard to non-conventional treatment and the medical establishment itself has recognized some aspects of folk healing as efficacious. There are those who see in the publication of Dr. D.C. Jarvis's book, *Folk Medicine*, a contributing factor: It became a best seller in the United States in the 1960s.[16] Yet another was the visit of former President Richard Nixon to People's China at the beginning of the 1970s, during which one of his party was operated on according to Chinese medical practices. Interest in medicinal plants, which grew in the 1970s with the "back to nature" movements, has resulted in research into their chemical composition. The cultivation of certain plants for the pharmacological industry is now being examined by international bodies with the support of the United Nations. The

Earth Summit Conference in Brazil in 1992 noted the importance not only of protecting medicinal plants but also of gathering and preserving information about their varied uses from folk healers. At the Third International Conference for Leech Science, held in Jerusalem a few years ago, a paper on the positive results of using leeches was presented. In various cities in the Western world, folk healers – formerly known as "witch-doctors" – are now permitted to enter hospitals if so requested by patients or their families. Data collected in northern Russia and published in St. Petersburg a year ago confirmed twenty-year-old reports from Siberia and Germany that incantations and traditional magical ceremonies connected, i.a., to healing were still deeply rooted among the people, even after seventy years "underground."

In this respect, the upsurge of interest in Jewish folk medicine in Israel today is not unique, but part of a world-wide readiness to take a sober look at old traditions and rediscover their relevance to life.

~

NOTES

1. D. Yoder, "Folk Medicine," in R. Dorson, *Folklore and Folklife*, University of Chicago Press, Chicago and London, printed in U.S.A., 1972; A. Kleinman, "Indigenous Systems of Healing, Questions for Professional Popular and Folk Care," in J.W. Salman, ed., *Alternative Medicines*, Tavistock Publications, 1985.

2. W.H. Rivers, *Medicine, Magic and Religion*, London, 1924, AMS Press, New York, 1979.

3. See articles on relevant subjects by Y.T. Levinsky, M. Bernstein, M. Gruenwald, Y. Zlotnik-Avida, and others, in the journals *Edot* (Hebrew) and *Yeda Am* (Hebrew).

4. See for example, I. Jakobovitz, *Jewish Medical Ethics*, Mossad Harav Kook, Jerusalem, 1966, ch. 2; and articles by Y. Riani and Z. Kurt in *Machnayim* (Hebrew), vol. 123, pp. 200-206 (1970).

5. T. Schrire, *Hebrew Amulets, Their Decipherment and Interpretation*, Routledge and Kegan Paul, London, 1966; J. Trachtenberg, *Jewish Magic and Superstition, A Study in Folk Religion*, A Temple Book, Atheneum, New York, 1979.

6. A. Daphne, *Folklore of Israel Plants* (Hebrew), Haifa, 1980; Hochberg, *A Guide to Medicinal Plants*, (Hebrew) Tel Aviv, 1980; P. Tal, *Medicinal Plants*, Tel Aviv, 1981. Exhibitions and catalogs of the Israel Museum: Feuchtwanger Collection with comments by Y. Shachar on amulets, Jerusalem, 1971; *Jewish Life in Morocco*, Jerusalem, 1973; *The Jews of Kurdistan*, Jerusalem, 1981. Studies from the Center for Folklore Research, Y. Bilu, "Traditional Psychiatry in Israel" (Hebrew), Ph.D thesis, Jerusalem, 1978; I. Ben-Ami, "The Folk Veneration of Saints among Moroccan Jews: Tradition, Continuity and Change" (Hebrew), in S. Morag, I. Ben-Ami and N. Stillman, eds., *Studies in Judaism and Islam*, The Magnes Press, Jerusalem, 1981; *Saint Veneration among Moroccan Jews* (Hebrew), Jerusalem, 1984.

7. Y. Bilu and A. Witstum, "Peered In and was Hurt" (Hebrew), about the mystical beliefs and practices of people seeking psychological treatment, *Alpayim*, 9, 1994; "Evil Spirits – the 'Zar' among Ethiopian Jews" (Hebrew), *Ha-refu'ah*, 1994.

8. R. Barkai, *Science, Magic and Mythology in the Middle Ages* (Hebrew), The Van Leer Jerusalem Institute, Jerusalem, 1987; S. Shaked, "On Jewish Magical Literature in Moslem Countries" (Hebrew), *Pe'amim*, Jerusalem, 1983; J. Naveh and S. Shaked, "Amulets and Magic Bowls," Jerusalem, 1985, R. Patai, *The Jewish Alchemists, A History and Source book*, Princeton University Press, 1994.

9. Y. Dan, *The Esoteric Theology of Ashkanazi Hassidim* (Hebrew), Bialik Institute, Jerusalem, 1968; G. Scholem, *Elements of the Kabbalah and its Symbolism* (Hebrew), Bialik Institute, Jerusalem, 1980; Schrire, *Amulets*; Trachtenberg, *Jewish Magic*.

10. M. Idel, *The Uses of the Psalms* (Hebrew); "Psalms," (Hebrew), *Hebrew Encyclopedia*; M. Grünwald, "Bibliomancy," *Jewish Encyclopaedia*.

11. H. Matras, "Forms and Intentions of Contemporary Printed Charm Books," *Proceedings of the XI World Congress of Jewish Studies*, Jerusalem, 1994.

12. A. Ben Yaacov, *Folk Medicine of the Babylonian Jews* (Hebrew), Jerusalem, 1991; Y. Bilu, *Without Bounds: The Life and Death of Rabbi Yaacov Wazana* (Hebrew), Magnes Press, Jerusalem, 1993; G.M. Foster and B.G. Anderson, *Medical Anthropology*, John Wiley & Sons, New York, Toronto, 1978, pp. 56; A.E. Elbaz, "Baby Kidnapped by a Jnun," in *Elbaz, Folktales of the Canadian Sepharadim*, Fitzhenry and Whiteside, Canada, 1982.

13. Y. T. Levinsky, *Yeda Am*, (Hebrew), 1, 5-6.

14. See Frazer, *The Golden Bough: A Study in Magic and Religion*, Macmillan and Co., London, 1922 [1890]; W. Hand, *Magical Medicine*, University of California Press, 1980.

15. The source of this practice is in Y. Sperling, *Customs and Laws* (Hebrew).

16. New York, 1958.

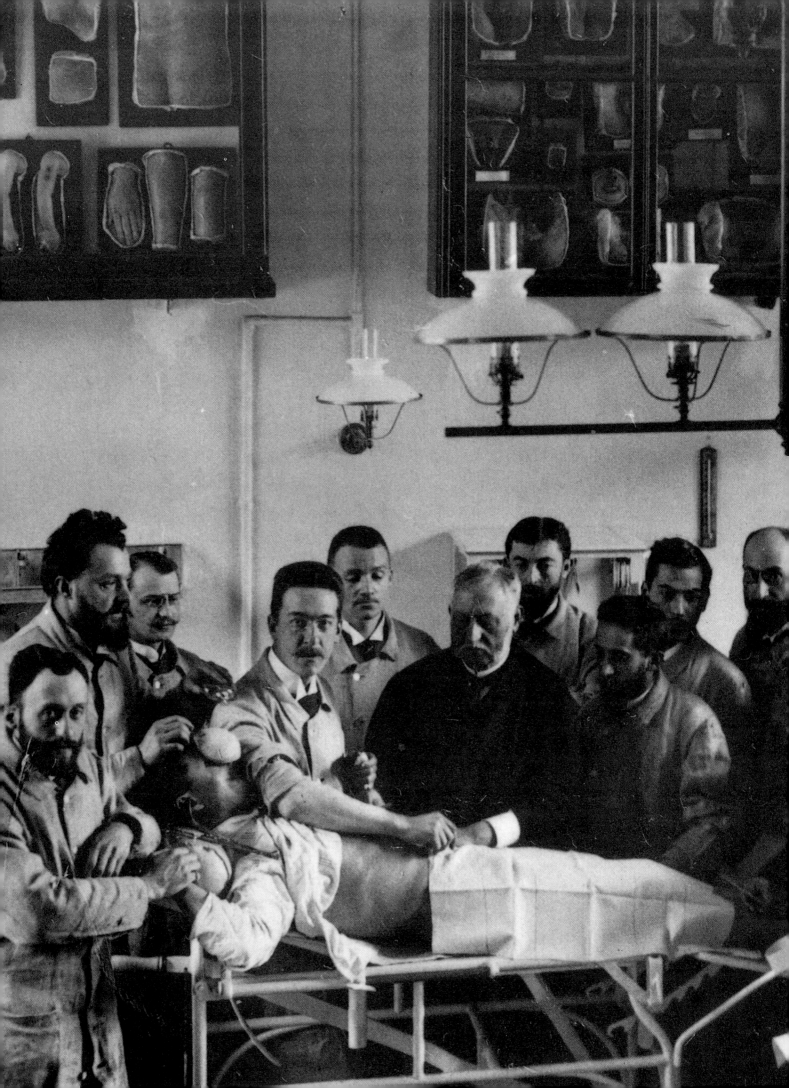

THOMAS SCHLICH

THE JEWISH DOCTOR IN THE ERA OF MODERN MEDICINE

If we think of Jewish doctors in modern times a number of generalizations occur to us. First of all, medicine seems to have been a typical Jewish occupation. Secondly, though Jewish doctors were discriminated against, their success in the field was overwhelming. Finally, Jewish doctors were in the forefront of the creation of modern medicine, excelling not only in the practice of medicine but in medical research and teaching. The quality and quantity of their contribution is reflected in rosters of Nobel laureates and winners of other awards, dictionaries of eponymic syndromes and diseases, and lists of medical authors and investigators.

Towards the end of the 18th century, the medical profession became increasingly dominated by the university-trained physician, a rare phenomenon among medical practitioners until then. This significant change naturally affected Jewish medical practitioners as well. Jews began to look into the medical aspects of non-Jewish secular education while, concomitantly, more and more European universities began to open their doors to Jews.[1] But it was not until the Emancipation, with its social, intellectual and political changes, that Jewish doctors really joined in the development of medicine in general.[2] This period, roughly from 1790 to 1870, marked a turning point in the history of European Jewry. And though the majority of the Jews lived in eastern Europe, developments in Germany were of crucial importance for these changes.[3]

The dermatologist Isidor Neumann examining a patient, surrounded by his assistants and the hospital staff, c.1900.

Isidor Neumann (1832-1906) was born in Moravia and studied in Vienna. He served as professor of dermatology at the University of Vienna and was responsible for the establishment of the Chair of Dermatology and Syphilis there. He was the first to describe pemphigus vegetans, called Neumann's disease. Neumann was knighted and became known as Isidor Neumann von Heilwart.

Institut für Geschichte der Medizin, Wien.

David Gruby

Born in Hungary, Gruby (1810-1898)
became one of the pioneers of modern
microbiology and parasitology. He
studied medicine in Vienna and
received his degree in 1834. Despite
being a Jew, he was appointed a
surgeon at the university medical school.
The university proposed that he be made
a professor on condition that he convert
to Christianity. Gruby rejected this
proposal, left Vienna and settled in
Paris (1839). From 1841-1852 he made
a number of discoveries, from which
evolved the new branch of mycology in
both human and veterinary medicine,
advancing the development of
microbiology and parasitology. He was
the private physician of Chopin, Liszt,
Heine, and Dumas.
Bibliothèque de l'Academie Nationale
de Medecine, Paris.

The Situation in Germany

The tendency towards academic studies in general and medicine in particular was part of an occupational shift to the free professions among Jews. From the 18th century on, the number of Jewish medical students studying at German universities rose continually. At Berlin University in 1826, for example, 7.4 to 9 percent of medical graduates were Jewish. By 1890, although only 1.2 percent of the German population were Jewish, 16 percent of the doctors were Jews (in Berlin the figure was more than 30 percent). There were several reasons for this steady increase. Firstly, secular studies in medicine were more readily tolerated because, according to Jewish tradition, preserving life is a divine commandment. Secondly, only the medical faculties at the universities were ready to accept Jews. Thirdly, taking up medicine was a means of improving one's social standing. Other vocations, valued more highly by the average German Christian – army, law, civil service – were still closed to the unbaptized.[4]

The preponderance of Jews in medicine was not only a German phenomenon. By 1925 Jews formed more than 10 percent of physicians in Hungary, the Soviet Union and South Africa.[5] Nevertheless, true emancipation and integration, desired by many Jews, was never fully realized, not even within the medical profession. In Germany, for example, there was a discrepancy between admission to medical school and openings in various fields of professional activity.[6] Though up to 1933 many Jews studied and worked at the universities, they were massively discriminated against at the top of the university hierarchy and excluded from the civil service.[7] Even when setting up private practice, Jews encountered discrimination – by the authorities, by their Christian colleagues, and sometimes by sectors of the Christian population.[8] The situation of Jewish doctors was, in fact, no different from that of other Jews who tried to become part of the middle or high German bourgeoisie from the end of the 18th century on. Despite these obstacles, however, only a minority, perhaps 25 percent, of the Jewish doctors in 19th-century Germany gave up their Jewish identity and joined one of the Christian denominations.[9] Some notable Jewish doctors found a solution to

Hermann Senator (1834-1911) *who was born in Gnesen, a province of Posen, became professor of internal medicine at the Augusta Hospital in Berlin. Later, he was appointed a director of the Charité Hospital in Berlin. Senator carried out research on the treatment of diabetes, on albuminuria and its significance in health and disease, on renal diseases and hemorrhagic disorders of the spleen, on polycythemia and plethora, and on peripharyngeal phlegmon.*

Institut für Geschichte der Medizin, Wien.

their predicament by emigrating. The famous physiologist, Gabriel Gustav Valentin of Breslau (1810-1883), is one example. Despite his early fame as a medical scientist, no German university was ready to make him a professor unless he converted. He refused and eventually the University of Bern, Switzerland made him the first full professor in a German-speaking university.[10] David Gruby (1810-1898) is another. Gruby was born in Novy Sad (then Hungary) and studied medicine in Vienna. Despite the fact that he was a Jew, he was appointed as a surgeon at the university medical school. He

Benjamin de Lemos.

Portrait, 1755. Anton Graff.

Oil on canvas. 80 x 64.5 cm.

Benjamin de Lemos (1711-1789) was of
Portuguese Jewish origin. He practiced
medicine in Halle and settled in Berlin
where he was highly esteemed as a
physician. From 1735 he devoted himself
to treating the Jewish community. He
was the first director of the Jewish
Hospital in Berlin. He was the father
of Henriette, who married the physician
Marcus Herz.

The Israel Museum, Jerusalem.

Marcus Herz.

Portrait, 18th century.

Friedrich Georg Weitsch.

Oil on canvas. 115 x 110.4 cm.

*Born in Berlin, Herz received his
degree from Halle in 1774. He was a
favorite pupil of Kant and became
renowned as a great philosopher and
teacher. He lectured on Kantian
philosophy and later delivered discourses
on physics. His lectures on the laws of
nature were illustrated with
experiments. In 1774 he was appointed
physician at the Berlin Jewish Hospital.
Herz was reputed to be one of the best
doctors of his time. He married
Henriette, the daughter of Benjamin de
Lemos, and their home was the
gathering place of Berlin's intellectuals.
The Israel Museum, Jerusalem.*

MICHEL LEVY 1809~1872

Michel Levy.

Portrait by A.A. Hirsch.

Oil on canvas, 1893.

80 x 75 cm.

Born in Strasbourg, Michel Levy (1809-1872) became professor of hygiene in Val-de-Grâce in 1836 and in 1845 he became the first professor of pathology in Metz but returned to the Val-de-Grâce after 2 years and became director of its medical school. His Traité d'Hygiène Publique et Privée (2 vols. 1843-45) was widely acclaimed and went through five editions. In recognition of his accomplishments in the field of hygiene, he was elected a member of the French Academy of Medicine.

Bibliothèque de l'Academie Nationale de Medecine, Paris.

The Politzer family, 1870.

Oil on canvas.

Painting by Hugo Charlemont.

Museum der Stadt, Wien.

A royal charter of Czar Alexander III enobling David Rosenthal, senior physician of the Jewish Hospital, Warsaw, September 1881.

David Rosenthal (1808-1889) was the the best known Jewish physician in Poland.

He received several imperial honors culminating in the title of a Polish nobleman in recognition of the outstanding talent and courage he demonstrated during the typhus and cholera epidemics in Poland.

The Library of the Jewish Theological Seminary of America, New York.

was subsequently offered a professorship on condition that he convert. Gruby rejected the proposal, left Vienna and settled in Paris in 1839. There he lectured on normal and morbid anatomy at the Museum of Nature and became famous for his work on the pathogenic role of fungi.[11]

In general, Jewish medical students and doctors comprised a kind of avant-garde in the process of acculturation. They were in closest touch with the Christian environment, the first to be confronted with the difficulties entailed in maintaining their traditional way of life. Like other sectors of the Jewish population, Jewish physicians tended to give up those aspects of traditional life that appeared anachronistic to them.[12] But for most of them Jewish religion remained the nucleus of their heritage.

In the last quarter of the 19th century, traditional anti-Jewish sentiments were expanded by a new "racial" anti-Semitism. Based on what was called "scientific" evidence, the Jews were regarded as being biologically, intellectually and morally inferior to the "Aryan" race. Assimilation or even baptism could no longer prevent discrimination. During this upsurge of anti-Semitism Jewish students and doctors, who were now legally equal, became the target of anti-Semitic propaganda. A repertoire of anti-Jewish stereotypes emerged, dealing specifically with Jewish physicians and derived in part from earlier stereotypes.[13] Nonetheless, Jewish physicians continued to be held in high esteem by many of their German patients – until the exclusion of Jewish doctors from the medical profession in 1938.[14]

The Situation in England

In England until 1871 the universities of Oxford, Cambridge and Durham were restricted to Anglicans only. But University College London, opened in 1827, accepted dissenters, such as Catholics and Jews. By the middle of the 19th century, increasing numbers of Jews were seeking entrance into the professions. Because of the difficulties encountered in entering fields such as the army and the law, the primary goal of Jewish professional ambition was medicine. If an English Jew wished to graduate in medicine at university in the 18th or early 19th century his options were limited to Scotland (particularly

Portrait of Dr. Haustein.

By Christian Shad, 1928.

Oil on canvas.

80.5 x 55 cm.

Dr. Haustein was a sexologist and
dermatologist in Berlin in the 1920s.
Museo Thyssen-Bornemisza, Madrid
1995.

Poster for the film *Prostitution*, produced
by Richard Oswald, in collaboration with
Dr. Magnus Hirschfeld.

By Josef Fenneker, 1919.

141 x 95 cm.

Magnus Hirschfeld (1868-1935) was a
renowned authority on sexology.
Stiftung Deutscher Kinemathek, Berlin.

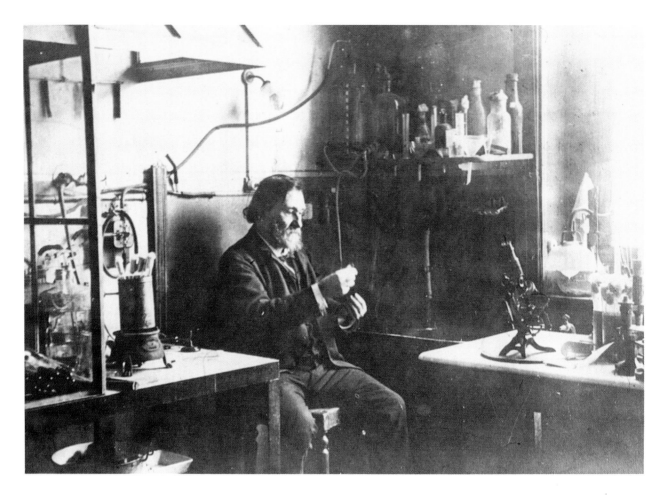

Elie Metchnikoff (1845-1916), *who was a half-Jew, became a teacher of zoology at the University of Odessa in 1867 and a professor in 1870. In 1882 he resigned his position due to the ordinances of the Czarist regime. In 1888 he left Russia and moved to Paris, where he worked in bacteriology and immunology at the Pasteur Institute. In 1904 when Pasteur died, Metchnikoff succeeded him. His most important contribution to medicine is his theory of phagocytosis, which influenced the science of immunology. Later, in collaboration with Emile Roux, he succeeded in inoculating anthropoid apes with syphilis. He described the effect of lactic acid on bacteria, e.g., in kumiss, as counteracting intestinal auto-intoxication and prolonging life. In 1908 Metchnikoff shared the Nobel Prize for medicine with Paul Ehrlich for their work on immunity. Institut Pasteur, Paris.*

Aberdeen) or to one of the continental universities (Holland or Germany). Liberal conditions in Scotland permitted a small immigrant group to improve their social status by entering the medical profession. Jewish doctors did not, however, enter the elite echelons of the medical profession but found careers in the provinces, in the army and colonial service and within the Jewish community.[15]

In Czarist Russia

Toward the end of the 19th century almost half of all European Jews lived in Czarist Russia. Czar Alexander I had opened the schools and colleges to the Jews in the early 19th century and before long there was a disproportionate number of Jewish lawyers, doctors and other professionals in Moscow and St. Petersburg. In the Russo-Turkish War of 1877-78, many Jewish doctors in the army received military decorations. There was a drastic change in policy towards the Jews after the waves of pogroms in 1881 and this led to the imposition of anti-Semitic quotas in university admission. As of July 1887, a numerus clausus limited Jews to 10 percent of student bodies at universities in the Pale Settlement, 5 percent outside the Pale, and 3 percent in St. Petersburg. Towards the end of the century Jewish physicians were restricted to private practice and excluded from all government posts. Yet up until the time of the 1917 revolutions, there was a large movement of Russian Jews to colleges and universities, both domestic and foreign, and the number of Jewish professionals increased greatly. While there were an estimated 4,500 Jewish doctors in the country in 1879, by the mid-1930s there were 21,000 in the Ukraine and White Russia alone.[16]

Jewish Sick Care and Jewish Hospitals

Because Judaism considers caring for the sick a religious duty, health care was always part of the social services organized by the Jewish communities or by specialized associations. Similar to the traditional Christian hospital, the traditional Jewish hospital, the *hekdesh*, was an institution where the impoverished sick in the 17th and 18th centuries could obtain shelter. In the

Alexander Besredka (1870-1940) *was an immunologist, known for his research on anaphylaxis, local immunization, and immunization in contagious diseases. He first studied in Russia then moved to France. He completed his medical studies in Paris and was appointed a member of the Pasteur Institute of which he later became director. Besredka maintained his contact with Judaism all his life, was active in Jewish organizations and wrote for Jewish scientific journals. His desensitization method was accepted throughout the world as the pretreatment of patients who had acquired a sensitivity toward a serum, in order to prevent anaphylactic shock. He was appointed professor at the Pasteur Institute in Paris in 1910. Institut Pasteur, Paris.*

Israel. Kinder-Hospiz, Duhnen.

Lwów. Szpital izraelicki.
Lemberg. Israelitisches Spital.

Postcards.

From the collection of Ammy Ben Yakov, New York.

E. V. PARIS (XIX) — Institut, fondation de Rothschild

47. TUNIS — Hôpital d'Israélites

FEZ. — Dispensaire Israélite

Breslau
Israelitisches Krankenhaus mit Wasserturm

Israelitische Kinderheilstätte
im Soolbade Königsdorff-Jastrzemb.
Verwaltung zu Gleiwitz.

Glückwunsch
zum
neuen Jahre!

Częstochowa. Szpital Żydowski.

Middle Ages the *hekdesh* had served as a shelter for wandering peddlers, strangers and, eventually, sick people from the poorer classes of society. With the wide-spread movement in Europe to improve hospitalization at the end of the 18th century, the Jewish hospital too changed its character from a social to a medical institution. It ceased to be a shelter for the poor and became an institution devoted solely to the sick, efficiently administered by competent technicians, staffed by scientifically trained physicians and surgeons.[17] From the middle of the 18th century on, numerous Jewish hospitals were founded in German-speaking countries.

The most important change to occur in medical care was the rise of specialized societies and semi-private associations that dealt with the health care of the middle class. Simultaneously, mutual aid sick-funds were organized by young people, influenced by the Enlightenment, as a means of achieving better standards in hospital care. This, however, was done in the framework of strictly religious societies. The "new" Vienna Jewish Hospital that opened in 1793 had been planned as early as 1784 but nine years of discussions followed, involving the authorities and the Jewish community. With the growth of secular culture among the Jews, secular Jewish hospitals began to appear and continued to be established up until the beginning of the 20th century. By the second half of the 19th century new Jewish hospitals were founded, i.e., in Paris, Metz, London, Budapest, Jerusalem, and in the United States. By 1933 they existed in most countries around the world and usually enjoyed a fine reputation.[18] Yet what happened inside the secularized Jewish hospitals was not, for the most, specifically Jewish.

Why did Jews found and maintain their own hospitals instead of seeking care in the newly created modern Christian institutions?[19] One reason was that the general hospitals did not cater for the special needs of Jewish patients, such as

Charity box from the Jewish hospital in Amsterdam, 1918.

The Jewish Museum Amsterdam.

Opposite:

Visiting the Sick.

Prague, c.1780.

Oil on canvas, 55 x 110 cm.

First painting from a series of fifteen paintings that decorated the hall of the Burial Society. In 1780 the society ordered a set of paintings depicting the customs related to death and burial. Dr. Jeitteles is the central figure. Jeitteles's main achievement was the propagation of a small pox vaccination. In 1784 after an audience with Joseph II he was permitted to treat patients regardless of their religion.

Jewish Museum, Prague.

The *JERUSALEM*
Alias, a JOURNEY *to the Vall*

inv. Ribi Tarfon

Pinx. Ribi Zador

1	Well said Rabby, Notary Public, and Soldier.	
2	Fine Sentence, Proud madman —	
3	A Scotsh Harp Player,	
4	A near Relation to Judescos —	
5	The wisast Governor —	
6	Hypocrates —	
7	Galenus —	
8	Doct.r Caga Fuego —	

9	A Famous Operator	
10	A Stutus —	
11	Matrona —	
12	A Pedler selling Gloves against Merc	
13	The Clerk —	
14	The Beadle —	
15	The Apothecary —	

154

The Jerusalem Infirmary.

Engraving, 1749.

An anonymous satire referring to the Beth Holim, the hospital for the poor of the Spanish and Portuguese Jews of London, founded in 1747. It attacks the exclusive character of the institution and brings out a number of irregularities which occurred soon after it was opened.

The chief figures in this caricature represent prominent members of the English Sephardi community and the medical staff of the infirmary. All are clean-shaven and wear contemporary dress.

The Jewish Museum, London.

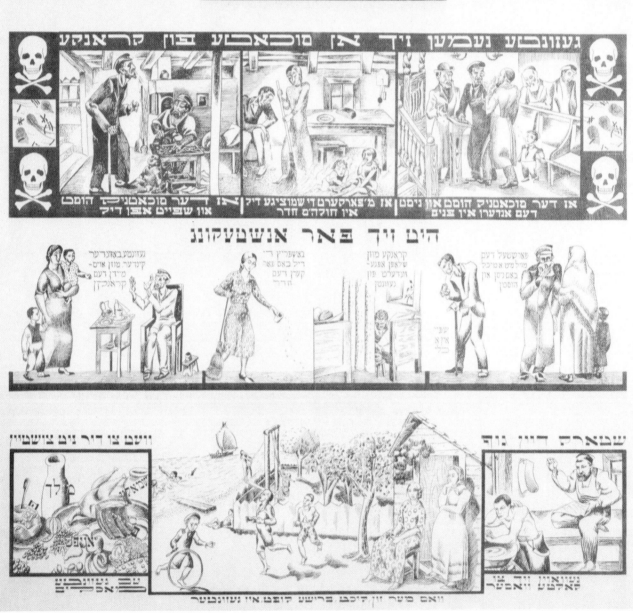

ritually prepared food. Another was the fact that adherence to Jewish customs concerning the handling of the dead was difficult in a non-Jewish setting. There was also the justified fear of proselytizing among Jewish patients. This does not mean, however, that Jewish hospitals were established in order to segregate Jews from Gentiles. They were, on the contrary, conceived as a contribution to the process of emancipation and the integration of the Jews. For example, representatives of the Berlin Jewish Hospital, one of the city's most renowned hospitals, believed that a modern Jewish hospital was evidence of successful emancipation. But the specific Jewish identity of the Jewish hospitals remained a contentious issue, and different hospitals dealt with the problem in different ways.

Nonethless, the needs of Jewish patients was not the only reason for setting up Jewish hospitals. The needs of the Jewish professionals was no less a factor. Anti-Semitic tendencies in other hospitals often resulted in the exclusion of Jewish medical students and young doctors from training opportunities and specialization in fields such as surgery, which were only available in hospitals. The same was true for nurses. The Jewish hospitals thus became places where Jewish doctors and nurses could develop their professional potentials. Without the Jewish hospital, for example, the chief surgeon of the Berlin Jewish Hospital, James Israel, might never have become one of the great surgeons of his time. Israel was famous for his work in kidney surgery and plastic surgery and is still known for his discovery of the infectious agent of actinomycosis.

Health Care and Immigration

In the 19th and the early part of the 20th centuries masses of European Jews began emigrating to other parts of the world, in search of a better life and in reaction to anti-Semitic outrages. Health care issues were particularly pressing for them during the initial years of their arrival and motivated them to develop forms of help not provided in the host society. In London, for example, the Jewish Board of Guardians (J.B.G.), the most important Jewish charitable institution, which had been established in 1859, provided numerous forms of

Yiddish health poster warning against lice.

"Blood, Frogs, Lice - The Third Plague is the Worst ...Beware of Lice!"
50 x 35 cm.
Illustrated by Joseph Tchaikov.
Printed by OSE. London/Berlin 1923.
YIVO, New York.

Yiddish preventive medicine poster.

Stressing the importance of preventive medicine and a healthy life-style.
"You Can Protect Yourself from Tuberculosis (Consumption)! To Heal the Sick is a Great Deed; To Prevent Illness is Greater Still!"
98 x 68 cm.
Printed by OSE. London/Berlin 1923.
YIVO, New York.

Cesare Lombroso (1836-1909) *was born in Verona and studied medicine in Italy and Austria. In 1862 he became professor of psychiatry at the University of Pavia, where he devoted himself to criminology. He believed in "born criminals" and advanced the theory that criminality is due to the survival of primitive physical and psychological traits in man. He thought that physical, nervous, and mental abnormalities appeared more often in criminals than in non-criminals and credited this in part to atavism and in part to degeneration. Lombroso was the author of many controversial books on criminology.*

National Library of Medicine, Bethesda.

medical aid and welfare relief for poor Jews. By the 1890s, women could seek a multitude of services during and after confinement not only from the J.B.G. but from the Sick Room Help Society and, later, its Jewish Maternity Home. Most people feared that care at non-Jewish institutions would lead to cultural isolation or even conversion, especially as charity for Jews was frequently combined with missionary work.[20]

Jewish Doctors after World War II

Between 1933 and 1945 Jewish doctors in Germany and other countries occupied by the Germans were forced out of the profession. Many of them perished in the Nazi Holocaust.[21] Most of them, however, an estimated 9,000 – 10,000 German-speaking doctors, succeeded in emigrating, the majority of them to the United States.[22] Initially Jewish emigrant physicians favored Palestine but British policy and the political and socio-economic constellation there militated against a substantial influx of Jews. By the end of World War II, the majority of the Jewish physicians who were successful in escaping from Germany and Austria found their way to the United States and to a system that was characterized by the quota system of admission to medical schools. The quotas aimed at limiting the number of Jews in medicine roughly to their proportion in the population. It was not before the end of the 1940s and after enormous material sacrifices and personal suffering that most immigrant Jewish physicians in the United States were doing well.[23]

England was lower in the hierarchy of receiver nations of German-Jewish doctors.[24] The situation there was also characterized by "protectionism" in the medical establishment. Regulations were much harsher than either in the United States or Palestine. No German-Jewish physician in England was allowed to practice without repeating years of study and a university medical examination. After the war the refugee physicians gradually entered British medical practice and many of their children followed them into medical careers. The marginal position of the Jewish immigrants improved markedly and Jews eventually obtained important positions in British medical life. Apart from Britain, however, very few European countries accepted Jewish doctors

Fernand Widal

Widal (1862-1929) was born in Dellys, Algeria and graduated from Paris Medical Faculty in 1889. He was an outstanding clinician and creative investigator. In 1888 he studied with Chantemesse the problem of preventive vaccination against typhoid fever, known as Widal's polyvaccine. In 1911 he was appointed professor of pathology and in 1918 he became professor of clinical medicine at the University of Paris. In recognition of his great medical achievements he was the recipient of many honors.

Nobel Prize Laureates for 1965.

From the right: André Michel Lwoff, Jacques Monod and François Jacob. Institut Pasteur, Paris.

Eugene and Elizabeth Wollman. *Eugene (1883-1943) was born in Russia, studied in France and in 1910 started to work at the Pasteur Institute together with his wife Elizabeth. In 1940 after the defeat of France he did not escape but continued his research. In 1943 Wollman and his wife were arrested by the German police at the Pasteur Institute and sent to Drancy and from there to Auschwitz.*
Institut Pasteur, Paris.

Der Doktor.

Issue of Yiddish medical newspaper published in Warsaw between 1930–1933.

Aaron Feingold Collection, New Jersey.

as practicing physicians after the war and then only with reservations.

The emigration of Jews from Central Europe in the wake of the rise of Hitler entailed a considerable loss of talent, knowledge and expertise for these countries. Six Jewish Nobel prize winners were forced by the Nazis to leave

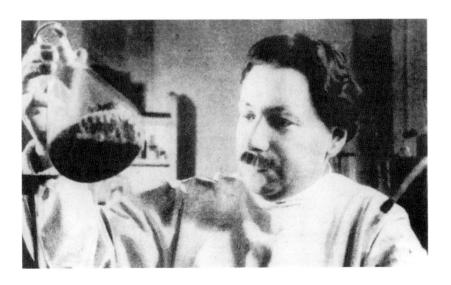

Dr. Boris E. Chain in his laboratory, c.1939.

Chain was born in Russia and graduated from Friedrich Wilhelm University as a chemist in 1931. After graduation he worked in the Department of Chemistry of the Pathological Institute of the Charité in Berlin. In 1933 he left Germany for England, where he worked as a chemist with Sir Gowald Hopkins at Cambridge University. Three years later he was appointed as a chemist to the Chemical Laboratory of Oxford University under the pathologist, Prof. Howard W. Florey. In July 1939 Dr. Chain started his investigations of penicillin. The latter was discovered by Prof. Fleming in mold in 1929, and it was used as a disinfectant for external wounds.

Dr. Chain, with the aid of his co-workers, succeeded in isolating penicillin, and he presented it to Professor Florey in order to determine its curative effect as a bactericidal agent. The experiments established its property as a bactericide. Dr. Chain was co-winner with Sir Alexander Fleming and Sir Howard W. Florey of the 1945 Nobel Prize for physiology and medicine in recognition of their great discovery. In 1949 Dr. Chain became head of the Biological Department of the Weizmann Institute in Rehovot, Israel.

National Library of Medicine, Bethesda.

Lina Solomonova Stern.

Lina Stern (1878-1950) a Russian physiologist and biologist was born in Lithuania. She qualified in Geneva. In 1932 she was elected to the German Academy of Natural Sciences and in 1939 she became the first woman to be admitted to the U.S.S.R. Academy of Sciences. She was the recipient of the Stalin Prize and several Orders of Merit. During the 1948-49 purges in the Soviet Union she was accused of "rootless cosmopolitanism" and removed from her positions, but after the death of Stalin all her honors were restored. Lina Stern made significant contributions to the study of the physiology of the central nervous system.

National Library of Medicine, Bethesda.

Germany alone. Heidelberg University lost a fourth of its medical faculty and the Berlin Charité 31 percent of its doctors.[25]

In the Soviet Union, following the war and up to the time of Stalin's death in 1953, "the Black Years", characterized by the oppression of the Jews and of Jewish culture, prevailed. Zionism was denounced as being an anti-Soviet espionage system. This period culminated in the so-called "doctor's plot". Nine eminent Moscow physicians, of whom six "happened" to be Jewish – among them Dr. Wofsi, president of the Academy of Medicine – had allegedly conspired to poison Stalin and other Soviet leaders and thus prepare the way for an internal revolution. But Stalin died and in the scuffle for succession the accused doctors were released and life seemed to return to normal. Despite official denials, however, it would appear that anti-Semitism continued to play a great role in shaping Jewish destinies in the post-Stalin era in the Soviet Union as well.[26]

Conclusion: General Patterns

If we review the history of Jewish doctors in the 19th and 20th centuries the general patterns we noted at the outset reemerge. There was a striking preponderance of Jews in the medical profession, although today this is true (apart from Israel) only in the United States.[27] The reasons are roughly the same everywhere. Apart from the medical tradition of Judaism it was a viable way to abandon traditional Jewish occupations, gain in social status, and join the modern culture of the non-Jewish environment. And even after Jews were actually admitted to the medical profession discrimination continued to be a central factor. In consequence, immigration was typical for Jewish doctors in modern times as it was for the general Jewish population. The distribution of Jewish doctors in the world today is the result of migrations in the last 200 years. Although for many the results of migration were tragic, for others it turned out to be a golden opportunity, at least for subsequent generations.

~

Ex Libris.

Book plates belonging to Jewish physicians.

Early 20th century.

Yitzhak Einhorn Collection, Tel Aviv.

NOTES

LEWIS J. SIEGAL, M.D., L.L.B.

1. See Samuel Kottek, "Sur l'ouverture progressive des universités d'Europe centrale aux étudiants en médecine juifs aus 18e siècle", in *Acta Congressus Internationalis XXIV Historiae Artis Medicinae*, vol. 2. Budapest 1976, pp. 1171-1177. See also *Encyclopaedia Judaica*, vol. 15, col. 1677.

2. For the time before emancipation in the German lands see Monika Richarz, *Der Eintritt der Juden in die akademischen Berufe. Jüdische Studenten und Akademiker in Deutschland 1678-1848*, J.C.B. Mohr, Tübingen, 1974, pp. 1-82.

3. Reinhard Rürup, "The Tortuous and Thorny Path to Legal Equality. 'Jew Laws' and Emancipatory Legislation in Germany from the Late 18th Century", in *Yearbook of the Leo Baeck Institute 31 (1986)*, pp. 3-33. Charles Singer, "Science and Judaism" in Louis Finkelstein, ed., *The Jews – Their History, Culture and Religion*, Harper and Bros., New York, 1949, vol. 2, pp. 1038-1091.

4. Werner Friedrich Kümmel, "Jüdische Ärzte in Deutschland zwischen Emanzipation und 'Ausschaltung,'" in Gert Preiser, ed., *Richard Koch und die ärztliche Diagnose*, Olms Weidmann, Hildesheim, 1988, pp. 15-47. Richarz, *Eintritt*, pp. 9-14, 172-178; Erwin H. Ackerknecht, "German Jews, English Dissenters, French Protestants: 19th-century Pioneers of Modern Medicine and Science", in: Charles Rosenberg, ed., *Healing and History*, Dawson Science Publications New York 1979, pp. 86-96; Michael H. Kater, "Professionalization and Socialization of Physicians in Wilhelmine and Weimar Germany", in: *Journal of Contemporary History 20 (1985)*, pp. 677-701.

5. Kenneth Collins, *Go and Learn. The International Story of Jews and Medicine in Scotland*, Aberdeen University Press, Aberdeen, 1988, p. 84.

6. Richarz, *Eintritt*, p. 87.

7. Shulamith Volkov, "Soziale Ursachen des Erfolgs in der Wissenschaft. Juden im Kaiserreich", *Historische Zeitschrift 245* (1987), pp. 329-330; Kümmel, *Jüdische Ärzte*, pp. 26-30; Hans-Peter Kröner, "Die Emigration deutschsprachiger Mediziner im Nationalsozialismus", *Berichte zur Wissenschaftsgeschichte 12* (1989), Sonderheft, pp. 6-9.

8. Thomas Schlich, *Marburger jüdische Chirurgie- und Medizinstudenten 1800-1832, Herkunft-Berufsweg Stellung in der Gesellschaft*, N.G. Elwert, Marburg 1990.

9. Kümmel, "Jüdische Ärzte", p. 19.

10. Erich Hintzsche, *Gabriel Gustav Valentin (1810-1883). Versuch einer Bio- und Bibliographie*, Bern, 1953; Thomas Schlich, "Religion und Universität: Der Streit um die Berufung jüdischer Professoren an der Universität Marburg im Vormärz", *Zeitschrift für Religions- und Geistesgeschichte 45 (1993)*, pp. 248-251.

11. *Encyclopaedia Judaica*, vol. 7, col. 941-942.

12. Richarz, *Eintritt*, pp. 74-90, 157-163, 172-178.

13. See Nicoline Hortzitz, *Der "Judenarzt." Historische und sprachliche Untersuchungen zur Diskriminierung eines Berufsstandes in der frühen Neuzeit*, Universitätsverlag, C. Winter, Heidelberg, 1994.

14. Kater, *Professionalization*, pp. 692-694; W.F. Kümmel, "Die Ausschaltung rassisch und politisch missliebiger Ärzte", in Fridolf Kudlien, *Ärzte im Nationalsozialismus*, Köln 1985, pp.57-63; Kümmel, "Jüdische Ärzte", pp. 21-26, 30-37.

15. Collins, *Go and Learn*, p. xiv, xvi, 76, 159; *Encyclopaedia Judaica*, vol. 15, col. 1677.

16. Salo W. Baron, *The Russian Jews under Tsars and Soviets*, Macmillan Publishing Co. Inc, New York, Collier Macmillan Publishers, London, 1976, second ed; rev. and enlarged, pp. 53, 94, 136-147; Haim Hillel Ben-Sasson, ed., *Geschichte des jüdischen Volkes*, Verlag C.H. Beck, München, 1980, vol. 3, pp. 111-125, 195-207.

17. Jacob R. Marcus, *Communal Sick-care in the German Ghetto*, The Hebrew Union College Press, Cincinatti, 1947; *Encyclopedia Judaica 14*, col. 1498-1499. Mayer A. Halévy, "Die Idee der Caritas in der jüdischen Religion", in *Historia Hospitalium. Mitteilungen der Deutschen Gesellschaft für Krankenhausgeschichte*, Sonderheft, Michael Triltsch Verlag, Düsseldorf, 1970, pp. 10-19; Dieter Jetter, "Zur Geschichte der jüdischen Krankenhäuser", *Ibid.*, pp. 28-59.

18. *Encyclopaedia Judaica 8*, col. 1033-1040. Marcus, *Sick-Care*, pp. 195-208.

19. See as an example: Dagmar Hartung-von Doetinchem, Rolf Winau, eds., *Zerstörte Fortschritte. Das Jüdische Krankenhaus in Berlin*, Edition Hentrich, Berlin, 1989, see especially the contributions by Jessica Jacoby (pp. 28-67) and Hartung-von Doetinchem (pp. 75-145).

20. Lara Marks, "'Dear Old Mother Levy's': The Jewish Maternity Home and Sick Room Helps Society 1895-1939", *Social History of Medicine 3* (1990), pp. 62-87.

21. Medicine and the Holocaust is dealt with in another contribution to the catalogue.

22. Stephan Leibfried, "Stationen der Abwehr. Berufsverbote für Ärzte im Deutschen Reich 1933-1938 und die Zerstörung des sozialen Asyls durch die organisierten Ärzteschaften des Auslands", *Bulletin des Leo Baeck Instituts 62* (1982), pp. 3-39; Michael Hubenstorf, "Österreichische Ärzteemigration 1934-1945 – Zwischen neuem Tätigkeitsgebiet und organisierten Rückkehrplänen", *Berichte zur Wissenschaftsgeschichte 7 (1984)*, pp. 85-107; Kümmel, "Jüdische Ärzte", p. 38; Michael H. Kater, *Doctors under Hitler*, Chapel Hill and London, 1989, pp. 199-221.

23. Kathleen M. Pearle: "Ärzteemigration nach 1933 in die USA: der Fall New York", *Medizinhistorisches Journal 19* (1984), pp. 112-137; Leon Sokoloff, "The Rise and Decline of the Jewish Quota in Medical School Admissions", *Bulletin of the New York Academy of Medicine 68* (1992), pp. 497-518.

24. Collins, *Go and Learn*, pp. 133-154; Kater, Doctors under Hitler, pp. 217-218.

25. Kümmel, "Jüdische Ärzte", p. 77; Alex Sakula, Jewish Nobel Prize-winners in Medicine and Physiology, *Koroth 9* (1989), pp. 684-699.

26. Baron, *The Russian Jews*, pp. 216-217, 269-285, 307-323.

27. *Encyclopaedia Judaica 11*, col. 1199.

GERHARD BAADER

THE CONTRIBUTION OF CENTRAL EUROPEAN JEWISH DOCTORS TO MEDICAL SCIENCE

Between the years 1933-1938 Jewish doctors comprised a high percentage of the medical profession in Germany and Austria. In 1932 of the 52,000 doctors in Germany, 6,000 were Jewish and another 2,000 were of Jewish origin, as defined by Hitler's racial laws. In Austria the situation was similar. The largest concentration of Jewish doctors was in Berlin and Vienna, the cities with the largest Jewish communities. In Berlin there were at one time 6,800 doctors of whom 2,300 were Jewish or of Jewish origin. In Vienna, from a total of 4,900 doctors, 3,200 were Jewish or of Jewish origin. Numbers, however, provide only a superficial picture of the importance of this group of physicians. For a more comprehensive understanding of their innovative contribution to medical science we must look at the high number of eponyms of Jewish doctors from this period still in use today in clinical and pre-clinical terminology. Among them are the Henle-Curve; the Auerbach-Plexus; the Edinger-Nucleus; the reaction according to Karl Herxheimer (1861-1942 – an increase in syphilis symptoms sometimes following the initial dose of arsphenamine); the Wassermann tests; and the Romberg experiments. We must also mention the discovery of Salvarsan by Paul Ehrlich (which was the foundation of chemotherapy), the clinical use of digitalis by Ludwig Traube, of cocaine by Carl Koller and chloral hydrate by Oskar Liebreich (1838-1908). Since Berlin and Vienna were the two major centers of world medicine at this time, without the innovations of these Jewish doctors, medical progress at the end of the 19th and beginning of the 20th centuries would have advanced at a much slower pace.

Theodore Billroth operating in the lecture hall.

A.F. Seligmann, 1890.

Oil on canvas, 113.5 x 86.5 cm.

Professor Billroth performs an operation; the anaesthetist is Dr. Leopold von Dittel (1815-1898), associate professor of surgery at the University of Vienna. Österreichische Galerie, Wien.

The Emperor Joseph II established the
Academy of Surgery and Medicine,
Vienna, 1785.

Vienna, Bundesdenkmalamt.
Institut für Geschichte der Medizin,
Wien.

Historical Background

Jews in Germany and Austria had participated in the movement for equal civil
rights for all members of society from the time of the Enlightenment in the
18th century. This attempt at emancipation, which in France had led to a new
constitution and equal civil rights, was much less successful in Germany. In
the most important German state, Prussia, for example, although all Jews had
been declared "natives and Prussian citizens" by 1812, they were still
excluded from becoming officers in the army or civil servants. This meant that
they were unable to hold positions as teachers or professors at universities
unless, of course, they were baptized. The situation remained this way with
few exceptions until 1918, when German Jews attempted to join the German
bourgeoisie. Slogans like "Be a Jew at home and a citizen abroad" blazed the
path to assimilation.

Although legal equality was part of the new constitution of the German
Empire in 1871, complete social integration of Jews never took place. Jews
could only hope to rise on the social ladder by belonging to the free

professions: i.e., medicine, journalism or law. It is well known that medicine had always been a profession of high repute among Jews and that Gentiles often thought highly of Jewish physicians. Despite all the attempts to ostracize them or accuse them of the maltreatment of Gentiles – for which they were often driven out of cities, persecuted and even killed – Jewish doctors practiced widely, as barber-surgeons, or city physicians or physicians to the kings and aristocracy, from the Middle Ages on.

In 1678 German Jews were admitted, for the first time, to the academic study of medicine in Frankfurt-am-Oder and, in 1721 allowed to graduate as medical doctors. From the end of the 18th century Jewish students were studying in Berlin and Halle, yet even though a law was passed in 1847 allowing Jews to obtain degrees in medicine and science and appointments as associate professors (that is, without tenure) or full professors – this rarely took place. In 1847 Robert Remak was the first Jew to become a lecturer at the University of Berlin. In 1851 he was appointed associate professor and that was as far as he got. The famous Berlin internist, Ludwig Traube, received recognition as a teacher of medicine only after the revolution of 1848 and was appointed associate professor only in 1857. He became full professor in 1872, the only unbaptized Jewish full professor at the Medical School in Berlin. Between 1882-1901, the number of Jewish full professors in medicine, most of whom were baptized, remained restricted to twenty-five. By 1917 the number had dwindled to thirteen. During the Weimar Republic, however, the number increased again to thirty.

Although during the time of the Weimar Republic non-baptized Jews could be appointed full professors, anti-Semitism was intensifying, affecting both Jewish students and professors. One could really speak in these years of a social boycott of Jewish colleagues by non-Jews. There is yet another aspect to this. Traube had been one of the few Jewish professors with a place in traditional medicine, i.e, internal medicine or surgery. All the other Jewish associate professors were in the so-called marginal branches of medicine, those that were only beginning to be professionalized, such as neurology, ophthalmology, dermatology, urology, social hygiene or sexology. But it was

Ludwig Traube (1818-1876) *was a pioneer in the field of experimental pathology; he was born in Silesia and graduated from the University of Berlin. In 1849 he was appointed lecturer and research worker at the Charité Hospital in Berlin and his clinic soon achieved a high reputation for precision and thoroughness in diagnoses and therapy. He was one of the first Jewish physicians to attain the title of professor in Germany. Traube was the first to introduce the use of the thermometer in his clinic for routine checking of his patients' temperature. Institut für Geschichte der Medizin, Wien.*

James Israel (1948-1926) *was born in Berlin and received his M.D. from the University of Berlin in 1870. In 1872 he became physician to the Jewish Hospital in Berlin, in 1875 he pursued studies in England and Scotland and finally, in 1880 he was made the director of the Surgical Department of the Jewish Hospital in Berlin. He was a pioneer in the fields of urology, and won international recognition as an authority in renal surgery. In recognition of his important medical achievements a Festschrift was published in his honor on the occasion of his seventy-fifth birthday.*

Institute für Geschichte der Medizin, Berlin.

precisely in these fields that Jewish doctors proved to be the most innovative.

Jewish Doctors at Work

Since work at the universities and the university hospitals was limited, it was only natural for many Jewish doctors to open private clinics where they could give full scope to their medical interests and ambitions. Indeed, it was their work at private clinics, beginning towards the end of the 19th century, which eventually brought them international recognition.

Most of these clinics, in which physicians and most of the staff were Jewish, were opened initially in the vicinity of Berlin's famous Charité Hospital. Among them, Julius Hirschberg opened an ophthalmological clinic in 1869; in 1876 Leopold and Theodor Landau opened a private gynecological and obstetrics clinic as did Paul Strassmann in 1900; Oscar Lassar opened a dermatological clinic in 1880, as did Max Joseph in 1887; in 1888 Hugo Neumann founded a polyclinic for child diseases; and Theodor Rosenheim ran a clinic for gastrointestinal diseases from 1886 on. In addition to treating patients and training medical students, these clinics served as research laboratories for their owners and directors.

But there were two other institutions which must be mentioned with regard to the innovative work of Jewish doctors: the Jewish hospitals and the municipal hospitals.

The Jewish hospitals were founded and supported by the Jewish communities. The Jewish Hospital in Berlin, for example, developed from a *hekdesh* into a medical institution of high standing at a time when most other hospitals were still institutions for the care of the poor. By the end of the 18th century the famous doctor, Marcus Herz, whose wife Henriette had one of Berlin's most famous salons, had already begun to make a name for himself at the Jewish Hospital. The hospital treated non-Jews as well as Jews in its attempt to serve as an instrument of emancipation and integration. In 1861 and again in 1914, the hospital had to move to larger premises. Always equipped with the most modern equipment, it provided Jewish doctors with a place to practice and to

BERLIN N.
Auguststrasse 14/16

Krankenhaus der
Jüdischen Gemeinde

The Jewish Hospital, on Augustus Street, Berlin.

Ammy Ben Yakov Collection, New York.

develop new methods. The noted Ludwig Traube served as its director of internal medicine, and James Israel became the pioneer of nephrologic surgery there. One of Traube's most significant discoveries was the pneumatic cabinet which was constructed by Nathan Zuntz for the treatment of chronic bronchitis and asthma. Zuntz, who had done pioneer research on high altitudes but, as a Jew could not find work at the university, worked at an agricultural high school.

From the time the new buildings of the Jewish Hospital in Berlin were planned in 1890 until they were finally erected the situation for Jews in Germany had changed. Anti-Semitism had made its way into society. The newly-enlarged hospital which had been planned to cater to the needs of Jews and non-Jews now took on different aims. As Hermann Senator, the director of the medical polyclinic at the Charité Hospital, (who himself was never appointed full professor there), pointed out, it was becoming difficult for Jewish doctors to find jobs at general hospitals, in addition to which attempts were made in such hospitals to convert Jewish children. Jewish nurses also found it increasingly difficult to obtain positions at non-Jewish hospitals, and for this reason the Jewish Nurses' Training School, which had been established in 1895 and affiliated to the Jewish Hospital, was enlarged.

As for municipal hospitals, from 1869 on Berlin witnessed the growth of new neighborhood hospitals to deal with the poverty and social problems of the overcrowded city, generated by the development of capitalism. In 1883, with Bismarck's health insurance laws, these hospitals stopped caring for the poor and turned instead to treatment of the ill.

From the very beginning Jewish doctors were appointed to important positions at these hospitals, the most famous of which was the Moabit. Founded in 1872 as a barracks-hospital during the cholera epidemic, it later became a regular municipal hospital. Georg Klemperer, who had received his degree at the Charité in internal medicine and was appointed associate professor in 1905, took over the Department of Internal Medicine at the Moabit in 1906 and remained there until 1933. Klemperer was also well-known for his interest in psychosomatics (see below). Carl Benda, who had been chief pathologist at the Urban Hospital, another city hospital, since 1896, joined the staff of the Moabit Hospital in 1908. From the opening of the Urban Hospital in 1890, Albert Fraenkel became one of its two medical directors and made important contributions to internal medicine.

With the structural changes in Berlin's health system after World War I, the Moabit was in part attached to the Charité. Still, there were no restrictions on the careers of Jewish doctors at those sections of the Moabit which remained under the social-democratic city administration. Klemperer remained in his job, Moritz Borchardt, a pioneer in neurosurgery, taught there from 1919 (he had formerly worked at another of the city hospitals, the Rudolf Virchow Krankenhaus), and Rudolf Jaffe was pathologist there in 1925.

Social Health Care

As Germany changed from an agrarian to an industrial society, the pauperization of the proletariat and the other crises of capitalism which appeared at the end of the 19th century intensified the problems of diseases like tuberculosis, along with new occupational diseases. It became clear that medical measures alone could not solve these problems. Their solution required the reorganization of the health care system by the city administration. From 1888 on municipal physicians were given positions on municipal councils. The Jewish social-hygienist, Adolf Gottstein, who later became responsible for public health in Prussia, was the first medical alderman in Charlottenburg. As the social democrats took over political responsibility in Berlin after World War I, the system of social welfare was enlarged. In nearly all districts of Berlin, municipal physicians were appointed and a network of welfare organizations established, serving infants, pre-natal and post-natal mothers, school children, tuberculosis patients, people suffering from venereal diseases and drug-addiction, and the elderly. Advisory boards were established for people with sexual problems or disorders, and for the mentally disabled. These organizations gave many Jewish doctors the possibility of pursuing medical careers. Many had already been dealing with social problems within Jewish welfare organizations and soon became active within the labor movement and the Social Democratic Party. But even before many of these organizations had been established, Jewish doctors had been engaged in these problems. At the end of the 19th century, for example, Ignaz Zadek was practicing in Berlin-Neukoelln, a working-class district. Aware of the terrible situation among the poor, he combined his medical work with a deep commitment to social-political activities. In 1893, he wrote a study on the housing situation among the working class in Berlin. In 1894, he joined the board of doctors that advised the Central Organization for Local Health Insurance. In 1893 and again from 1905 until 1919, he was a member of the Berlin Municipal Council, on the social democratic ticket. In 1913, together with other social democratic doctors, most of whom were Jewish, Zadek founded the Social Democratic Medical Association, a political tool for promoting social politics and for disseminating medical and hygiene information among the proletariat.

Jewish Physicians in the Various Branches of Medicine

Although the following are not comprehensive surveys, they provide the reader with an indication of the importance of Jewish doctors in the various branches of medicine in Germany and Austria from the end of the 19th

Oskar Minkowski (1858-1931) *was born in Lithuania. He was an outstanding investigator and clinician, and carried out extensive physiological and chemical research in the field of metabolism at various centers in Germany. Among his most important medical achievements is his discovery of the endocrine nature of diabetes. Minkowski demonstrated that the removal of the pancreas in a dog causes diabetes, which made him one of the originators of modern therapy for diabetes with the use of insulin. National Library of Medicine, Bethesda.*

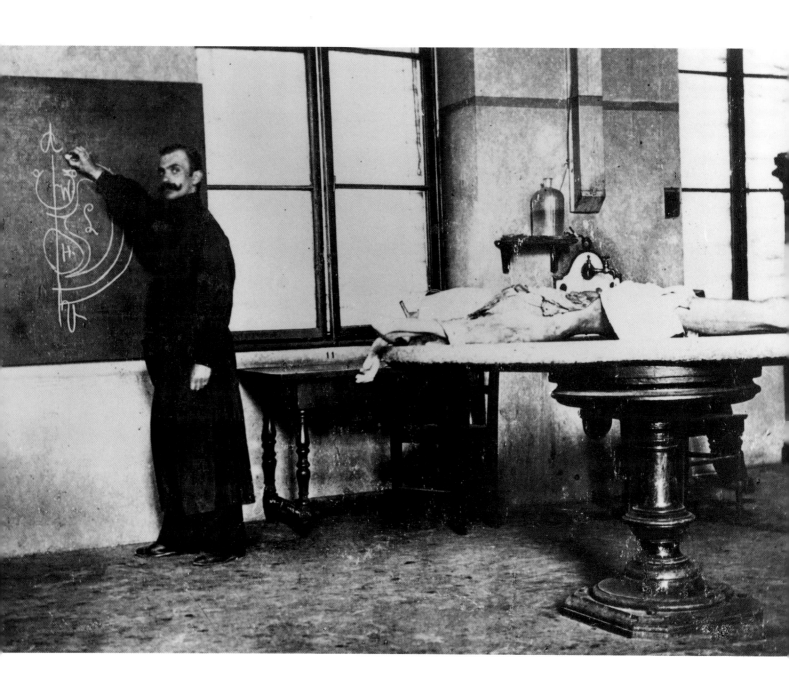

century until the end of the 1930s.

In *internal medicine*, Georg Klemperer established his own school on psychosomatic tendencies which opened itself to new and different fields of social hygiene. Drug addiction and alcoholism were serious problems after World War I. Two pupils of Klemperer, Ernst Joel and Ernst Haase, dealt with these problems, later heading the advisory board for drug addicts in Berlin-Tiergarten. Lilly Ehrenfried also trained under Klemperer and worked afterwards as a welfare doctor and head of a sexual advisory board in Berlin-Prenzlauer Berg. Hermann Strauss, who trained under Hermann Senator at the Jewish Hospital in Berlin from 1911 onwards, was considered a pioneer in nephrology. In Vienna, Julius Bauer worked in endocrinology and constitutional pathology, founding his own school, and when Hans Eppinger became head of internal medicine at the first Medical Clinic in 1933, the situation had become unbearable for Jews.

In *surgery* the pioneer neurosurgeon, Moritz Borchardt, headed the Department of Surgery at the Moabit. Among his pupils were Max Marcus who became famous for his skill in abdominal and vascular surgery, James Israel who performed pioneering surgery of the kidneys at the Jewish Hospital and, later, Paul Rosenstein in the same field.

In *gynecology* we find a high percentage of Jewish practitioners. In Vienna, 58 percent of all gynecologists were Jewish. In Berlin the famous gynecologists Samuel Kristeller, Ernst Groefenberg and Paul Strassman were all Jewish. The Department of Gynecology at the Moabit was staffed in the main by Jewish gynecologists, among them Siegbert Joseph and Erwin Rabau. Hertha Nathorff-Einstein, who studied with Joseph, was gynecologist and head of the advisory board for marital and family problems in Berlin-Charlottenburg until 1933. Bernhard Zondek was head of the Department of Gynecology at the municipal hospital in Berlin-Spandau from 1929-1933. Zondek was in fact more a scientist than a practitioner and was one of the leading figures in hormone research. There were innovations in this field by Max Hirsch, and Wilhelm Liepmann founded the branch of social gynecology on the basis of constitutional medicine.

Julius Tandler at the blackboard drawing anatomic details of the human body during an anatomy lecture at the Medical School of the University of Vienna.

Vienna, 1905 (?).

Julius Tandler (1869-1936) was born in Moravia, and studied in Vienna. In 1902 he became professor of anatomy and in 1910 he took over the Chair of Anatomy at the University of Vienna.

Museen der Stadt Wien.

The pioneers of *nephrology* and *urology* were mainly Jewish doctors from Berlin as were those who performed surgery on the kidneys and the urogenital system. Besides James Israel and Hermann Strauss, there were Eugen Joseph, who became head of urology at the Surgical University Clinic in Berlin, and Alexander V. Lichtenberg, assistant professor of urology at the university in Berlin in 1921, who is better known for his work as a surgeon at the Catholic Hedwigs Hospital where he invented the chromocystoscopy.

In *orthopedics* Julius Wolff in Berlin and Adolf Lorenz in Vienna were among the founders of this branch. In *ophthalmology* Julius Hirschberg was a pioneer and this too remained predominantly a Jewish field until 1933. The same can also be said for *dermatology*. In Vienna 68 percent of dermatologists were Jewish. Moritz Kaposi was a professor of dermatology at the University of Vienna. Paul Ehrlich discovered Salvarsan for the treatment of syphilis and August von Wassermann developed tests for the disease. Dermatologists were often closely connected with social medicine since they treated venereal diseases. Georg Loewenstein was a municipal physician in Berlin-Lichtenberg, engaged in controlling sexual diseases and working for sexual reform.

In *pediatrics* Adolf Aron Baginski and Leopold Langstein were two of the most important pediatricians of their time in Berlin. In Vienna, Clemens Pirquet did research in allergies and child psychology, and Josef Friedjung did research in sexual medicine.

Psychiatry, neurology and *psychoanalysis* should be considered jointly here since this was the time when the professionalization of neurology took place and psychoanalysis emerged. Jewish doctors were pioneers in this field and most of the important neurologists of the time were Jewish. Gustav Aschaffenburg and Wilhelm Sonder, the director of the largest asylum in Berlin, were pioneers in forensic psychiatry. Emanuel Mendel, Edward Levinstein and Moritz Jastrowitz all operated private asylums in Berlin and were famous for their therapy. Hermann Oppenheim managed a private neurological polyclinic in Berlin that became the center of neurology, and not for Germany alone. Sigmund Freud was originally a neurologist. Psycho-

analysis was a field almost totally dominated by Jews and the same can be said for child psychoanalysis, pioneered by Anna Freud.

Among the many Jews in *pharmacology* was Otto Loewi, a full professor in Graz, famous for his discovery of Adrenalinmydriasis (*Loewisches symptom*). In Vienna were Ernst Pick and Hans Molitor, the latter known for combining pharmacology with serology. In Berlin Oskar Liebreich invented chloralhydrate and Louis Lewin was the founder of toxicology.

Psychosomatic medicine really began to flourish only after 1945. However, in the Weimar Republic Jewish doctors in internal medicine and gastroenterology had already begun work in this field. Doctors like Klemperer and Leopold Alkan contributed to this field. In Berlin neurologist Kurt Goldstein from the Moabit Hospital also contributed to this new field.

Jewish doctors were the pioneers in *social hygiene* and *social* and *occupational medicine*. They were for the most social democrats but

Paul Ehrlich (1854-1915) *was one of the greatest, most original and profound investigators of his time. He revolutionized biochemistry, hematology, immunology and chemotherapy. As a medical student he became interested in chemistry and bacteriological research. He was named director of the Institute for Experimental Therapy at Frankfurt-am-Main in 1899 and professor at the University of Frankfurt fifteen years later. By discovering the existence of antibodies, Ehrlich established the doctrine of immunobiological relations and founded the vitally important science of hematology. He also created a new branch of chemotherapy with the introduction of Salvarsan (1910) in the treatment of syphilis, thus marking a new era in the long history of the struggle against this disease. In 1908 Ehrlich shared the Nobel Prize for medicine with Elie Metchnikoff for work on immunity. Many future advances were due directly to his investigations and discoveries.*

Paul Ehrlich Institute, Langen.

German bacteriologists, Berlin 1913.

From the left: Neufeld, Hartmann,

Wassermann, Gaffki, Lockermann.

Institute für Geschichte der Medizin,

Berlin.

Käte Frankenthal (1889-1976) *Activist of social hygiene and in charge of health affairs in the SPD (German Socialist Party), was nominated in 1928 as deputy city-physician and school physician in Berlin-Neukolln. She inaugurated a station for marital and sexual counseling, where contraceptives were dispensed free of charge. She was active in solving housing problems and procuring clothing and food for needy families, all within the framework of health welfare. In 1933, because of her "non-Aryan" origins, Frankenthal was dismissed from her position, and emigrated, via Prague, Zurich and Paris to New York, where she practiced psychoanalysis.*

Leo Baeck Institute, New York.

some were communists and others were liberals, like the last president of the Jewish Reform Congregation in Berlin, Arnold Peyser, a laryngologist, and Adolf Gottstein, a leading public health officer in Prussia. Engaging in social medicine gave Jewish doctors an opportunity to advance their careers outside of the universities. In Berlin nearly all of the municipal doctors we have mentioned, like Georg Loewenstein, were Jewish. Benno Chajes, Julius Moses and Käte Frankenthal were engaged in all aspects of social medicine in the Weimar Republic. Moses and Chajes were pioneers in the ambulatory service of the health insurance in the Weimar Republic. Franz-Karl Meyer-Brodnitz was a representative of occupational medicine who worked on behalf of the workers and in the service of the trade unions. In Austria three of the most important social hygienists were Jews and Austrian Marxists. Julius Tandler, professor of anatomy at the university, established the exemplary welfare system of so-called "red Vienna." Ludwig Teleky was active in preventative medicine (tuberculosis and occupational diseases), social security and trade hygiene.

Like psychoanalysis, the field of *sexual medicine* was dominated by Jewish doctors. Iwan Bloch, Albert Moll, Max Marcuse and the famous Magnus Hirschfeld were pioneers in this field in Berlin.

Medical Journalism

Two types of medical journals can be distinguished in Central Europe during the 19th and 20th century: journals which published the results of new research and journals in which forthcoming books or papers of interest were reviewed. Since Jews were restricted in the kind of positions they could hold, it was common for them to engage in medical journalism. They were the most frequent reviewers in Virchow's important *Jahresberichte ueber die Fortschritte der Medizin* [Annual reports of progress in medicine], especially in those new fields of specialization in which they were the innovators and practitioners. Jewish scholars participated in, and often founded, review journals focusing on books and papers dealing with one specialty alone – the so-called *Zentralblaetter*. Julius Hirschberg was involved in the *Zentralblatt fuer Augenheilkunde* [Central organ for ophthalmology]. Leo Langstein, an eminent pediatrician, was editor of the *Zentralblatt fuer Kinderheilkunde* [Central organ for pediatrics). Sigmund Exner from Vienna was involved in the *Zentralblatt fuer Physiologie* [Central organ for physiology] from its very first number in 1887. The well-known Hermann Senator was a member of the editorial board of the *Zentralblatt fuer die medizinischen Wissenschaften* [Central organ for medical sciences) from the time it first appeared in 1887. Josef Jadassohn was the co-editor of the *Zentralblatt fuer Haut- und Geschlechtskrankheiten* [Central organ for dermatology] until 1934 when the journal ceased publication, a year after the Nazis overthrew the Weimar republic.

Jews were also engaged in founding or expanding general medical journals. The *Wiener medizinische Wochenschrift* [Viennese medical weekly], founded in 1850, had two Jewish editors: Hans Adler from 1889-1909 and Adolf Kronfeld from 1909-1938. In Berlin, Louis Posner, who had been in charge of the *Allgemeine medizinische Zentralseitung* (the main medical journal for the whole country) from 1849, founded his own journal, the *Berliner klinische Wochenschrift* [Berlin clinical weekly] in 1864, a journal famous for the innovative and often prophetic papers it published.

All this came to a sudden end – in Berlin in 1933 and in Vienna in 1938. In Berlin on March 27, 1933, the S.S. attacked the Moabit Hospital and took many of its Jewish doctors to so-called wild concentration camps where they were tortured. Jewish doctors who worked as civil servants were relieved of their positions and taken to concentration camps. Universities were forced by the government to withdraw the degrees of associate professors, which meant that nearly all Jewish doctors were excluded from working at the universities. On April 1, 1933, there was a boycott of all Jewish shops, doctors and lawyers. The law which reshaped the civil service meant that Jews and opponents of National Socialism were excluded from working in the civil service. After April 7, 1933, this law was extended to include all doctors who were working within

The Jewish Hospital, Berlin, 1938.

The sign at the entrance to the Clinic for Women's Diseases reads: "As of October 1, 1938, only Jewish patients will be treated."

Bildarchiv Abraham Pisarek, Berlin.

the framework of the health insurance, and as of July 25, 1933, it covered all Jewish doctors. The right to practice was cancelled and only 1,082 Jewish practitioners were permitted to continue to practice medicine, but only for the care of Jews still living in Germany.

Some 80 percent of Jewish doctors succeeded in emigrating. The rest suffered the fate of the Jewish people as a whole and were murdered by the Germans. I shall only mention a few of them. The social hygienist, Julius Moses, and the Berlin municipal doctor, Manfred Bejach, perished in Theresienstadt. The social-hygienist Felix Koenigsberger was killed in Dachau by the S.S. because he refused to participate in medical experiments on Jewish children in the camp. Walter Oettinger was killed in the Riga Ghetto. Between the years 1933 to 1938 many Jewish doctors committed suicide, among them, pediatrician Leo Langstein, the social-hygienist Theodor Plaut, Ludwig Jaffe and the famous Magnus Hirschfeld.

For many of those who emigrated, life was very difficult and often meant the end of their careers. Georg Loewenstein, who immigrated to the United States said that although he was able to work again in public health, his work was never again as interesting as when he had been a municipal doctor in Berlin-Lichtenberg. Many of those who emigrated to Palestine – which absorbed the greatest number of doctors until 1935 – succeeded. Benno Chajes continued to work as a social hygienist in Palestine, contributing to occupational medicine at the Histadrut. Bernhard Zondek continued as a gynecologist at the Hebrew University, as did Erwin Rabau. Max Marcus worked as a surgeon at the Hadassah Hospital in Tel Aviv and served as a doctor in the War of Independence for the Haganah.

Nazi medical practices overthrew the progressive work of all the Jewish doctors. After 1945 no doctors were invited to return and their ideas were not revived. People who now study the history of medicine speak of a deleted alternative in medicine in Germany. Jewish doctors and their work are often forgotten. To remember them and to use their achievements to further medicine is a duty for Jews and all human beings today.

~

BIBLIOGRAPHY

ERNA LESKY, *The Vienna Medical School in the 19th Century*, The Johns Hopkins University Press, Baltimore and London, 1976. Translated by L. Williams and I.S. Levij (German original 1965).

ROLF WINAU, *Medizin in Berlin*, Walter de Gruyter, Berlin and New York, 1987.

STEPHAN LEIBFRIED AND FLORIAN TENNSTEDT, *Berufsverbote und Sozialpolitik, 1933* [Forbidden professions and social politics,1933], Working papers, No. 2, Bremen University, 3rd ed., 1981.

CHRISTIAN PROSS AND ROLF WINAU, eds., *Nicht misshandeln. Das Krankenhaus Moabit, 1920-1945* [Don't mistreat. The Moabit Hospital, 1920-1945], Places in Berlin's History, vol. 5, Hentrich, 1984.

DAGMAR HARTUNG-VON DOETINCHEM, ed., *Zerstoerte Fortschritte. Das Juedische Krankenhaus in Berlin 1756-1861-1914-1989* [Progress destroyed. The Jewish Hospital in Berlin 1756-1861-1914-1989], Places in Berlin's History, vol. 35, Hentrich, 1989.

ERWIN H. ACKERKNECHT, *A Short History of Medicine*, The Ronald Press Company, New York, 1968.

"He keeps on saying 'Science knows no frontiers' - and he hasn't a passport."
Punch cartoon of August 1938 graphically illustrates the problems faced by refugee scientists and physicians.
From Go and Learn by Kenneth Collins, Aberdeen University Press, 1988.

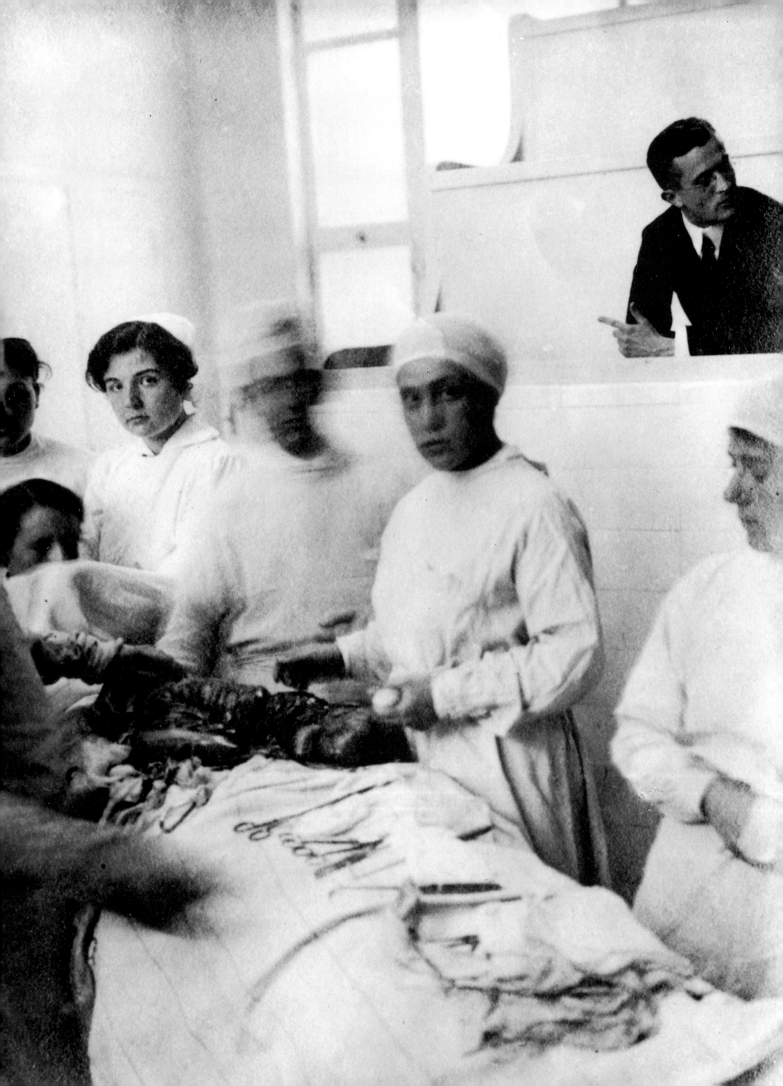

HARRIET PASS FREIDENREICH

JEWISH WOMEN IN MEDICINE IN THE EARLY 20TH CENTURY THE CASE OF CENTRAL EUROPE

Jewish women made up a disproportionately large percentage of the female physicians in Central Europe before the Nazi era. When German and Austrian universities began opening their doors to women around the turn of the century, Jewish women eagerly took advantage of the opportunity to enter the previously all-male professional world of medicine. At first the major difficulties they had to surmount were related to the fact that they were women. After 1933, they shared the fate of all Jews in Nazi Europe and were compelled to emigrate in order to continue their interrupted lives and careers.

Overcoming Obstacles

At the end of the 19th century few professions were readily accessible to educated middle-class women, who were expected to follow their mothers' example by marrying and raising a family, and not working outside the home. Teaching was by far the most popular career choice for women, but Jews faced dismal employment prospects in both public and private schools. Even the finest education then available to girls in Germany and Austria did not prepare them to pass the matriculation examinations (*Abitur* or *Matura*) which would enable them to attend universities as regular students. Before girls' academic Gymnasia or Realgymnasia became widespread, young women had to receive private tutoring or take special courses to catch up in mathematics, science and Latin, subjects which were not taught in girls' schools. They had to pass the matriculation examinations as external students in boys' Gymnasia. But even passing the *Abitur* did not smooth the way for the early pioneers.

Johanna Hellmann operating on a patient.

Berlin, 1930s.

Johanna Hellmann was born in Nuremberg, Germany in 1898 and studied in Berlin and Kiel. In a report in 1974 to the International Association of Women in Medicine in Stockholm, she wrote about her hardships at the university:

"The best opportunities for studying anatomy were in Berlin, and so I went there. Professor Virchow's lectures attracted a large crowd of students – men and women, although dissection courses were strictly separate for male and female students. After a year and a half, I moved to Kiel. Out of sheer curiosity I attended a lecture in surgery - and it struck me immediately that surgery was my goal."

Leo Baeck Institute, New York.

Frauenstudium - Women taking their medical examinations.

"Miss X (a medical student), what is interesting about this patient?"

"That she's wearing a silk petticoat."

Caricature by Th. Heine for Simplicissimus, 1901

Bildarchiv Preussischer Kulturbesitz, Berlin.

Irma Klausner (later Cronheim) was among the six women who completed the first organized "cram" courses in Berlin and passed her *Abitur* exam in 1896. She then had to obtain special permission from each of her professors to attend lectures at the University of Halle, and the Prussian legislature had subsequently to pass a special law, nicknamed "Lex Irma" after her, to enable her to take medical examinations. Similarly, Rachel Goitein (later Strauss), a member of the first graduating class of the new Girls' Gymnasium in Karlsruhe in 1899, required special authorization to study medicine in Heidelberg and then to obtain her medical degree six years later.

Although Jewish women sometimes met with anti-Semitism in one form or another during their medical studies, they tended to encounter greater discrimination because of their gender rather than their religious affiliation. Women students often had to contend with ridicule from their professors during lectures and oral examinations, as well as heckling from male students, behavior today classified as sexual harassment. For example, women who studied medicine in Vienna almost invariably mentioned Julius Tandler, a prominent professor of anatomy and a renowned Social Democratic welfare reformer, who regularly poked fun at the women in his classes – although he did not usually fail them. Most Jewish university women came from fairly assimilated, non-observant households, yet several who came from modern Orthodox homes managed to complete their medical training without veering from Orthodox practices. In at least one case this meant switching universities in order not to have to take required courses or examinations on the Sabbath.

Medicine was the most expensive and most rigorous field of study, requiring a minimum of five years of training, including passing a preliminary examination or *Physikum* after two years, and then writing a dissertation after completing six clinical semesters. But acquiring the degree of doctor of medicine was only the first major hurdle a woman had to overcome before embarking on a successful medical career; internships, research assistantships and residencies were often difficult for women to obtain, especially if they were Jewish, and the work was frequently unpaid.

Doctorate discussion by a female student in Berlin, 1902.

Berlin, Landesbildstelle.

Nonetheless, more and more women set their sights on a medical career. They often decided to study medicine at a very early age, sometimes before they were even aware that women could actually become physicians in Central Europe. Few considered nursing as an alternative career. As one women reported: "I was born with the wish to become a doctor. My dolls were always sick." Their role models were almost always male – fathers, brothers, uncles or the family physicians of their childhood. Some women articulated a strong desire to help others as the motivation behind their choice of a medical career, others were clearly rebelling against their mothers and the conventional roles prescribed for middle class women. While some women received strong parental encouragement and financial support for their medical studies, others had to overcome stiff opposition at home, generally based on a parent's fear that if their daughter became a doctor she might never marry and have a family of her own.

Medicine: A Choice for Jews

On the eve of World War I, shortly after German and Austrian institutions of higher learning began admitting women, Jewish women comprised 11 percent of all women students in Prussian universities and almost 30 percent

Rachel Hirsch at the medical clinic of the Charité Hospital, 1911.

In 1913 Rachel Hirsch (1870-1953) became the first woman to be nominated professor of medicine in Prussia. She worked at the Charité Hospital, and was the first to describe the absorption of starch grains into the blood vessels through absorption from the intestine. At that time nobody took her seriously and, disappointed, she discontinued her research. The phenomenon was "rediscovered" fifty years later and the process was name the Rachel Hirsch effect.

Rachel Hirsch was the granddaughter of Samson Raphael Hirsch. She left Berlin in 1933 and emigrated to England. She died in London in 1953.

Institut für Geschichte der Medizin, Berlin.

of women medical students. At the University of Vienna, where Jewish women accounted for 43 percent of the women students, they constituted nearly 60 percent of women studying medicine. After the war, the absolute number of Jewish women studying medicine continued to increase although their percentage within the female student population decreased. According to the 1925 German census, 330 Jewish women were practicing medicine in Prussia, comprising more than 20 percent of all female physicians. In 1932 almost 40 percent of the women physicians in Berlin were Jewish. In Vienna the percentage was even higher.

Medicine has always been a highly respected occupation for Jewish men. It is among the free professions which allow its practitioners self-employment, upward mobility and economic security. But the first generation of Jewish women who embarked on medical careers did not do so for strictly economic reasons. For the most part they already came from upper middle class homes: their fathers were either professionals or well-to-do businessmen. They often sought liberation from their mother's lifestyle and personal independence. Medicine was also a profession which could be combined with home and family.

While it was not uncommon for their male Jewish counterparts to enter academia at least as lecturers, it proved extremely difficult for Jewish women with medical degrees to obtain even entry-level positions in academic medicine, although a few managed to attain the rank of untenured associate professor. In general, Jewish women physicians found themselves in less prestigious and economically less successful areas when compared with Jewish male physicians with the same educational background. Nevertheless, nearly all of the women who became physicians seem to have been gainfully employed within the medical profession until the advent of the Nazi regime. Most Jewish women physicians maintained private practices, often in their own homes, occasionally in conjunction with their husbands or fathers. Although some were specialists and treated affluent patients, men and women alike, the majority were general practitioners. Their clientele was mainly women and children, while much of their case load came from working-class insurance patients. Many seem to have developed a loyal following of devoted patients who turned to them for personal advice as well as medical care.

Women who decided to specialize generally chose among a relatively limited number of fields – pediatrics, gynecology, psychiatry and ophthalmology, but never surgery or orthopedics. After World War I there was already a marked tendency among Jewish women with medical degrees toward psychotherapy. In this respect, as well as in their active involvement in the sex reform movement and their strongly leftist political orientation, female Jewish physicians differed significantly from most of their non-Jewish women colleagues.

Home and Family

Among the 100 Jewish women physicians included in this study, 80 percent married and two-thirds of those who married had children, although relatively few married before obtaining their medical degrees. More than half of those who married did so within five years after graduation, while about a fourth married later in life. Very few of these women intermarried; the vast majority married Jews with medical or other university degrees. Most of them had

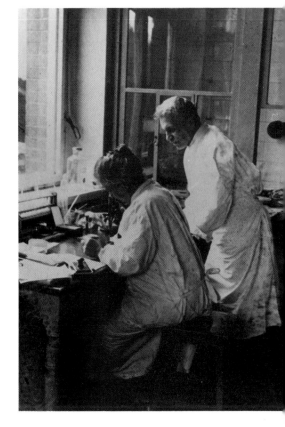

Lydia Rabinowitz-Kempner at the microscope with Martin Jacoby.

Berlin, c.1930.

Lydia Rabinowitz-Kempner (1871-1935), born in Kovno, studied in Berne and carried out post-graduate studies at the Institute for Infectious Diseases in Berlin. From 1898 she was associated with Robert Koch in his research. She was the first woman to receive the title of professor in Prussia, 1912.

Bildarchiv Preussischer Kulturbesitz, Berlin.

small families with one or two children, although there were those who had three or more. It is striking to note that although physicians had fewer children than women in my sample who left university without obtaining a doctorate, as a group, women medical doctors had larger families than those women who obtained degrees in non-medical fields. Within a sample of some 400 women, there appears to be a much higher incidence of married women physicians working in their profession when compared to women with doctorates in other subjects. The latter seem to have been more likely to discontinue their careers after marriage and childbirth. Private medical practice was evidently compatible with child-rearing, especially since most professional Jewish households in early 20th-century Central Europe could well afford child care and housekeepers.

Unmarried women enjoyed some professional advantages over their married colleagues in the fields of public health and medical research. However, while single women gained economic independence from their families, they did not necessarily desire or achieve financial success or higher status as a result of their careers.

The Advent of Hitler

As a result of Nazi legislation, more than 600 "non-Aryan" women in Germany and several hundred more in Austria lost their right to practice medicine. Jewish women physicians with German civil service status – even if they had officially left the Jewish community – were dismissed from their positions by May 1933. Those in private practice, including women who had intermarried, were harassed by the S.A. during the April economic boycott and thereafter. Once Jewish physicians, men or women, were excluded from insurance plans, it became increasingly difficult for them to continue their medical careers.

Many of these women saw the writing on the wall fairly early on and were fortunate enough to be able to emigrate before the outbreak of war, though some of them reached dead ends in neighboring countries. Among those who survived the Holocaust, several claim it was due, at least partially, to their

medical expertise. Very few Jewish women physicians returned to Germany or Austria after the war; most chose to remain in the United States, Great Britain or Israel.

Young Jewish women whose medical studies were interrupted due to Nazi restrictions found it virtually impossible to complete their training elsewhere. Those who emigrated with medical degrees in hand did not have an easy adjustment either. Re-accreditation as physicians depended on when and to where they emigrated and their ability to overcome bureaucratic obstacles. In Brazil, for example, they had to start their training all over again once they had learned Portuguese and Brazilian geography. As one women wrote to her relatives: "At age fifty-two I am professionally at the exact point I was at twenty-six in Germany." Although a majority of the women in this study succeeded in resuming their medical careers in some form, often as psychoanalysts, many of the older women never requalified as physicians but worked instead alongside their physician husbands or as overqualified nurses. Among the younger emigrant women physicians, some eventually attained higher academic or professional positions in the United States than would have been possible in their native countries. Most, however, continued to maintain private practices in family medicine or in pediatrics. In Israel women physicians often worked in clinics within the public health sector.

In conclusion, the evidence shows that those Jewish women who studied medicine in Central Europe in the early part of the 20th century were a highly

Johanna Hellmann taking part in a lecture of the German Society of Surgery. Johanna Hellmann joined the North-West German Surgical Society in 1920, and in 1925 became the first female member of the German Society for Surgery.
Berlin, April 1931 (?).
Photo: Welt Photo Bericht, Berlin.
Leo Baeck Institute, New York.

motivated and courageous group who succeeded in acquiring medical degrees and practicing medicine despite the considerable odds against them, both as women and as Jews. Although very few attained financial success or high status, most of them did achieve many of their personal goals: they utilized their professional skills to help others and at the same time they supported themselves and contributed to the well-being of their families. Medicine was a difficult profession for women to enter, yet it offered the best chance for Jewish women with a university degree to continue working in their chosen field, both after marriage and – in many cases – after emigration. As a lifetime career, it proved more practical and more portable than law, education or other professions more closely linked to language and culture.

This article is an abridged version of a conference paper presented at the annual conference of the Association for Jewish Studies in Boston in 1993. It is based on information gleaned from published and unpublished memoirs, biographical dictionaries, questionnaires and interviews and is part of a larger study in progress, a collective biography of 400 women of Jewish origin who studied at German or Austrian universities between 1897 and 1938.

BIBLIOGRAPHY

ELISABETH BOEDEKER AND MARIA MAYER-PLATH, *50 Jahre Habilitation von Frauen in Deutschland*, Göttingen, 1974.

EVA BRINKSCHULTE, ed., *Weibliche Ärzte*, Berlin, Hentrich, 1993.

BARBARA COHORS-FRESENBORG, *Frau Onkel Doktor: Untersuchung über die Anfänge des Frauenstudiums in der Medizin anhand von Fragebögen und Interviews mit Ärztinnen*, Münster, Lit Verlag, 1989.

HELENE ROSENBACH DEUTSCH, *Confrontations with Myself*, New York, W.W. Norton, 1973.

KÄTE FRANKENTHAL, *Der dreifache fluch*, Frankfurt, 1981.

ANITA GROSSMANN, "Berliner Arztinnen und Volksgesundheit in der Weimarer Republik: Zwischen Sexualreform und Eugenik," in Christiane Eifert and Susanne Rouette, *Unter allen Umständen: Frauengeschichte(n) in Berlin*, Berlin, 1986.

ANITA GROSSMANN, "German Women Doctors from Berlin to New York: Maternity and Modernity in Weimar and in Exile," *Feminist Studies*, 19/1 (Spring 1993).

WALTRAUD HEINDLE AND MARINA TICHY, eds., *Durch Erkenntnis zu Freiheit und Glück: Frauen an der Universität*, Wien, Vienna, WUV-Universitätsverlag, 1990.

IRMA KLAUSNER-CRONHEIM, "Dornenweg der Medizinerin," *Vossische Zeitung*, December 25, 1929.

MARIE LANGER, *Von Wien bis Managua*, Frankfurt, Kore, 1986.

MAGARET SCHOENBERGER MAHLER, *Memoirs of Margaret S. Mahler*, New York, Free Press, 1988.

ELKE MUHLLEITER, *Biographisches Lexikon der Psychoanalyse*, Tübingen, Diskord, 1992.

HERTHA NATHORFF, *Das Tagebuch der Hertha Nathorff*, Munich, 1987.

RACHEL STRAUS, *Wir lebten in Deutschland*, Stuttgart, 1961.

YAAKOV AND HADASSAH WEHL, *House Calls to Eternity: The Story of Dr. Selma Wehl*, Brooklyn,: Mesorah Publications, 1987.

CHARLOTTE WOLFF, *Hindsight*, London, Quartet Books, 1980.

INTERVIEWS AND QUESTIONNAIRES

IRMA KLAUSENER-CRONHEIM, questionnaire, completed by her son, Georg Cronheim, .

HANNAH E. LAZARUS FRAENKEL, questionnaire and letter, September 1992.

PAULINE GLANZBERG-RACHLIS, interview, November 1991.

RUTH ZALOSCER GUTMANN, interview, August 1992.

EDITH POPPER HACKER, questionnaire.

ELEANOR HADRA, interview, June 1992.

FRANZISKA GRUNHUNT HARTLE, questionnaire.

HEDI ROTHCHILD KANDEL, questionnaire.

RITA SMRCKA KRAUSE, interview, July 1991.

KATHARINA WEINER LÖFFLER, information provided in letters by daughter, Inge Zornig, May 4, 1993 and niece Lore Jonas, January 3, 1993.

SELMA MAYER, letter from Peter Voswinckel, August 16, 1992.

JULIA OPPENHEIMER RAHMER, questionnaire.

HANNA HEDWIG KOHN STRIESOW, questionnaire.

SARAH LIBON WEINER, questionnaire.

ALISA (ELISABETH) CZEMPIN YALLON, questionnaire.

UNPUBLISHED SOURCES

SUSANNE M. BATZDORFF, "Reflections in a Rearview Mirror" (Santa Rosa, Cal., 1984).

CLAUDIA HUERKAMP, "Jüdische Akademikerinnen in Deutschland, 1900-1938" (courtesy of author).

HENRIETTE (HENNY) MAGNUS NECHELES, "My Life in Germany" (Houghton Library, Boston, bMS Ger 93, #163).

PAULA TOBIAS, "My Life in Germany" (Houghton Library, Boston, bMS Ger 93, #235), pp.3-5.

PETER GAY

SIGMUND FREUD

The author can, with due moderation raise the question of whether his own

personality as a Jew who never tried to conceal his Judaism did not play

a part in the antipathy his milieu felt toward psychoanalysis. Only rarely has

an argument of this kind been mentioned aloud; we have, sadly, become

so distrustful that we cannot help suspecting that this circumstance has not

remained totally without effect. It is perhaps no mere coincidence that

the first representative of psychoanalysis was a Jew. Advocating it demanded

a substantial degree of readiness to accept the fate of being isolated in the

opposition, a fate more familiar to the Jew than to anyone else.

Sigmund Freud

At the turn of the century Vienna boasted a disparate yet closely associated army of freedom fighters, of liberators who must have inspired one another in important ways: Arthur Schnitzler, Karl Kraus, Ludwig Wittgenstein – and Sigmund Freud. It is certain that Freud was very much aware of Vienna and that (though to a much smaller degree) Vienna was aware of Freud. He conducted many of his scientific skirmishes here; his earliest detractors, though not his earliest admirers, were Viennese. He admired Schnitzler – his tribute to Schnitzler as a "colleague" in the investigation of the "underestimated and much-maligned erotic" has often been quoted. He was in turn derided by Kraus, and gave Wittgenstein food for tortured reflections. But it would be rash, and I think wrong, to conclude that the boldness of his fellow-Viennese somehow infected Freud with a boldness of his own, or that their observations shortened or in any way eased his own laborious descent to the foundations of human behavior. I want to argue that Freud lived far less in Austrian Vienna than in his own mind; he lived with the international positivist tradition, with

Sigmund Freud.

National Photo Library, Vienna.

the tantalizing triumphs of classical archeologists, with the admirable and moving model provided by that great French scientist of the mind, Jean-Martin Charcot, with the consolations of his far-flung correspondence, and with the infinitely instructive surprises of systematic introspection. Naturally, his introspection fed, often casually and quite unconsciously, on materials Freud gathered up in Vienna, on visits to his cigar merchant or during his regular card game, in the slow progress up the academic ladder and with his experience of Austrian anti-Semitism. After all, like many of his early patients, Freud was brought up in Vienna and permanently settled there; Vienna's often bizarre politics impinged on his awareness, daily, with his reading of the newspaper.

Yet it is, I think, scarcely claiming too much to say that "Vienna," that distinctive, impalpable, all-pervasive, electric atmosphere in which everyone knew everyone who counted, and everyone who was anyone acted both as teacher and pupil in an intense, continuing seminar on Modernist culture – that Vienna is an invention of cultural historians in search of quick explanations. There were indeed opulent salons in Vienna, fostering surroundings for new poems, new ideas, new compositions. Poets recited to each other, composers visited their rivals' concerts, philosophers formed working circles. And some of the physicians with whom the young Freud worked attended these schools for culture. Yet Freud himself went to the theater less and less, and never became a habitue of Viennese salon life; his Vienna was medical Vienna, and that city rarely frequented the hospitable mansions of Vienna's patrons. Besides, that medical Vienna was only partially Austrian; instead it represented, late in the 19th century, a microcosm of German scientific talent: the physiologist Ernst Brücke and the clinician Hermann Nothnagel, two distinguished medical men whose influence on Freud's scientific mode of thinking was decisive, were both Germans who had assumed their posts in Vienna after training and working in the "north." Freud, then, had relatively little to do with the "prison" he sometimes loved and often hated, and reached out beyond it. His mind, it will emerge, was as large, as free, as his physical habitat was constricted.

Third International Congress of Psychoanalysis, Weimer, Germany, 21-22 September 1911.

1. Sigmund Freud, 2. Otto Rank, 3. Ludwig Binswanger, 4. Ludwig Jekels, 5. Abraham A. Brill, 6. Eduard Hitschmann, 7. Paul Federn, 8. Oskar Pfister, 9. Max Eitingon, 10. Karl Abraham, 11. James J. Putman, 12. Ernest Jones, 13. Wilhelm Stekel, 14. Eugen Bleuler, 15. Lou Andreas-Salomé, 16. Emma Jung, 17. Sandor Ferenczi, 18. C.G. Jung.
The Freud Museum, London.

Berggasse 19, where Freud lived for nearly half a century, is an unpretentious apartment house on a respectable residential street in northern Vienna. When he moved there in the summer of 1891 to take a small apartment, Freud was a promising young neurologist with unorthodox ideas and a future to make; when he left the house and Nazi-occupied Austria in June 1938 "to die in freedom," he was a world-famous old man, founder of a science as pervasive in its influence as it was controversial in its claims. He enacted much quiet drama in this building; the silent struggles and private triumphs that mark the lives of all intellectual innovators marked this innovator more than others. Here, at Berggasse 19, Freud wrote most of his books and analyzed most of his patients; here he gathered his library, collected his art, met his associates, raised his children, and conducted a voluminous correspondence in which he rehearsed his momentous ideas and kept the threads of the psychoanalytic movement from twisting or from disintegrating altogether. His apartment is now a museum, and a plaque informs the passer-by that Sigmund Freud "lived and worked" here. The celebration seems modest enough for one of the decisive discoverers in history, for the Columbus of the mind. Nor does the plaque represent an effusion of local pride: it was put up in 1953 by the World Federation for Mental Health. In fact, most of the recognition Freud received in Vienna has been the work of foreigners: his bust, which now stands in the University, was presented by Ernest Jones. There is in Vienna, crisscrossed with streets named after its great, or at least prominent, residents, no Freudgasse. Guidebooks and leaflets advertising the city, though in their accustomed way assiduous in rescuing once-famous Viennese from oblivion, barely mention his name. The public indifference, the latent hostility, are chilling. Freud, the first psychologist to chart the workings of ambivalence, had in this city abundant materials for the exercise of mixed feelings. Vienna, it seems, has largely repressed Freud.

But Freud is irrepressible. He has scattered rich and rewarding clues to himself, to his way of thinking and his mode of working, to his habits and his aversions. His living quarters were a museum in the figurative sense – a crammed, instructive storehouse of ideas, tastes, and convictions – long before they were elevated into an official place of pilgrimage for foreign psychoanalysts and foreign analysands. His autobiographical writings are terse but informative. His letters are abundant, energetic and, wholly characteristic. Best of all, his scientific works provide sketch maps to his innermost nature. Considering the kind of science he founded, they could not do anything less: psychoanalysis is controlled and deep autobiography, and as the first psychoanalyst, compelled as he was to use himself as material, Freud found it necessary to publish some of his most private fantasies. His life was among his best documents.

For a healer, it has been justly observed, Freud had a strikingly low opinion of the human animal. Much happened to him across the years, much happened that pleased him. But the unreceptive world of Vienna never changed; neither did the hatred of that larger mob, educated and uneducated, for Freud the unrepentant Jew. "Something in me rebels against the compulsion to go on earning money which is never enough," he wrote glumly to his trusted Sàndor Ferenczi in early 1922, "and to continue with the same psychological devices that for thirty years have kept me upright in the face of my contempt for people and the detestable world. Strange secret yearnings rise in me – perhaps from my ancestral heritage – for the East and the Mediterranean and for a life of quite another kind: wishes from late childhood never to be fulfilled."

The two sides of Freud's work, the psychoanalytic writings and the cultural-historical speculations, were not identical; but they were consistent with, in fact implied, one another. And, I must add, to deny that one has a *Weltanschauung* does not mean that one is, in fact, without one. Freud, in taking the part of science against authoritarianism or mysticism, at least implicitly supported some philosophies of life and opposed their opponents.

One side of Freud's thought has been emphasized at the expense of the other. Freud has often been hailed as a great liberator of men – and, despite that fatal phrase, "biology is destiny", of women, too. The accolade is fully deserved, and at least once Freud himself suggested that he thought so, too. In the summer of 1915, writing to the distinguished American neurologist, James

J. Putnam, he described himself as a highly moral man who accepted the ethical rules of modern civilization without question – all except those governing modern sexual conduct. "Sexual morality as society, in its most extreme form, the American one, defines it, seems to be very contemptible. I stand for an incomparably freer sexual life, although," he confessed, "I myself have made very little use of such freedom: only in so far as I myself judged it to be allowable." It was a part of Freud's inner freedom that he did not need to impose his private preferences on culture as a whole. Whatever his own practices, he reiterated that modern man enjoyed himself too little and punished himself too much. In a much-quoted essay of 1908 on the effects of modern sexual restraint on mental health, he insisted that the pressures of civilization had become excessive. "Experience teaches that there is for most people a limit beyond which their constitution cannot comply with the demands of culture. All those who want to be nobler than their constitution permits, lapse into neurosis." And he adds, with his characteristic reasonableness, "They would have been healthier if it had remained possible for them to be more wicked – *schlechter zu sein*." Freud's writings are pervaded with invitations to be more wicked: to accept eccentric behavior as normal, to give up punitive attitudes toward what were called the perversions – to accept, in short, instinctual life.

In a remarkable letter of 1935, written from Berggasse 19 to a woman, a stranger, who had confessed that her son was a homosexual, Freud chided her gently for not being able to bring herself to write the dreadful word.

May I question you why you avoid it? Homosexuality is assuredly no advantage, but it is nothing to be ashamed of, no vice, no degradation, it cannot be classified as an illness; we consider it to be a variation of the sexual function, produced by a certain arrest of sexual development.

He added, as consistent as he was being humane to the anguished mother:

Many highly respectable individuals of ancient and modern times have been homosexuals, several of the greatest men among them (Plato, Michelangelo, Leonardo da Vinci, etc.). It is a great injustice to persecute homosexuality as a crime - and a cruelty, too.

The group of psychiatrists who made up the core of the psychoanalytic movement, 1922.

Standing from left: Otto Rank, Karl Abraham, Max Eitingon, Ernest Jones. Seated from left: Sigmund Freud, Sandor Ferenczi, Hanns Sachs. Institut für Geschichte der Medizin, Wien.

When he addressed himself to more conventional sexual behavior, his liberalism was equally pronounced. At fourteen, "Dora" had responded with disgust to the sexual advances of an older man, a man she loved; Freud, in his report on the case, judged this rejection to be not praiseworthy moral conduct but a neurotic symptom: "I should certainly consider every person hysterical, in whom an occasion for sexual excitement elicits feelings preponderantly or exclusively unpleasurable." Dicta such as these, delivered in Freud's most matter-of-fact voice, could only serve to enlarge the sphere of the permissible. His very theories pressed modern society to substitute clinical neutrality for high-minded condemnation. After all, if every human being is subject to the urges of infantile sexuality and the most murderous wishes against the most beloved persons, moral canons and cultural habits must be adjusted to take account of these overwhelming truths about human nature. And once again, style served substance. Freud was not Nietzsche; he was not, as Hartmann has said, "'a transvaluer of values' – not in the sense, that is, that he wanted to

Sigmund Freud in his study.

Max Pollack, 1914.

Aquatint, 80 x 61.5 cm.

The Freud Museum, London.

impress on his fellow men a new scale of moral values." But intentions and influence are two different things. Freud was no philosopher; he was just more effective than the philosophers. He was, partly without his active cooperation, a moral liberator.

Facing up to things as they are characterizes Freud's life. It was not easy to be a Jew in Imperial Austria, especially a Jew with aspirations. In Vienna, especially at the end of the century, anti-Semitism was more than the confused broodings of psychopaths; it pervaded and poisoned student organizations, university politics, social relationships, medical opinions. To be the destroyer of human illusions, as Freud was by intention and by results, was to make oneself into a special target of the anti-Semite. "Be assured," Freud wrote in the summer of 1908 to his brilliant disciple Karl Abraham, "if my name were

Oberhuber, my innovations would have encountered far less resistance, despite everything." Yet Freud persisted, both in doing psychoanalytic work and in calling himself a Jew. There is, in this loyalty, a kind of defiance. Freud was the opposite of religious: his view of religion as an illusion akin to neurosis applied to the faith of his fathers as much as any other. He granted the existence of some mysterious bonds that tied him to Judaism, and he attributed his objectivity and his willingness to be in a minority at least partly to his Jewish origins. But there was another element in this equation. "My merit in the Jewish cause," he wrote to Marie Bonaparte in 1926, after B'nai Brith had honored him on his seventieth birthday, "is confined to one single point: that I have never denied my Jewishness." To deny it would have been senseless and, as he also said, undignified. The Jewish bond he felt was the recognition of a common fate in a hostile world.

Individualistic and problematic as it was, Freud's Jewishness made an intimate bond between him and Vienna. For Vienna, never in reality the city of operettas and flirtations, was, even in Freud's time, a city of ugly rehearsals; it made Freud the Jew suffer even more because he was a Jew than because he was Freud. A laboratory for every known species of anti-Semitism, Vienna virtually compelled Freud to see himself as one among a band of potential victims, as one among Vienna's Jews. It was a role that he took upon himself with his accustomed courage. But the core of that courage was neither sectarian nor local. It was intellectual. Freud was, first and last, the scientist, bravely following the evidence wherever it led.

~

Excerpted from Peter Gay, Freud, Jews and Other Germans - Masters and Victims in Modernist Culture, New York, 1978; by permission of Oxford University Press. Compiled by Natalia Berger.

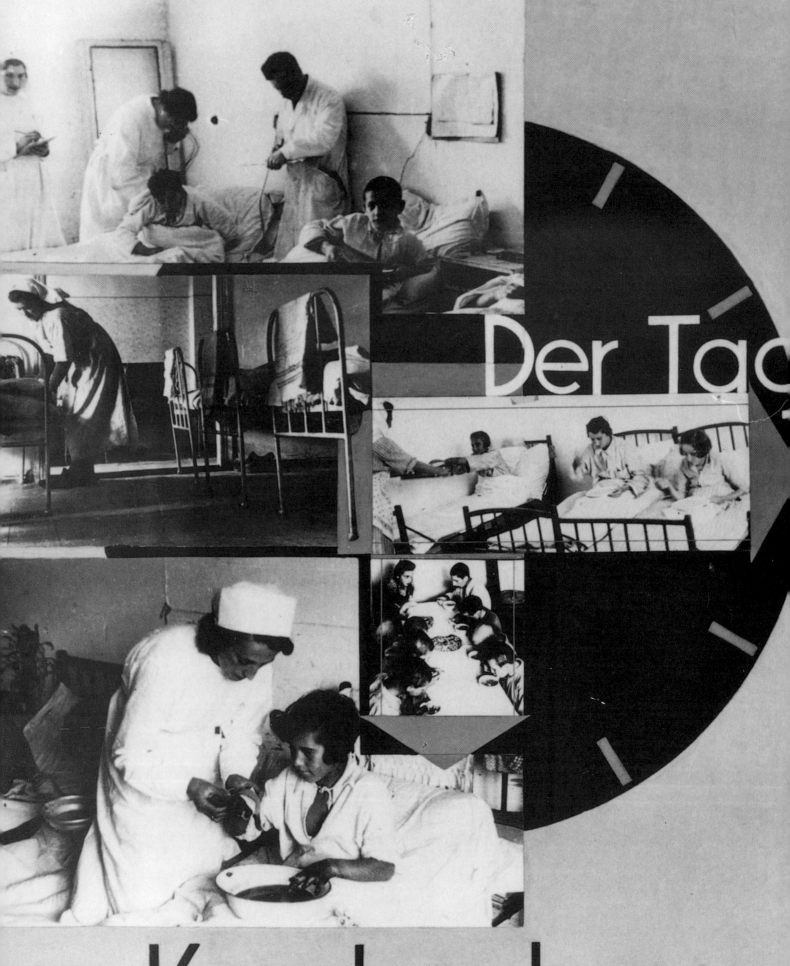

Der Tag

im Krankenhaus

DANIEL NADAV

JEWISH MEDICINE DURING THE HOLOCAUST IN THE GHETTOS AND FORESTS

The persecution and displacement of Jewish physicians in Nazi Germany during the 1930s were merely a foretaste of the horrific events which were to transpire during the Holocaust.[1] Dr. Julius Moses, whose medical license was revoked in July 1938, saw the handwriting on the wall even before Hitler took power. In 1932 he wrote:

Everything considered sacred in the medical profession until now - concern for the ill regardless of race, full attention to every disease, the provision of relief to the ill wherever they may be - are considered by the Nazis as complete balderdash. The only thing worthy of their attention is waging an all-out war against so-called "inferior people".

Dr. Moses concludes with a warning that if the Nazis succeed in their plans, "German medicine will lose its moral standards ... the doctor will kill his patients, the doctor will become a murderer."[2]

Many others, and foremost among them Dr. Marek Dworzecki, called attention to the decline of medical morals in Nazi Germany.[3] Immediately upon Hitler's accession to power, a law was passed which resulted in the sterilization of hundreds of thousands of people suffering from genetic diseases. This category included such "diseases" as chronic alcoholism and others, such as epilepsy, which have since been shown to be treatable.

Hitler and his cronies were not yet satisfied, however, and simply waited for an opportune moment in which to employ more brutal means against "inferior people."

And indeed, after the outbreak of World War II, they began the systematic

The Jewish Hospital in the Lodz Ghetto.

Photographs taken between 1940-44 by Harry Cross, Mendel Grossman and Nachman Sonnebend.

Yad Vashem, Jerusalem.

La Difesa della Razza [The defense of the Race].

Journal.

Published in Italy between 1938-1943.

Library of the Jewish Theological

Seminary of America, New York.

elimination of mentally disturbed or retarded Germans within the framework of alleged "mercy killings," authorized personally by der Fuehrer. In a secret operation, thousands of unfortunate people were assembled in a number of institutions in which gas pipes had been installed and cruelly executed by gassing with carbon dioxide.[4]

This operation was not necessarily directed against Jews. According to reliable estimates 70,000 German "Aryans" lost their lives until the operation was stopped under pressure from the church in August 1941. But the physicians who supervised the killings, usually S.S. members, had acquired enough experience to stand them in good stead in executing the Jews once the decision had been taken to implement "the final solution to the Jewish question."

Even before this, with the German occupation of Poland in the fall of 1939, Nazi doctors played a key role in undermining the existence of the three million Jews who lived there. At the head of the German Health Authority stood Dr. Jost Walbaum who had joined the Nazi party as early as the 1920s. His chief assistant was Dr. Josef Rupprecht. In 1940 the two prepared memoranda in which the Jews were blamed for the rapid spread of contagious diseases, foremost among them typhus. According to the memoranda, the Jews spread the disease because they were lice-infested and did not observe the most elementary rules of bodily hygiene. Instead of improving the diet and living conditions of the Jews, which had already been severely impaired by a variety of German ordinances, they proposed confining all the Jews in ghettos. By quarantining the Jews, they would decrease the danger of their infecting non-Jews with the disease. Of course they were not really worried about the Poles, who were also considered an inferior race, destined at the most to serve members of the German "master race." But they were concerned that German soldiers and other German nationals residing in Poland might become infected. The recommendations made by these doctors were highly instrumental in furthering the idea of ghettoization, which reached its peak in November 1940, with the establishment and cordoning off of the Warsaw Ghetto.[5]

True, the idea of the "ghetto" per se was not a new one. It had been partially implemented immediately following the German occupation, primarily at the insistence of the S.S. The concentration of the Jews in one place, as in the Middle Ages, was intended both to humiliate them and prepare the ground for additional measures, such as rounding them up for forced labor. The Jews were evicted from their apartments in areas outside the ghetto and brought to the ghetto with the assistance of the local Judenrat, which had been set up earlier in all those places where Jews lived in large numbers.

The fact that the Jews were suddenly cut off from services which they and the

Cartoon from a rare anti-Nazi pamphlet, issued in Paris, shortly before its fall in 1940.

It shows the effects on those who have abjured the use of whatever has been discovered, invented or developed by the Jews. One stone reads "Here rests a Nazi, who could not use Salvarsan, discovered by the German Jew Paul Ehrlich." Other stones refer to the Wasserman reaction discovered by August von Wasserman, Digitaline by Ludwig Traube, Cocaine by Salomon Stricker and Insulin by Oskar Minkowsky.

The William Helfand Collection, New York.

rest of the Polish population had enjoyed before resulted in a modicum of self-rule naturally under the auspices of the Germans. The Germans often prided themselves on the autonomy which they granted the Jews. The organization of alternate institutions and services, among them health services, was undertaken by the various divisions of the Judenrat.

In this way, a fairly ramified network of health services developed in many ghettos although, obviously, their task was an onerous one, considering the crowding, hunger and impossible conditions imposed by the Germans.

In November of 1939 the S.S. tried to concentrate the Jews of Warsaw in the ghetto but failed, primarily because the local Judenrat, which was opposed, succeeded in persuading the German commander in the city to their point of view.[6] In this way ghettoization was deferred, but in March 1940 the area most densely populated by Jews was declared a contaminated area, and in the months that followed plans were set in motion to construct a wall around it. In the meantime, all the Jewish refugees streaming into Warsaw from other towns and cities were directed into the area, which had been somewhat enlarged since the original plan from November. Slowly but surely, Jews living in other parts of the city were evicted and forced to move into the area which the ghetto would encompass. In October 1940 the German commander of Warsaw issued an official ordinance on the establishment of the ghetto. It should be mentioned that by this time the excuse of the "Jewish epidemic" was not tenable since there had been only a dozen cases of typhus in August, compared with the hundreds of cases in April. The incidence of enteric fever had also plummeted. It was only with the dense crowding in the ghetto after it was sealed off in November that the figures again rose dramatically. Professor Ludwig Hirschfeld, a distinguished physician who had converted to Christianity but was nevertheless forced into the ghetto, wrote the truth in his autobiography:

The authorities allegedly wanted to quarantine people infected with the dangerous disease. Persons calling themselves physicians gave credence to this version. Science had already eliminated quarantines, as far back as the Middle Ages, not only because of their brutality but because they were inefficient.

Yellow star for Jewish doctors.
Aaron Feingold Collection, New Jersey.

Mara poses in front of a device (plastometer) for measuring the difference in size between Aryan and non-Aryan skulls. Berlin, 1933.
Photographer: Roman Vishniac. International Center for Photography, New York.

Children in the Warsaw Ghetto.

Yad Vashem, Jerusalem.

"I would like to be a dog, because the Germans like dogs, and I would not have to be afraid that they would kill me."

This was the response of a Jewish girl in the Warsaw Ghetto when asked what she would like to be. Being a child in the ghetto was a lethal condition, nearly all children died before the war ended.

From **Courage Under Siege** *by Charles G. Roland, Oxford University Press, 1992.*

Inefficient? After all, their intention was not to eliminate the epidemic but to eliminate the Jews.[7]

Indeed, the number of deaths among the Jews was shockingly high, primarily because of the appalling lack of nutrition which lowered their resistance to disease. The number of deaths rose steadily from 445 in November, reaching 5,560 in August 1941. During the year 1941 one-tenth of the population of the largest ghetto in Europe, which originally numbered a half a million Jews, died. Marek Dworzecki testified at the Eichmann Trial that according to his calculations all the Jews in the ghetto would have died within a period of eight years had the Nazis not been in such a hurry to ship them off to the death camp in Treblinka.[8]

Sanitary conditions in the Warsaw Ghetto might have deteriorated even more rapidly were it not for the Jews themselves who tried to improve the situation. Under the guise of courses in sanitation, approved by the German authorities, hundreds of young people received extensive medical training, similar to that acquired by medical students. Professor Charles Roland of Canada discovered the existence of this "medical faculty", most of whose students perished later in Treblinka.[9]

These para-clinical studies were held in the building of the high school, equipped for the purpose with the help of the Judenrat. At the beginning and end of every lesson, powdered disinfectants were sprayed in all the rooms in order to forestall any possible German complaints. Among the teaching staff were former faculty members of Polish universities, such as the aforementioned Professor Hirschfeld. Dr. Julius Zweibaum, a lecturer at Warsaw University before the war, headed the "faculty." Clinical studies were held at the various medical facilities which still existed and functioned in the ghetto. The members of the "faculty" did not limit themselves to teaching alone. They also conducted research, most of which focused on the characteristic symptoms of starvation in its various forms. Dr. Israel Milejkowski, who headed the Judenrat's Health Department, coordinated this study in which many of the students participated. The results of the study were published after the war, when most of the participants were no longer alive.[10]

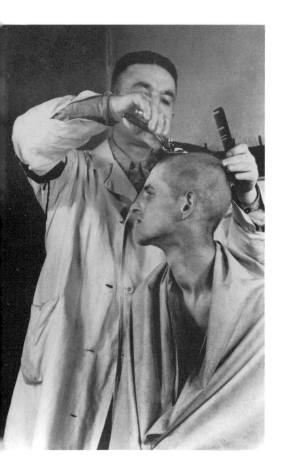

Haircut for disinfection purposes.

Warsaw Ghetto, c.1941.

Yad Vashem, Jerusalem.

The practical work of the students and teachers centered on the sanitization of the ghetto and the treatment of the sick insofar as it was possible. The Jewish hospital in Warsaw, Czyste, which had been in operation before the war and was the most modern hospital in Poland, was outside the walls of the ghetto and had been sequestered by the Germans. Permission had been received to transfer a number of its departments to the ghetto but the modern equipment was left behind (although some equipment was smuggled into the ghetto by numerous stratagems, one of which was hiding it under the bedclothes of the patients while they were being transferred). The departments were scattered throughout the ghetto and housed in unsuitable buildings. In any case, they were unable to hospitalize everyone in need. The severe shortage of medication exacerbated the difficulties, though efforts to assist were being made by the American Joint Distribution Committee and other bodies, most of whose efforts went to improving nutrition. Overcrowding – two to three patients per bed – and the inevitable spread of infection exacted a terrible price in death during hospitalization, reaching 25 percent and more every month.

With the beginning of the deportations to Treblinka, many of the physicians were taken, despite the variety of permits which were supposed to protect them. A number of physicians who could have saved themselves by escaping to the "Aryan" part of the city in time, among them Dr. Anna Braude-Heller, a woman doctor who worked at the Berson and Bauman Children's Hospital in the ghetto, decided, instead, to remain with their patients until the bitter end.

In May 1943, after the ghetto uprising, those who still remained alive in the ghetto were herded to the Umschlagplatz. A number of physicians were among them, including Dr. Tadeuz Stabholz, who took part in the uprising. Only a very few, like Prof. Hirschfeld and Henrik Pfenigstein, survived to tell their story to the coming generations. Eighteen months of autonomous Jewish activity in the field of health and medical studies in the Warsaw Ghetto had come to an end.

Intensive medical activity was carried out in the Lodz Ghetto as well. This was the second largest ghetto in Poland, with 200,000 or more Jews in it from the time of its establishment in February 1940. A Council of Elders (*Ältestenrat*), headed by Mordechai Romakovsky, operated in the ghetto. Encouraged by the occupation authorities, the council believed that the Jews might be able to survive if they were economically useful to the Germans. About 100 workshops and factories were established in the ghetto, most of them in textiles. In 1942-1943, some 70,000 or more persons worked in them. They comprised almost the entire population after the elderly and the very young had been executed or died of starvation or disease.[11]

The factories and workshops were exceptionally profitable for the S.S. and the Gestapo. This fact provided the Jewish self-government with a convenient excuse for continuing to provide health services: they would maintain proper sanitation and thus assure the continuation of productivity. Dr. Yoram Sandhaus studied the history of this project which eventually expanded to an incredible degree.[12] It began even before the establishment of the ghetto when a number of Jews were stricken with infectious diseases. A health department was established under the auspices of the Council of Elders which included a medical staff of 1,000, among them 94 physicians. There were no less than five hospitals operating within the confines of the ghetto, among them a maternity hospital and a psychiatric clinic. Most were closed down in September 1942 during the period of the extended curfew and the deportations to Chelmno. Among the first victims of this mass action were 1,700 hospitalized patients.

Later, with the conversion of the ghetto into a gigantic labor camp, most treatment was carried out in relatively small infirmaries attached to the factories. Even the medical staff was obliged to work in the factories, in addition to their humanitarian activities. Horse-drawn carts marked with a red cross served as ambulances. The two most prevalent afflictions in the camp were tuberculosis – which spread in proportion to the decline in sanitary conditions, and starvation – which was the lot of even many of those working for the Germans. The average daily ration was no more than 1,100 calories and "natural" death rose six times to what it was before the war. The factory

Bronze plaque made by a young woman in the Lodz Ghetto and dedicated to Dr Epsztain who saved her life. The plaque is decorated with family jewellery and is engraved with a sketch of the ghetto. It reads:

"To the important physician from the Hospital 75 Dworskiej St.
To Dr. Epsztain with gratitude for the treatment.
Rela Sapiro, Lodz Ghetto, 28.12.1943."
Yitzhak Einhorn Collection, Tel Aviv.

infirmaries continued to operate for another two years until the summer of 1944, when, with the Soviet Army approaching the outskirts of the city, deportations were renewed. At the time of the liberation of the city, less than a thousand Jews remained in Lodz. Romakovsky's dream of saving "productive" Jews thus resulted in a bitter awakening.

Theresienstadt was another kind of ghetto altogether. It resembled a concentration camp more than a ghetto although it did not contain installations for mass executions. One of its significant characteristics was the presence of the highest concentration of physicians relative to the population anywhere in the world. Physicians comprised more than 1 percent of the ghetto population in the years 1942-1944.[13]

The reason for this was because this ghetto was intended, inter alia, for the more "venerated" Jews of Central Europe. The S.S. used the camp to camouflage its liquidation activities, which were taking place at the time in Eastern Europe. This also accounts for the existence of a relatively extensive health service to care for the thousands of elderly persons in the ghetto. The elderly were the majority of the population. The younger generation was being steadily decreased by frequent deportations to the death camps.

There were dozens of infirmaries, sick bays and hospitals scattered around the ghetto. No less than 11 percent of the population was employed by the local health services. They had at their disposal relatively up-to-date equipment, confiscated from Jewish hospitals in Germany and Czechoslovakia. Even the supply of medicine was fairly generous. Nonetheless, the mortality rate was very high, reaching in some months, as at the beginning of 1943, 5 percent of the ghetto population. One must take into account, however, the advanced age of the population. Those who died suffered mostly from digestive diseases (because even here the food was of poor quality), from tuberculosis, and, surprisingly, from children's diseases – because of a weakening of the natural immune system and manifestations of psychological regression.[14]

Dr. Erich Munk was appointed head of the health network and he was responsible to the ghetto's Council of Elders. In addition to his organizational capabilities, he had an icy temperament which suited the macabre nature of the place. Thus he collaborated in bringing candidates for deportation up to the proper standard of health: "German order" required that nobody taken from Theresienstadt should be ill.

A similar role was played by the director of the Jewish Hospital in Berlin, who survived in the capital of the Third Reich until the end of the war. It should be pointed out that Dr. Walter Lustig, despite the controversy over his character, succeeded in saving hundreds of Jews from the clutches of the S.S.[15]

This article is much too short to cover all of the camps and ghettos in which the Jews organized medical services during the Holocaust. In almost every place where they were, the Jews attempted in one way or another to change their fate or at least to slow down the tempo of slaughter. Here and there, they found themselves trapped in situations which, even relatively speaking, were exceptionally onerous. The example of the small ghetto of Shabli, in Lithuania, will suffice to illustrate this.

Just recently the diary of Dr. Aaron Pick came to light through the research of Miriam Ofer, a student at Haifa University. The diary was written in the ghetto in Hebrew. In addition to furnishing examples of the medical services in the city, including the existence of a small hospital, the diary enables us to penetrate the terrifying dilemmas which faced physicians during the Holocaust. The greatest difficulty of all was the prohibition on pregnancy and childbirth in the ghetto, as Dr. Pick writes:

It is hard to believe that we, civilized people with high moral principles, have degenerated to such a low level that we have become the murderers and destroyers of human souls. The edict prohibiting childbirth in the ghetto remains in force. Nevertheless, a number of births took place. It was incumbent upon us, the doctors, to destroy these normal, healthy living children (!) in order to save the ghetto from the danger of complete annihilation.[16]

With the gradual destruction of the ghettos most of their inhabitants were murdered. Only a tiny minority succeeded in escaping and taking up arms against the Germans. This occurred largely in the Soviet Union in areas under German occupation, with the formation of partisan units. A number of physicians, among them Dr. Yehezkiel Atlas, stood at the head of some of

Dr. E. Springer.
Caricature by Petr Kien, 1941-45.
Pencil, india ink, paper.
32.7 x 24.8 cm.
Kien did a suite of caricatures of prisoners who worked in the Terezin hospital. He included in each upper right-hand corner a depiction of what we surmise was that person's daydream. Terezin Monument, Terezin.

these units, which regularly raided German positions.[17]

In a few places, "family camps" of survivors with their wives and children were organized. Dr. Marek Dworzecki has documented the work of physicians in such camps in Estonia, for example.[18]

In a number of instances there were doctors who behaved in the most extraordinary fashion under the terrible conditions to which they were subjected. Dr. Shlomo Igilnik, for example, could have remained alive in order to serve the Germans as a doctor when, during a planned action in the town of Lachva (in eastern Poland), he was removed from the list of candidates for execution. The graves for the victims had already been dug when an uprising broke out in the town. This was on September 3, 1942. A number of German soldiers were killed and several more wounded. Dr. Igilnik was ordered to treat one of the wounded soldiers, but he refused and was executed on the spot.[19]

Other Jewish doctors continued to devote themselves to their medical responsibilities despite unbelievable hardships. Dr. Abraham Blumowitz (Atzmon), for example, succeeded in escaping from the Slonim Ghetto after having run the community clinic for some time. He joined a partisan unit in the summer of 1942 which was fighting in the forests of Byelorussia and many are the tales told about him, both as partisan and as physician. He was known to have performed operations in the thick of the forest with "surgical instruments" shaped by his own hand from kitchen knives and work tools.[20] According to official Soviet documents, Blumowitz saved the lives of dozens of fighters in the hundreds of operations he performed. With the Soviet re-occupation of the region, Blumowitz ran a large military hospital in the Brest area.[21] His experience proved useful when he was appointed as one of the commanders of the Military Medical Corps during Israel's War of Independence.

There is no doubt that the medical activites of the Jews during the Holocaust were not only that of treating the ill, extending life and fighting disease, the fundamental tenets of medicine everywhere. They were also engaged in actively fighting against Nazi plans to destroy the Jewish people, in protecting

Dr. Orenstein with members of his nursing staff and babies born in Germany within one week, in 1945, to parents who had survived the Holocaust.

Dr. Orenstein was a physician in Poland and spent several years in concentration camps.

Gift of Dr. and Mrs. Frederick Orenstein, Museum of Jewish Heritage, New York.

the lives of a persecuted people, and in making a valiant attempt to uphold the tenets of accepted medical ethics. All this they did in the face of unprecedented constraints in the history of medicine, constraints which often forced them to make miserable compromises with what they believed to be their professional ethos. They were unable to ward off the murderous decrees but they were able to relieve the pain beforehand and to extend a helping hand to their brothers and sisters in distress. Some of them were even able to continue their medical mission in the forests, fighting against the Nazi beast.

~

NOTES

1. Michael H. Kater, *Doctors under Hitler*, Chapel Hill, Sheed and Word 1989.

2. *The Sick-Fund Doctor*, a journal published by Dr. Moses in Berlin, February 1932.

3. *Europa bli yeladim: tochniot hanazim l'heres biologi* (Hebrew) [Europe without children: Nazi plans for biological destruction], Yad Vashem Jerusalem, 1958.

4. See my article in *Korot* (Hebrew), vol. 9, 1989, pp. 220-231.

5. From studies by the American scholar, Christopher Browning, whose important work was published in 1985: *Fateful Months: Essays on the Emergence of the Final Solution*, Holmes and Meier, New York.

6. The most important source material for this article: Y. Gutman, *Yehudei varsha 1939-1943: geto, machteret, mered* (Hebrew) [The Jews of Warsaw 1939–1943: ghetto, underground, revolt], Tel Aviv, Sifryat Poalim 1977, pp. 65 ff. See also M. Lanski, *Chayei hayehudim b'geto varsha: zichronot shel rofe* (Hebrew) [Jewish life in the Warsaw Ghetto], Jerusalem, 1961, Holocaust Library.

7. Y. Gutman, *Jews of Warsaw*, quoting Hirschfeld's memoirs, p. 197.

8. Dworzecki's evidence appears in: *Mishpat Eichmann, eduiot* (Hebrew) [Eichmann Trial, testimonies], vol. 1, Jerusalem, 1973, pp. 321-334. With regard to the Vilna Ghetto, see M. Dworzecki, *Yerushalyim d'lita b'meri ub'shoa* (Hebrew) [Vilna in revolt and during the Holocaust], Tel Aviv, 1951, pp. 286 ff.

9. Charles G. Roland, *Courage under Siege*, Oxford University Press, New York, 1991.

10. *Hunger Disease: Studies by the Jewish Physicians in the Warsaw Ghetto*, John Wiley & Sons, New York 1979.

11. *Entziclopedia shel hashoa* (Hebrew) [Encyclopedia of the Holocaust], Yad Vashem and Sifryat Poalim, Tel Aviv, vol. 3, 1990, pp. 661-617.

12. Under the supervision of Eran Dolev, Tel Aviv University.

13. H. G. Adler, *Theresienstadt 1941-1945*, J.C.B. Mohr, Tübingen, 1960, p. 511.

14. One of the victims was Dr. Julius Moses, mentioned at the beginning of the article.

15. See my article on Lustig in the anthology *Zerstörte Fortschritte*, Berlin, 1989. A comprehensive study on the hospital during the Nazi period was written by Rivka Elkin for an M.A degree at Beersheba University, 1989.

16. Published in Hebrew in the daily *Ma'ariv*, 8.4.94, p.14.

17. S. Bernstein, *Plugat hadoctor atlas: sipuro shel partizan yehudi* (Hebrew) [Dr. Atlas's company: the story of a Jewish partisan], Tel Aviv, 1975.

18. M. Dworzecki, *Machanot yehudim b'estonia: 1942-1944* (Hebrew) [Jewish Camps in Estonia: 1942-1944], Jerusalem, Yad Vashem,1970.

19. *Sefer zichron valodava v'hasviva, sobibor* (Hebrew) [A Memorial to Valodava and its environs], Sobibor, Irgun Yotzei Valodava, Tel Aviv, 1974, p. 487. See also *Rishonim l'mered: lachva* (Hebrew) [First to revolt: Lachva], Jerusalem,1957, *Entziclopedia Shel Galuyot*, pp. 62-64. I am grateful to Mrs. Lea Rubin of Tel Aviv for this information.

20. Sara Shneer-Nashmit, *Hapluga ha-51: korot hakvutza hapartizanit shel yehudei geto slonim* (Hebrew) [The 51st Company: the history of the Jewish partisans of Ghetto Slonim], Tel Aviv, Misrad Habitachon 1990, pp. 62-62. I was assisted here by members of the family.

21. I would like to thank members of the family of Dr. Abraham Atzmon who made the original documents available to me with the translation of Zvi Shefet.

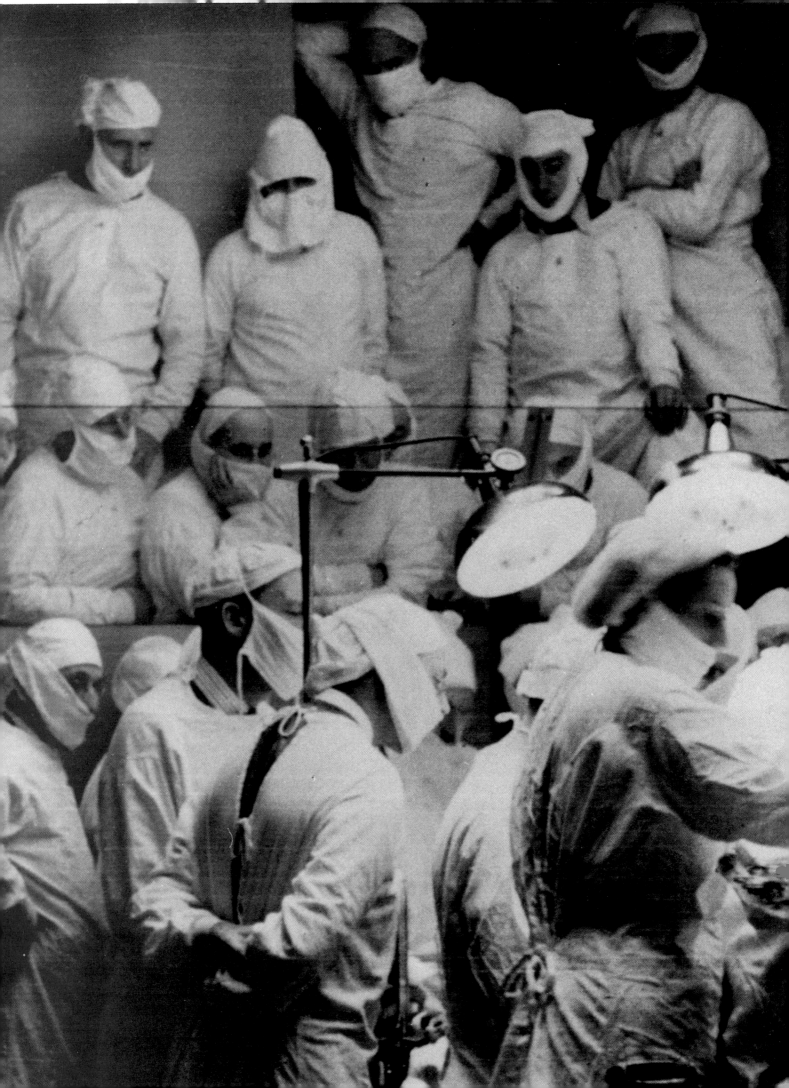

THEODORE M. BROWN

JEWISH PHYSICIANS IN THE UNITED STATES

Jewish physicians have been promi-
nent in all periods of American history, from earliest colonial times to the
present.[1] The first Jewish physicians probably arrived on the American
continent with Columbus, in the persons of Maestre Bernal, his ship's
physician, and Marco, his ship's surgeon. There is no doubt that Jewish
physicians were in active practice well before the founding of the republic, and
by the early 19th century Jewish physicians were well-established in all major
American cities. As the number of Jews dramatically increased in the United
States – with the influx of German-speaking immigrants from western Europe
in the mid-19th century and with the much larger waves of Russian and
Yiddish speaking immigrants from Russia and eastern Europe in the late 19th
and early 20th centuries – the number of Jewish physicians grew markedly.
Some had been trained abroad and made their careers in America; others
received all or most of their medical education in the United States, where
they pursued their new profession. Medicine was a very popular career choice
for first- and second-generation Jewish immigrants, and the number of Jewish
physicians increased even more rapidly than did the percentage of Jews in the
overall population. In New York City, for example, the number of Jewish
physicians grew more than sixfold from 1905 to 1936 while the percentage of
Jews in the city only increased from approximately 21.5 percent to roughly 27
percent during the same period. By 1970 Jewish doctors were about 9 percent
of the physicians in the United States, at a time when Jews were no more than
3 percent of the American population overall.[2]

Whether emigre or native born, Jewish physicians achieved great success and

Operation in Mount Sinai Hospital,
New York, 1938.
*The Archives of the Mount Sinai
Medical Center, New York.*

David Camden De Leon (1816-1872).

De Leon was the first surgeon general of the Confederate Army. He followed his father's profession, graduating from the University of Pennsylvania Medical School in 1836. He entered the US Army as an assistant surgeon in 1838. De Leon was twice cited for gallantry in action, gaining the sobriquet "The fighting doctor".

The Burns Archive, New York.

recognition in all fields and divisions of American medicine. In the 19th century, they already made significant clinical and scientific advances in internal medicine, ophthalmology, otolaryngology, pediatrics, surgery, gastroenterology and neurology. In the 20th century this record of achievement continued with major breakthroughs by Jewish physicians in these same fields as well as in dermatology, endocrinology, pathology, microbiology, pharmacology, biochemistry, immunology and physiology. Jewish achievements in 20th century psychiatry, basic research, public health and health policy have been perhaps most notable. While Jews have been particularly known for their progressive views, they have actually occupied positions all along the professional and scientific spectrum. In psychiatry, for example, Jews were prominent among the more radical Freudians, yet they were also represented among those psychiatrists who expressed considerable skepticism towards psychodynamic theories and continuing loyalty to biological approaches. Likewise in health policy, Jewish physicians have been notable for their support of organizational innovations, prepaid group practice and national health insurance, yet for many years the most vocal and effective representative of the conservative American Medical Association was Dr. Morris Fishbein of Chicago, who was also a Jew.

In general, Jewish physicians have enjoyed considerable prominence in the American medical mainstream. They held major posts in medical societies, academic institutions and the scientific establishment.[3] As just a few examples, Isaac Hays (1796-1879) edited the *American Journal of Medical Sciences* and was active in the development of the American Medical Association; Abraham Jacobi (1830-1918) served as president of the Association of American Physicians and the American Medical Association; Bernard Sachs (1858-1944) was president of the American Neurological Association and the New York Academy of Medicine; Howard Lilienthal (1861-1946) was president of the American Association for Thoracic Surgery; Simon Flexner (1863-1946) directed the Rockefeller Institute for Medical Research; Isaac Abt (1867-1955) served as president of the American Pediatric Society and was co-founder and president of the American Academy of Pediatrics; Milton Rosenau (1869-1946) was dean of the School of Public Health at the University of North Carolina and president of the American Public Health Association; Jay Schamberg (1870-1934) served as president of the American Dermatological Association; Sigismund S. Goldwater (1873-1942) was Commissioner of Health in New York City; Robert F. Loeb (1895-1973) was president of the American Society for Clinical Investigation; Milton Winternitz (1885-1959) served as dean of the Yale Medical School; and Soma Weiss (1899-1942) was Hersey Professor of the Theory and Practice of Medicine at the Harvard School of Medicine.

Major Jewish institutions have also been prominent features of the American medical landscape.[4] Mount Sinai Medical Center in New York City (founded in 1852) has grown in the 20th century to be a national and world center of basic research as well as clinical innovation. The Beth Israel Hospital of Boston (opened in 1917 and reopened in 1928 in expanded quarters near the Harvard Medical School) is one of the leading hospitals in the country.

Abraham Jacobi.

Born in Westphalia (1830-1918), Jacobi came to the United States in 1853. When the College of Physicians and Surgeons of Columbia University appointed him professor of infant pathology and therapeutics in 1860, the first systematic instruction in that field commenced. In 1862 he established the first pediatric clinic in the U.S.A. Jacobi served as president of the Association of American Physicians and the American Medical Association. National Library of Medicine, Bethesda.

**Horse-drawn ambulance of the Mount
Sinai Hospital, Philadelphia, c.1900.**
*The Albert Einstein Medical Center,
Philadelphia.*

Moreover, among the more than five dozen other important Jewish hospitals in the United States today are Michael Reese in Chicago (opened in 1882), Montefiore in New York City (founded in 1884), Cedars-Sinai Medical Center in Los Angeles (established in 1902), the Cincinnati Jewish Hospital (opened in 1854), the Touro Infirmary in New Orleans (opened in 1853), and Miriam Hospital in Providence, Rhode Island (founded in 1926). The Albert Einstein College of Medicine of Yeshiva University, which opened in 1955 in Bronx, New York, was the first medical school in the United States under Jewish auspices. It has since grown to be one of the country's leading medical institutions. In 1968 the Mount Sinai Medical Center in New York City opened the country's second medical school under Jewish aegis, in affiliation with the City University of New York. It too has become a nationally distinguished center for undergraduate medical education, adding to its earlier record of achievement in medical research and postgraduate training.

Despite this clear record of success by individuals and institutions, the history of Jews in American medicine is not without serious blemish. That blemish is the result of anti-Semitism, which was always present in some form in the United States, but most intense and damaging in the period between the two world wars. Writing in 1944, the Swedish author Gunnar Myrdal observed that anti-Semitism "in America during the last years before World War II probably was somewhat stronger than in Germany before the Nazi regime."[5] A recent scholarly study, *Anti-Semitism in America* by Leonard Dinnerstein, corroborates this view and notes that overt and often physically violent acts against Jews peaked in the late 1930s and early 1940s and did not begin to abate until the postwar period, when reaction to the Nazi atrocities made public anti-Semitism less socially acceptable.[6] The consequences of intensified anti-Semitism in the interwar period for Jews in American medicine were manifold. In the 1920s, 1930s, 1940s and even the 1950s, anti-Semitic attitudes and practices affected medical school admissions, postgraduate opportunities and career advancement, and the integration of emigre Jewish physicians and medical scientists fleeing the Nazi Holocaust.

With regard to medical school admissions, anti-Semitic attitudes created and sustained a variety of discriminatory practices. Medical schools established quotas and admitted students according to geographic patterns and the proportion of religious or ethnic groups in the state or national population. Since Jews clustered in the northeast, especially in New York, they were severely disadvantaged. In addition, medical schools refused to accept applicants from certain undergraduate institutions or accepted them in very small numbers. Schools known for their large number of Jewish undergraduates were very seriously handicapped.[7] At Columbia University's College of Physicians and Surgeons, the percentage of Jews among the matriculated medical students was about 50 percent in 1920 but dropped to 19 percent by 1924 and continued to drop throughout the 1920s and 1930s until it reached a low of 12 percent in 1938.[8] The situation only began to improve again in the postwar period. In the 1950s the Yeshiva University trustees decided to found the Albert Einstein College of Medicine, motivated

Beth Israel Hospital, Newark, New Jersey.

Aaron Feingold Collection, New Jersey.

Montefiore Sanatorium, Beford Hills, N.Y.

Aaron Feingold Collection, New Jersey.

Mount Sinai Hospital, New York City.

Aaron Feingold Collection, New Jersey.

to a very large extent by the need they felt to create additional medical school educational opportunities for Jewish students.[9] As late as 1959, an article on medical education published in the *Journal of the Mount Sinai Hospital* called discriminatory admissions practices in American medical schools still a "tender" subject for which "reliable statistics and genuinely unprejudiced discussion are hard to come by."[10]

The ways in which anti-Semitism affected postgraduate opportunities and career advancement was also a tender subject. It was generally understood that Jewish medical school graduates had great difficulties during the interwar period acquiring internships and increasingly important residency positions.[11] Sometimes Jewish graduates obtained hospital positions but were harassed, even driven out by their Gentile colleagues.[12] More often, they remained in general rather than specialty practice, or if very fortunate, they obtained a postgraduate staff position in one of the Jewish hospitals. In 1923 Dr. B.E. Greenberg of Boston wrote:

Out of the twenty-five to thirty [Jewish] men who graduate from medical schools [in Boston] each year, practically all of them are compelled to go into general practice, to become the sort of practitioner who does not carry much weight, who is not considered at the head of his profession, because they are not given the opportunity to get into hospitals to procure hospital experience.[13]

Jewish students who were forced to go abroad to pursue their undergraduate medical education had still greater difficulties when they returned to the United States because very often they failed even to obtain licenses to practice medicine as general practitioners.[14] Academic careers were almost impossible to pursue, even for those with American specialty or research training. In 1927 there was one Jew on each of the entire faculties of Yale University, Johns Hopkins University, and the University of Chicago, two at Columbia and three at Harvard.[15] The numbers did not improve much over the next decade, especially given the economic difficulties faced by American universities in the 30s.

During the 1930s it was also extremely difficult for emigre physicians and medical scientists to become established in America, even if they had long and

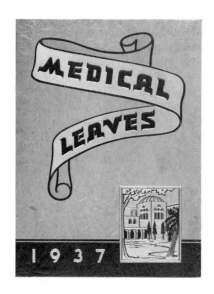

Medical Leaves

Jewish medical journal, 1937, Chicago.

Editor in Chief Joseph C. Beck M.D.

Published under the auspices of the

Histadrut, Chicago.

Aaron Feingold Collection, New Jersey.

distinguished careers before the rise of the Nazis drove them from Europe.[16] Most American physicians and medical organizations resisted the influx of refugee doctors, for both anti-Semitic and economic reasons. But even where American response was quick and positive, it was not often very effective. In New York City, Dr. Bernard Sachs announced in October 1933 the formation of the Emergency Committee in Aid of Displaced Physicians and outlined an ambitious set of goals. Almost a decade later, however, the Committee acknowledged that it had been able to grant scholarships to only 125 refugees and to find positions for a mere 100 others. This was in stark contrast to the approximately 6,000 physicians who emigrated to the United States in the same period, an estimated 75 to 80 percent of whom were Jews. In most states, emigre physicians were prohibited by law even from taking licensing exams because they were not citizens, and in some they were also expected to re-graduate from American medical schools or take internships in American hospitals. Most refugee physicians settled in New York and other liberal Atlantic coast states. Yet the backlash by New York physicians drastically curtailed the number of refugee doctors entering practice, especially after 1936. By 1939, a prominent National Committee for Resettlement of Foreign Physicians was formed under the chairmanship of Harvard Medical School Dean David Edsall, but this committee only began to enjoy modest success after America's entry into World War II created shortages at home that some emigres were allowed to fill.

Even during the most restrictive phase of the Depression decade, some Jewish emigre physicians succeeded in securing academic appointments.[17] Nobel Prize winners Otto Loewi (1873-1961) and Otto Meyerhof (1884-1951) obtained posts at New York University and the University of Pennsylvania, respectively. Future Nobel Laureate Fritz Lipmann (1899-1986) found successive positions at Cornell Medical School in New York and the Massachusetts General Hospital, and the distinguished neuropsychiatrist Kurt Goldstein (1878-1965) was appointed first at Columbia University in New York and then at Tufts Medical School in Boston. Several other investigators of great accomplishment and renown also acquired appointments, as did

Hermann Joseph Muller (1890-1967) *was born in New York. He received his Ph.D. from Columbia University in 1916 and his D.Sc. from the University of Edinburgh in 1940. He was research associate and visiting professor at the Department of Biology (1940-45) at Amherst College and from 1945 was professor of zoology at Indiana University, Texas. Dr. Muller took part in the development of the chromosome and gene theory of heredity, through investigations of the fruit fly, drosophila. He laid the basis of the modern theory of mutation and its relation to evolution. In 1946 Muller was awarded the Nobel Prize for medicine and physiology for the discovery of the production of mutations by means of X-ray irradiation.*

The Lilly Library, Indiana University, Bloomington.

Jonas Salk *received his B.S. from the City College of New York in 1934 and his M.D. from New York University five years later. He did important research on influenza vaccines and in 1949 became professor of bacteriology at the University of Pittsburgh and head of its Department of Preventive Medicine in 1954. In the latter years he became known throughout the world for his discovery of a preventive vaccine for poliomyelitis. Since 1957 Salk has been professor of experimental medicine at the University of Pittsburgh. A brilliant virologist, he is one of the truly great scientists of our time and is the recipient of many honorary degrees. In 1962 dedication ceremonies were held for the Salk Institute for Biological Studies, which opened in La Jolla, California in 1963, with Dr. Salk as director.*

National Library of Medicine, Bethesda.

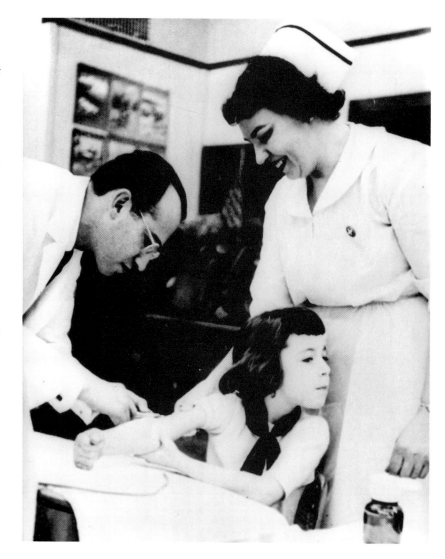

leading clinicians and quite a few psychoanalysts. These successfully relocated emigres joined the small number of distinguished American-born or American-trained physicians already holding posts at leading institutions. Together, however, they were largely "tokens", in the sense that most refugee Jewish physicians, like most American Jewish physicians, were unable in this period to advance in the American mainstream. A far larger number got stuck in their careers or were able to advance only at Jewish institutions, which, not accidentally, grew significantly during these same years.[18] Many major Jewish hospitals underwent growth spurts in the 1920s and 1930s that were partly motivated by the desire to create alternative professional opportunities for Jewish clinicians and investigators. Thus, massive interwar facility expansion at Jewish medical institutions was usually accompanied by dramatic growth in internship and residency positions, specialty training, and staff appointments. After World War II, Jewish physicians whose careers had developed exclusively at Jewish institutions had options to cross over to newly receptive mainstream American medicine.

In the past few decades, Jews have been more "at home in America" than in any earlier period. As a direct result, they have become increasingly integrated into the medical mainstream. Jewish students now compete quite successfully for medical school slots, and Jewish medical graduates have no special difficulty getting postgraduate positions in a wide variety of fields and at the most prestigious institutions. Jewish men and women also seem to encounter no particular barriers to career advancement, whether in office practice, major hospitals, or academic settings. At one prominent medical school known for its exclusionary admissions and hiring policies through the 1950s, the current dean, senior associate dean, Chair of Medicine and Chair of Surgery are all Jewish. There also seem to be no substantial differences these days between professional opportunities at Jewish-affiliated or at mainstream institutions, and, in fact, the two sorts of institutions are now more closely affiliated with one another than at any earlier time. It is quite telling that of the 12 Nobel Prizes awarded in Medicine or Physiology between 1975 and 1986, six were shared by American Jews who had fashioned their careers quite successfully at mainstream institutions and a seventh was shared by an American Jewish scientist who built her career at Jewish institutions.[19] The stain of anti-Semitism seems, at least for now, to have faded from American medicine, and Jews are enjoying unprecedented success in all aspects of professional life.

~

NOTES

1. Solomon R. Kagan, *Jewish Contributions to Medicine in America*, Boston Medical Publishing Company, 1939; Kagan, *American Jewish Physicians of Note*, Boston Medical Publishing Company, 1942; "Physicians" in *The Universal Jewish Encyclopedia*, Vol. 8 (1942); "Medicine," in *Encyclopedia Judaica*, Vol. 11 (1971).

2. "New York City," in *The Universal Jewish Encyclopedia*, Vol. 8 (1942), pp. 183-184; "Medicine," in *Encyclopedia Judaica*, Vol. 11 (1971), p. 1191.

3. Martin Kaufman, Stuart Galishoff, and Todd Savitt, eds., *Dictionary of American Medical Biography*, Westport, Conn., Greenwood Press, 1984.

4. Kagan, *Jewish Contributions*, pp. 462-476; "Hospitals," in *Encylopedia Judaica*, Vol. 8 (1971); Tina Levitan, *Islands of Compassion: A History of the Jewish Hospitals of New York*, New York, Twayne Publishers, 1964. See also Joseph Hirsh and Beka Doherty, *The First Hundred Years of the Mount Sinai Hospital of New York*, New York, Random House, 1952; Dorothy Levenson, *Montefiore: The Hospital as Social Instrument, 1884-1984*, New York, Farrar, Straus & Giroux, 1984; Arthur J. Linenthal, *First a Dream: The History of Boston's Jewish Hospitals, 1896-1928*, Boston, Francis A. Countway Library of Medicine, 1990; *Ten Brave Years: Albert Einstein College of Medicine of Yeshiva University*, New York, The College, 1966.

5. Quoted in Saul Jarcho, "Medical Education in the United States - 1910-1956," *Journal of the Mount Sinai Hospital*, Vol. 26 (1959): 358.

6. Leonard Dinnerstein, *Anti-Semitism in America*, New York, Oxford University Press, 1994, esp. pp. 112, 122, 126-127, 133, 136, 151, 154.

7. Ibid., p. 158.

8. Harold S. Wechsler, *The Qualified Student: A History of Selective College Admission in America*, New York, John Wiley & Sons, 1977, pp. 169-171.

9. *Ten Brave Years*, pp. vi-vii.

10. Jarcho, "Medical Education," p. 357.

11. George Rosen, *The Structure of American Medical Practice, 1875-1941*, Philadelphia: University of Pennsylvania Press, 1983, pp. 76-85. Cf. Dinnerstein, p. 89.

12. Dinnerstein, *Anti-Semitism*, pp. 100-101.

13. Quoted in Linenthal, First a Dream, p. 211.

14. Rosen, *American Medical Practice*, pp. 76, 78, 134; notes 123-128.

15. Dinnerstein, *Anti-Semitism*, p. 87.

16. Kathleen M. Pearle, *Preventive Medicine: The Refugee Physician and the New York Medical Community 1933-1945*, Bremen, University of Bremen, 1981, pp. 12-41.

17. For information on emigres who were successful in obtaining American academic appointments, see Donald Fleming and Bernard Bailyn, eds., *The Intellectual Migration: Europe and America, 1930-1960*, Cambridge, Harvard University Press, 1969, esp. pp. 675-718 passim; Laura Fermi, *Illustrious Immigrants: The Intellectual Migration from Europe 1930-41*, Chicago, University of Chicago Press, 1971, esp. pp. 299-311.

18. Barry A. Lazarus, "The Practice of Medicine and Prejudice in a New England Town: The Founding of Mount Sinai Hospital, Hartford, Connecticut," *Journal of American Ethnic History*, 10 (1991): 21-41. For the significant growth of Jewish hospitals during this period, see Kagan, *Jewish Contributions*, pp. 462-476 passim.

19. Daniel Fox, Marcia Meldrum, and Ira Rezak, eds., *Nobel Laureates in Medicine or Physiology: A Biographical Dictionary*, New York, Garland Publishing, 1990.

A visiting nurse from the Henry Street Settlement.

An intrepid nurse crosses rooftops to visit residents on the Lower East Side, c.1910.

Museum of the City of New York, New York. Lent by the Visiting Nurse Service of New York.

NOBEL PRIZE WINNERS

The Nobel Foundation was established under the terms of the will of Alfred Bernard Nobel, Ph.D. Since the inception of the Nobel Prize in 1899, thirty-nine Jews have been honoured with this prestigious award for their diverse contributions to scientific and medical research.

1908 Paul Ehrlich, *Germany*

1908 Elie Metchnikoff, *Russia*

1914 Robert Barany, *Austria*

1922 Otto Meyerhof, *Germany*

1930 Karl Landsteiner, *Austria*

1931 Otto Warburg, *Germany*

1936 Otto Loewi, *Austria*

1944 Joseph Erlanger, *U.S.A.*

1944 Herbert Spencer-Gasser, *U.S.A.*

1945 Ernst Chain, *U.K.*

1946 Hermann Joseph Muller, *U.S.A.*

1950 Tadeus Reichstein, *Switzerland*

1952 Selman A. Waksman, *U.S.A.*

1953 Hans Adolf Krebs, *U.K.*

1953 Fritz Albert Lipmann, *U.S.A.*

1958 Joshua Lederberg, *U.S.A.*

1959 Arthur Kornberg, *U.S.A.*

1964 Konrad Bloch, *U.S.A.*

1965 François Jacob, *France*

1965 André Lwoff, *France*

1967 George Wald, *U.S.A.*

1968 Marshall W. Nirenberg, *U.S.A.*

1969 Salvador Luria, *U.S.A.*

1970 Julius Axelrod, *U.S.A.*

1970 Sir Bernard Katz, *U.K.*

1972 Gerald M. Edelman, *U.S.A.*

1975 Howard Temin, *U.S.A.*

1975 David Baltimore, *U.S.A.*

1976 Baruch Blumberg, *U.S.A.*

1977 Rosalyn Yalow, *U.S.A.*

1978 Daniel Nathans, *U.S.A.*

1980 Baruj Benacerraf, *U.S.A.*

1984 Cesar Milstein, *U.K.*

1985 Joseph L. Goldstein, *U.S.A.*

1985 Michael S. Brown, *U.S.A.*

1986 Stanley Cohen, *U.S.A.*

1986 Rita Levi-Montalcini, *U.S.A.*

1988 Gertrude Elion, *U.S.A.*

1989 Harold Varmus, *U.S.A.*

Rosalyn Yalow.

Rosalyn Yalow (b.1921) was born in the Bronx, New York. She attended Hunter College in New York City and graduated Phi Beta Kappa and magna cum laude with a B.A. degree in physics and chemistry. She was then accepted as a teaching fellow in physics at the University of Illinois at Urbana, the only woman among 400 men in the faculty of the College of Engineering. In 1945 she became the second woman to receive a Ph.D. degree in physics from the university. Yalow joined the faculty at Hunter College as a physics lecturer from 1946-1950. Yalow was then hired as a consultant to the Radiotherapy Department in the Bronx. Yalow and Dr. Solomon Berson, who joined the staff and became chief of the radioisotope unit four years later, studied the use of radioactive iodine in the diagnosis and treatment of thyroid disease. It was through these studies that they came up with their revolutionary method of radioimmunoassay (RIA). This RIA technique made it possible to measure the insulin level in the blood of adult diabetics. Subsequently, Yalow and others have utilized RIA to resolve scores of medical problems in thousands of laboratories in the US and abroad. Blood collection centers used the RIA to prevent the inclusion of blood contaminated with hepatitis virus. Yalow was the first American woman to receive a Nobel Prize in Science, awarded this honor for medicine and pharmacology in 1977 for the development of radioimmunoassay of the peptide hormones.

AB Repartagebild, Stockholm.

Otto Loewi.

Photo: U.S.A., summer 1955.

Loewi (1873-1961) was born in

Frankfürt and studied in Strasbourg.

From 1909 to 1938 he was professor of

pharmacology at the University of Graz,

Austria. He was awarded the Nobel

Prize in physiology and medicine in

1936 (jointly with Sir Henry Dale),

"for discoveries relating to chemical

transmission of nerve impulses." After

the Germans took over Austria in 1938,

he was imprisoned for two months and

deprived of all his possessions before

being allowed to leave. During 1939-40

Loewi worked in Oxford. In 1949 he

went to the U.S.A. where he was

appointed professor of pharmacology at

the College of Medicine of New York

University.

Institut für Geschichte der Medizin,

Wien.

Selman A. Waksman.

Professor of microbiology and Director

of the Institute of Microbiology at

Rutgers University, Waksman

(1888-1973) made extensive

investigations on the nature and

physiology of the microbiological

population of the soil during the years

1915-50. From 1939 he devoted all his

attention to the study of antibiotics,

twelve of which were isolated in his

laboratory. Of these, streptomycin,

isolated in 1944, proved to be a highly

important life saving agent. Many

bacterial diseases heretofore incurable,

such as tuberculosis, dysentery,

tularemia, meningitis and others,

respond to streptomycin. His discovery

stimulated many investigators to search

for other effective antibiotics, and new

drugs were discovered as a result of Dr.

Waksman's pioneer work.

In 1952 Selman Waksman was

awarded the Nobel Prize for Medicine

for his discovery of streptomycin, the first

antibiotic effective against tuberculosis.

American Jewish Archives on the

Cincinnati campus of the Hebrew

Union College.

Baruch Blumberg.

After an undergraduate degree in physics from Union College in upstate New York, Blumberg (b.1925) began graduate work in mathematics at Columbia University. However, his father suggested that he go to medical school so he entered The College of Physicians and Surgeons of Columbia University in 1947. From 1955-57 he was a graduate student at the Department of Biochemistry at Oxford University. He did his Ph.D. thesis with Alexander G. Ogston on the physical and biochemical characteristics of hyaluronic acid. In 1957 Blumberg took his first trip to Nigeria. There he collected blood specimens from several populations and studied inherited polymorphisms of the serum proteins of milk and of hemoglobin. This approach was continued in many subsequent field trips and it eventually led to the discovery of several new polymorphisms and in due course, the hepatitis B virus. From 1957 until 1964 he worked at the National Institutes of Health. In 1964 started working in the Institute for Cancer Research. In December 1976 Blumberg was awarded the Nobel Prize. Fox Chase Cancer Center, Philadelphia.

Rita Levi-Montalcini (b. 1909).

Born in Torino, Italy, Levi-Montalcini graduated from Torino University and later worked there until 1939 when the racial legislation prevented Jews from doing research. She continued her work in an improvised laboratory in her bedroom. The results of her research were published in Belgium. In 1947 she moved to Washington University in St. Louis, Missouri where she worked in collaboration with Professor Victor Hamburger. In 1977 she went back to Rome and was appointed head of the Laboratory for Cell Biology by the National Council for Scientific Research. In 1986 she was awarded the Nobel Prize for medicine and physiology for her discovery of NGF. Becker Library, Washington University School of Medicine, St. Louis.

SHMUEL NISSAN

MEDICAL SERVICES IN THE HOLY LAND IN THE NINETEENTH CENTURY: 1842-1914

For 600 years, following the end of the Crusades, the Holy Land was a forsaken, plague-ridden country. The streets of its cities and villages were overrun with sewage, garbage and carcasses. Drinking water came from polluted wells, infested by malaria-carrying mosquitoes, and disease was rampant.

Until 1842, according to reports in *Lancet* by Dr. D.H. Yates, an English doctor who investigated the situation, there was not a single resident physician in the entire area from Gaza to Antioch, from Damascus to Beirut.

The 18th century was the Age of Reason which ended in the bloodletting of the French Revolution. In response, numerous religious and messianic movements sprang up among both Jews and Christians who saw in the revolution the convulsions which were to precede the coming of the Messiah. In the early decades of the 19th century, hundreds of disciples of the Vilna Gaon, known as the *Perushim*, left their families for an abstemious life in the Holy Land, where they awaited the coming of the Messiah, the son of David. At about the same time, the London Missionary society was founded to disseminate Christianity among the Jews in anticipation of the Second Coming, an event dependent upon the return of the Jews to their homeland and their acceptance of Jesus in the very place where he had been rejected. In the wake of the Apocalypse, a thousand years of peace – the millennium – would descend upon mankind. These Christian believers thus came to be known as the millenarians. Among the leading figures in the society were the Earl of Shaftesbury, a highly influential person in Victorian England, and the

The staff of Meyer Rothschild Hospital, Jerusalem, c.1919.

Israel Museum, Jerusalem. (The Anna Ticho Museum).

Viscount Palmerston, who eventually served as both prime minister and foreign secretary of Great Britain under Queen Victoria.

One of the first steps taken by the London Society was the dispatch of a missionary physician to Jerusalem. This was in 1824. Dr. George E. Dalton did missionary and medical work for a year but at the beginning of 1826 he fell ill and, in the absence of another physician to treat him, he died.

The greatest achievement of the London Society was the establishment of a joint Anglo-Prussian bishopric in Jerusalem in 1842. Under the patronage of Queen Victoria and the King of Prussia, Friedrich Wilhelm IV, the prime minister of Britain, Lord Peel, provided a steamer to carry Bishop M. S. Alexander, a converted Jew, to the Holy Land. On board the boat, accompanying the bishop, was Dr. Edward McGowan, who had worked for the London Society for eighteen years, proselytizing Jews in Jerusalem. It should also be noted that at this time, the European powers had begun to take an interest in the Middle Eastern countries, the Holy Land among them, both for political and strategic reasons: steamships had begun to ply the Mediterranean on their way to India, their cargos being transported overland from Port Said to Port Suez. On this background, too, medical services began to expand.

Sir Moses Montifiore, who had visited the Jewish community in Palestine a number of times, could not countenance the idea of missionary work being carried out under the guise of medical assistance. So in 1843 Montifiore brought Dr. Simon Frankel, a Jewish physician from Upper Silesia, to Jerusalem, where he began to work together with McGowan, treating the Jews of the city.

In 1842, a German reform rabbi from Magdeburg by the name of Ludwig Philipson proposed establishing a Jewish hospital in Jerusalem, but the idea was rejected both by the city's rabbis and community functionaries and by the administrators of the *haluka* funds in Amsterdam. But two years later the first Jewish hospital in the Holy Land was, indeed, established.

The First Jewish Hospital

The first Jewish hospital in Jerusalem was founded in reaction to the plan of the London Missionary Society to establish a hospital for the Jews, scheduled to open on December 12, 1844. Hassidic and Sephardic Jews, who had left Safed after the earthquake of 1837 and returned to Jerusalem, rented a three-story building in July of 1844 and turned it into a hospital. Dr. Simon Frankel was the physician in charge and Rabbi Israel Bak, the owner of the first printing house in Jerusalem, the chief administrator. The hospital has been described in great detail by John Nicolson, who was a missionary, and by Titus Tobler, a Swiss physician, one of the leading authorities on the Holy Land in the 19th century. It was the first hospital in the country since the days of the Crusaders.

Once there was a Jewish hospital in Jerusalem, the city's rabbis imposed a ban on the use of the missionary hospital and ostracized any Jew who used its facilities. A public notice to this effect was printed by Rabbi Bak's printing house and circulated among all the synagogues of Jerusalem.

But in 1848, the Jewish hospital was closed because of financial difficulties and poor standards, and the only hospital remaining in the Holy Land was the missionary hospital. In 1850, the Chief Rabbi of Jerusalem, Abraham Gagin, was treated there by Dr. McGowan, who also operated on Gagin's daughter, using chloroform, a general anesthetic only recently introduced into medical practice.

The German Hospital

The missionary hospital did not maintain its monopoly for long. In response to the request of the Protestant Bishop Gobat, Theodor Fliedner from Kaiserwerth, the founder of the Diakonissen movement of Rhine and Westphalia – a movement to help the poor and the sick – arrived in Jerusalem in 1851 and founded the German Hospital. Four deaconesses from the movement worked in the hospital. The German consul, E.G. Schultz, proposed that the German-Jewish physician, Simon Frankel, be in charge, but his proposal was rejected by Fliedner, who accepted Bishop Gobat's

The Misgav Ledach Hospital and Pharmacy, Jerusalem, 1893.

In the center, Rabbi H. Michlin who was the director of the hospital for forty years.

The Michlin Family, Tel Aviv.

suggestion that Dr. McGowan be employed. The first patient, by the way, was a carpenter called Frederich Steinbeck, the uncle of the well-known American writer, John Steinbeck. Until 1868 the physicians working in the German Hospital were all Englishmen from the mission hospital, among them Drs. McGowan, Atkinson and Chaplin.

The first German physician to work at the hospital was Dr. Max Sandreczky, a pediatrician and surgeon (see Children's Hospital, below). His appointment was accepted only after great difficulties, despite his exceptionally fine professional background and experience, and the fact that he was familiar with conditions in Palestine. He was the son of Karl Sandreczky who had worked in Jerusalem for twenty years as the secretary of the Ecclesiastical Missionary Society in Jerusalem and director of its school network, and was one of the leading authorities on Palestine. One reason for opposing Dr. Sandreczky's appointment, no doubt, was the fact that he was unalterably opposed to proselytizing in Palestine. Up until then both the missionary hospital and the German Hospital had devoted a good deal of effort in trying to convert patients and their families – though with relatively little success. In 1894 both hospitals transferred their facilities to places outside the walls of the Old City, to the Street of the Prophets (one at no. 82, the other at the corner of Strauss St.).

Rothschild Hospital

With the outbreak of the Crimean War in 1853, the Jewish community in the Holy Land was cut off from all sources of income and assistance, and people became easy prey to missionary activity. To stem this tide, the Rothschild family stepped in and, among other things, rented a Talmud Torah and turned it into a hospital. The Jewish medical director of the hospital, Dr. Bernard Neumann, unlike Dr. Frankel, refused to have any contact whatsoever with the missionary hospital and did not even invite Dr. McGowan to the opening, which took place in July 1854.

Dr. Neumann directed the hospital until 1862 when he returned to Europe for health reasons. Dr. Neumann's deputy was not up to the job and instead

Dr. B. Rothziegel was appointed in 1863. In 1865 a cholera epidemic broke out which lasted for a year. During that time Dr. Rothziegel's wife and only son came down with the disease and died. Nevertheless, Dr. Rothziegel continued to work indefatigably. The Turkish pasha evacuated his troops and civil servants, and imposed a quarantine on the city.

The German consul insisted that Dr. Rothziegel leave the city but he refused and continued to treat patients until he himself came down with the disease and died, in 1866. All in all, the Rothschild Hospital treated 438 cholera patients, 21 of whom died.

Dr. Neumann was recalled to take Dr. Rothziegel's place. He returned to Jerusalem but was again forced for health reasons to leave for Europe. Dr. Benjamin London, a Viennese Jew, was appointed in his place. Dr. London was twenty-six years old and worked at the hospital for eight years, until 1874. In 1869 Kaiser Franz Josef visited Jerusalem, following the ceremonial opening of the Suez Canal, and took this opportunity to ennoble Dr. London as a knight of the Order of Franz Josef.

In 1870, however, during the German siege of Paris, the hospital was cut off from its source of funds. The Rothschild family sent two letters by way of dirigibles: one to Lionel Rothschild of the Rothschild Bank in London, requesting him to transfer 5,000 francs to the hospital in Jerusalem; the second, to Dr. London in Jerusalem – it took twenty-six days to arrive – informing him of the transfer of the funds.

In 1875 Dr. London returned to Europe in the wake of unjustified criticism from Jewish circles in Jerusalem. In Europe he enjoyed success and esteem. His place was taken by Dr. Schwartz who persuaded the Rothschilds to purchase a 6,000m^2 plot of land outside the walls of the Old City (today 37 Street of the Prophets).

In 1877 the cornerstone was laid and in September 1888 the hospital was inaugurated. Attending were the Turkish pasha and representatives of France, Austria, Spain and Italy. Soon after the opening, Dr. Schwartz resigned and his place was taken by his son-in-law, Dr. Isaac Gregori D'Arbela (originally Amcyslowski). D'Arbela, a native of Poltava, Russia, was born in 1847 and completed his medical studies in Paris. He was a member of the early Zionist Hovevei Zion group and at some point in his life became the secret advisor and physician to the sultan of Zanzibar. In 1886, during a visit to Paris, he was persuaded by Baron Edmund de Rothschild to leave Zanzibar and settle in Rishon l'Zion as resident physician. Until D'Arbela's arrival in Rishon, Dr. Menachem Stein of Jaffa was the visiting physician. In 1888, D'Arbela moved to Jerusalem to direct the Rothschild Hospital and remained there until 1903. He later left the country for Palermo, Sicily and Tunis, where he died in 1910.

It was at D'Arbela's home in Jerusalem in 1889 that the "Committee for a Clear Language" was founded, headed by Eliezer Ben Yehuda and including several Jerusalem intellectuals. The committee soon became the "Hebrew Language Committee," the predecessor of Israel's Academy of the Hebrew Language.

Dr. Michaelovitz, who had worked at the Rothschild Hospital in Paris, succeeded Dr. D'Arbela as medical director of the Rothschild Hospital in Jerusalem. He worked only in medicine, however, and not in administration. In 1907 he was succeeded by Dr. Naftali Waitz, who directed the hospital until 1910. He was followed by Dr. Jacob Segal, a native of Safed (b. 1882) who, like Dr. Waitz before him, had completed his studies in Paris.

With the outbreak of World War I, Dr. Segal left the country and Dr. Moritz Wallach, the director of the Sha'arei Zedek Hospital (see below), took his place. In 1916 the hospital was sequestered by the Turkish pasha. Towards the end of the war, in 1918, the Rothschild family signed over the hospital to the American Zionist Medical Unit. In the course of time, the hospital, which was supported by the Rothschild family until the fall of France in 1940, became the Hadassah Hospital.

The French Hospital

In 1856 two more hospitals were added to the list of Jerusalem hospitals, an Armenian hospital and a French-Catholic hospital. The latter was called the Saint Louis Hospital after King Louis IX of France who, had participated in

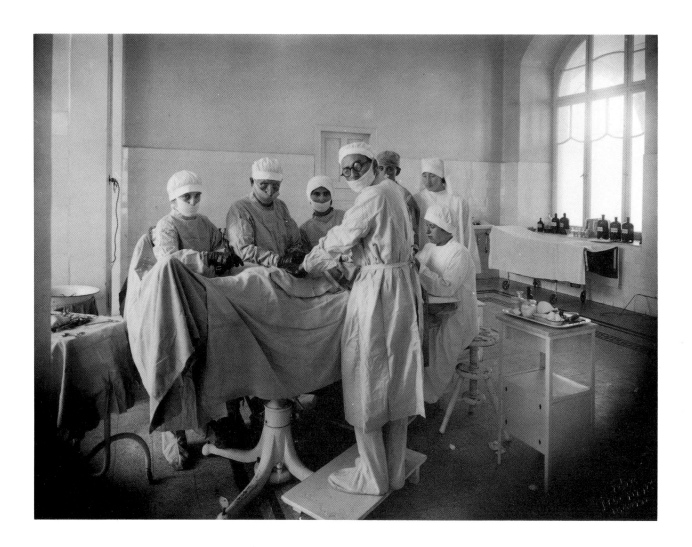

the fifth Crusade. Dr. A. Mendelssohn, a cousin of Felix Mendelssohn Bartholdi, worked at the hospital.

One of the people who contributed to the development of the hospital was Conte Marie Amadée de Piellat, a longtime founder and benefactor of Catholic institutions in the Holy Land.

Bikkur Holim Hospital

In 1867 another Jewish hospital was added to list of hospitals in Jerusalem – the Bikkur Holim Hospital. It was founded by disciples of the Vilna Gaon, the

Perushim, with the help of Sir Moses Montifiore, and most of its patients were Yiddish-speaking. The German Chancellor Otto von Bismarck, who considered Ashkenazic Jews to be propagators of German culture, ordered the German consul in Jerusalem to sponsor the hospital. As a result the hospital became known as the German Hospital Bikkur Holim in Jerusalem.

In 1873 Dr. Puffeles, who had studied in Vienna, was appointed medical director of the hospital. Although he was an orthodox Jew "in dress and in behavior," he was known to maintain exceptionally high medical standards. He found it difficult to adjust to conditions at the hospital, however, and in 1875, after disagreements over the budget, he was forced to resign. The hospital was closed for some time. Another physician, Dr. Nadache, remained in the job only one month. The hospital was assisted by a number of foreign physicians, among them, Dr. G. Carpani and Dr. E. Einzler. The latter was the physician of the German Consulate and the son-in-law of the architect, Conrad Shick (see below). After the death of Dr. Einzler, his place was taken by Dr. A.M. Mazie (1858-1930), one of the founders of the Association of Jewish Physicians in Eretz Yisrael, the author of the *Hebrew Dictionary of Medicine and Science*, and the president of the "Hebrew Language Committee."

Dr. Wallach, who directed the Rothschild Hospital during the war, also worked at Bikkur Holim prior to the establishment of the Sha'arei Zedek Hospital (see below).

Operation in Bikkur Holim Hospital, Jerusalem, c.1910.
The Central Zionist Archives, Jerusalem.

The Russian Hospital

At the end of the Crimean War the Russians acquired a large plot of land called the "Medan," now known as the Russian compound and, among other institutions, established a hospital. The hospital treated large numbers of Russian pilgrims as well as the Arab community but refused to accept Jewish patients. Among the hospital's own physicians were Drs. Rechetyllo and Severin. They were assisted by outside physicians such as Dr. Max Sandreczky. The Russian Hospital was closed at the beginning of World War I.

The Lepers' Hospital

Dealing with leprosy was one of 19th-century Jerusalem's most difficult problems. Large numbers of people suffering from the disease lived in hovels located between Zion Gate and Dung Gate. In 1865 a leper hospital-hospice was planned through the joint efforts of Bishop Gobat, Dr. Chaplin and Karl Sandreczky. They acquired a plot of land (today 20 Agron Street) and in 1867 the hospital, designed by Conrad Shick, was opened. In 1882 a larger tract of land was acquired in the Valley of Rephaim (17 Marcus Street) and a new lepers' hospital, also designed by Shick, was erected. The patients were treated by Drs. Chaplin and Einzler.

The Greek Hospital

Feeling threatened by the vigorous activity of the English and Prussians, the Greek Orthodox community, upon the initiative of the Patriarch Cyrillus II, established the Greek Hospital in 1871. Like the patients, the physicians were, for the most, Greek Orthodox: Dr. H. Mazaraky, who finished his studies in Greece, and Dr. Spyridon, who studied at Constantinople.

Marienstift Children's Hospital

The crowning medical achievement in the Holy Land at the time was, without doubt, the Marienstift Children's Hospital. It was founded under the directorship of Dr. Max Sandreczky. Dr. Sandreczky had come with his father Karl (see above) to Jerusalem as a youngster and later gone to Munich for medical studies. He completed his studies in Wirtzenburg in 1865 and joined the staff of the children's hospital in Munich. After completing his military service with the Prussian army at a field hospital, he returned to Jerusalem to work at the German Hospital. In 1872 the Duke and Duchess of Mecklenburg-Schwerin came to visit Jerusalem and were so impressed with Dr. Sandreczky and his wife, Johanna, a Dutch woman from the court of Princess Marianna, that they agreed to sponsor a pediatric hospital which would treat all the children of the country free of charge, refraining entirely from proselytization. Dr. and Mrs. Sandreczky agreed to work without

recompense. After a year it was decided to call the hospital "Marienstift," in honor of the Duchess of Mecklenburg-Schwerin.

Children's hospitals were just beginning to appear in the Western world in the second half of the 19th century, yet here in Jerusalem a first-rate children's hospital and children's surgery was already in operation. Max Sandreczky won the trust of the Jewish community and his reputation reached beyond the

249

borders of the Holy Land. Children from Safed, Hebron, Gaza and, naturally, Jerusalem were treated at the hospital. From various Hebrew journals of that period, among them *Hatzvi, Halevanon*, and *Hahavatzelet*, it appears that Sandreczky was highly esteemed by all the Jews of Eretz Yisrael, young and old alike.

Unfortunately, without the backing of any establishment – either Catholic, Russian, English or the German Diakonissens – Dr. Sandreczky was unable to acquire land to build a permanent, more viable children's hospital. After thirty-two years of dedicated work, sacrifice and endless criticism from the missionaries, Dr. Sandreczky fell ill with a disease of the joints and the kidneys. This was the tragic end of the children's hospital. On June 22, 1899 Max Sandreczky descended into the Valley of Yehoshafat, the alleged site of Judgment Day, and in the burial cave of the sons of Hezir, popularly known as "the prophets' graves," he gave up his soul to his Creator. In his will he requested from the German bishop to look after his wife and children and the Jewish pharmacist, Ze'ev Yerusaleminsky, who had faithfully served him. His wife succumbed to advanced diabetes and his oldest daughter to tuberculosis.

His funeral was attended by hundreds of people. The Jewish community mourned the death of this distinguished physician who was buried in the Protestant cemetery on Mount Zion. On his tombstone was inscribed: "Blessed be the merciful." Almost 100 years later, on June 23, 1984, the Israeli Society for Pediatric Surgery and the Council for the Preservation of Public Sites put up a plaque on the building of the Marienstift Hospital (29 Street of the Prophets), relating the history of the hospital and its director, Dr. Max Sandreczky. Mrs. Tamar Kollek, the wife of the mayor of Jerusalem, unveiled the plaque in the presence of a large gathering of people, including physicians and members of the diplomatic corps.

St. John Ophthalmic Hospital

In 1883, in the rush to set up medical institutions, the British decided to revive and enlarge the Order of St. John the Baptist. They established the

Ophthalmic Hospital near the railway station. The hospital is still functioning today in Sheikh Jarach, serving the entire Arab population.

Misgav Ladach Hospital

The name of the hospital comes from Psalms 9:10: "The Lord is a stronghold for the oppressed (*misgav ladach*), a stronghold in times of trouble." In 1888 the Rothschild Hospital moved to its new home on the Street of the Prophets. In 1891, in the old building, previously a Sephardic Talmud Torah, the Sephardic city elders established the Misgav Ladach Hospital. They were helped by a Salonikian Jew. The physicians who worked at the hospital were the Greek Dr. Mazaraky, the Jewish Dr. A. Cohen, and the Arab Dr. Abu Shadid. During World War I the hospital was sequestered by the Turks. It reopened after the war. The hospital was destroyed by Arabs from the Old City during the War of Independence in 1948. Today the hospital operates in West Jerusalem as a maternity hospital.

The Municipal Hospital

In 1891, the same year that Misgav Ladach Hospital was established, a Christian Arab donated a magnificent building (across from the Police Station in Machane Yehuda, 86 Jaffa Street) to the Turkish authorities in order to set up a municipal hospital. The building had been intended for the donor's son who died on the eve of his wedding. This bad luck inflamed superstitious beliefs and people refused to enter the hospital. Eventually it was used to serve the prison population of the city. It was here that Dr. Helena Kagan, who arrived in the country just prior to World War I, after completing her medical studies in Bern, began to practice medicine. Because women were not allowed to practice medicine in the Ottoman Empire she was permitted to work only at the Municipal Hospital. She was also allowed to treat women in the harems of Jerusalem's wealthy Muslims.

Ezrat Nashim Mental Hospital

In 1895 three publicly active women, led by Chaya Zippa Pines, founded the

Ezrat Nashim (Women's help) society, whose purpose was to provide medical assistance to poor women and mothers. In 1895 they founded the first mental hospital in the country in a rented house in the Old City. In 1902, under the patronage of the Baroness de Rothschild a building for the hospital was erected outside the walls, at the entrance to Jerusalem. The hospital was first staffed by general practitioners, among them Drs. Yitzhak Krishevsky, Moritz Wallach and Aaron Yermans.

Sha'arei Zedek Hospital

In 1897 there were four Jewish hospitals in Jerusalem which had a Jewish population of 30,000: Bikkur Holim with forty-four beds; Misgav Ladach with twenty-two beds; Rothschild with twenty-four beds; and Ezrat Nashim. Occupancy was 100 percent and another hospital was needed. For other reasons, such as differences in outlook and behavior, Central European Jews decided to have a hospital of their own.

The name of the hospital, which means "the gates of justice," was taken from the name of the neighborhood in which it was established (161 Jaffa Street). The land was purchased, with the assistance of the German Consul Von Tichendorf, from a Swiss banker in the middle of bankruptcy proceedings. The committee for the establishment of the hospital in Jerusalem was made up of members of Jewish congregations in Hamburg, Mainz, Frankfurt and Amsterdam. In 1891 Dr. Moritz Wallach (1866-1957), the son of the head of the Edat Yisrael Congregation in Cologne, was sent to Jerusalem, as medical director. The hospital was designed by the architects Shick and Sandel. The inauguration of the hospital was scheduled for the birthday of Kaiser Wilhelm II, who had approved of the hospital's bylaws.

The opening ceremony took place on January 27, 1902. It was an up-to-date facility and included an isolation ward, a sterilization unit and hot running water. Dr. Wallach, who was close to the Agudat Yisrael, an orthodox movement, ran the hospital for forty-five years in accordance with strict Orthodox law.

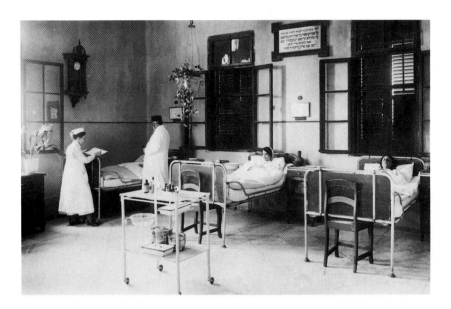

Dr. Moritz Wallach and Schwester Selma at the General Jewish Hospital, Sha'arei Zedek, Jerusalem, c. 1910.

Ammy Ben Yakov, New York.

Sha'arei Zion Hospital in Jaffa

The first waves of *aliya* in the years between 1882 and 1890 resulted in the growth of the Jewish community in Jaffa and the establishment of the Baron Rothschild settlements in Judah. In the summer of 1891 a malaria epidemic erupted in Jaffa and its environs. The English Mission Hospital which had been operating in the city closed for the summer. The city elders, the Bnei Brith lodge and the *L'ma'an Zion* society – a German-based Jewish philanthropic society which sought to improve conditions among the Jews of the Holy Land, particularly in the area of health – rented a two-story building and turned it into a hospital with twenty beds. It was called Sha'arei Zion, after the Bnei Brith lodge. Dr. Menahem Stein was appointed head physician and director and he was assisted by Dr. A. Mazie, who worked in the settlements of the baron. Among the physicians who eventually worked at the hospital were Drs. Hillel Joffe, an outstanding public figure as well as Chaim Chissin, a laborer-turned-doctor, and Sonia Belkind, the first woman physician in the country.

The hospital served the Jewish population of Jaffa and the Jewish workers from the baron's settlements, but also treated Arab patients. Because of the growth in the population being cared for by the hospital it was decided to

acquire a larger building, one which had served as the residence of the Austrian consul. To this end, the Baroness Hirsch and the Baron Rothschild, among others, were mobilized, and the new hospital was inaugurated in 1898. With the eviction of the Jews from Jaffa in 1917 by the Turks, the hospital was closed. It was reopened after the British conquest of Palestine a year later. After the disturbances of 1921, the hospital was closed for the last time. Its place as regional hospital was taken over by the Hadassah Hospital, which was opened on Balfour Street in Tel Aviv in the 1920s.

L'ma'an Zion Ophthalmic Hospital

In 1908 the *L'ma'an Zion* Society founded a Jewish ophthalmic hospital in Jaffa. The physician in charge was Dr. M. Ehrlanger of Lucerne, Switzerland. When he retired his place was taken by Dr. A. Ticho (1883-1960) from Moravia. He had completed his medical studies in Prague and Vienna in 1912. Dr. Ticho worked tirelessly among the Jewish and Arab populations until his death. His wife, Anna Ticho, who worked alongside him, was one of the leading artists in the *Yishuv* and in Israel.

In Conclusion

During the 19th century hospitals were established in the Holy Land primarily for three reasons: religious, messianic or missionary purposes; imperialist policy; or because of the particularism of the various communities who feared outside influence – Jews, Armenians and Greek Orthodox (who also established their own school systems). In the second half of the 19th century, the various European powers provided services for their own nationals who flocked to the Holy Land as pilgrims.

An exception to this reasoning was the founding of the Marienstift Pediatric Hospital under Dr. Max Sandreczky. Dr. Sandreczky was of the opinion that religion was a personal matter and that his duty was to fulfill his own potential by service, sacrifice, dedicated work, modesty and integrity. Furthermore, he believed it was preferable to perform such services in what was then an undeveloped, disease-ridden country. He also believed that Jews and Christians were equal and that there was no justification for converting Jews.

The medical history of the Holy Land cannot be rivaled. Until 1842 there was not a single resident physician in the entire area. On the eve of World War I nineteen hospitals had been established in Jerusalem alone, during a period when the population never exceeded 70,000, and hospitals were opened in other cities such as Jaffa, Haifa, Nazareth, Nablus, Gaza and Tiberias.

~

The first medical convention on trachoma, Jerusalem, 1914.
First row (from right): Dr. Naftali Weitz, Dr. Goldberg, Dr. Jacob Segall, Dr. Pochowski, Dr. A. Mazie, Dr. Weisbord, Dr. Shimoni. Middle row, standing: Dr. Jermans, Dr. Baron, Dr. Sonia Alexander-Belkind, Dr. Kronkin, Dr. Haya Weitz (wife of Naftali Weitz), Dr. Blasskind, Dr. Krapkot. The Central Zionist Archives, Jerusalem.

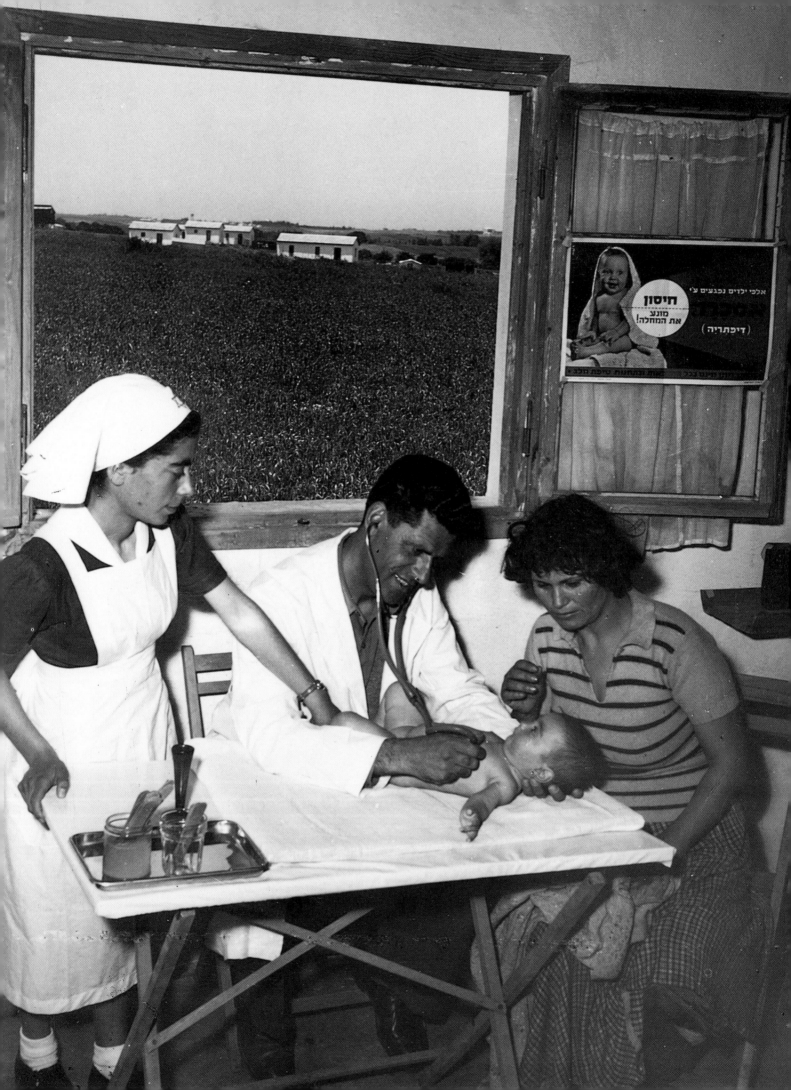

SHIFRA SHVARTS

THE DEVELOPMENT OF THE JEWISH HEALTH CARE SYSTEM IN PALESTINE AND ISRAEL DURING THE TWENTIETH CENTURY

In December 1903, the first group of survivors of the Kishinev pogroms arrived in Jaffa, marking the beginning of the Second Aliya of Jewish immigrants to Palestine which was to continue until the outbreak of World War I. Among them were a few thousand young socialists whose goal it was to become workers in the Jewish agricultural settlements. The difference in climate, primitive living conditions, hard labor and poor nutrition adversely affected the young people's health, resulting in recurrent attacks of paratyphus, malaria and cholera. Many of the young people fell ill and died due to the lack of proper medical treatment. In the large villages, some medical services were available, but accessibility was dependent upon the good will of the Baron Rothschild, patron of the settlements. The village councils themselves felt no obligation to provide health care for their workers. Medical services were available only at high prices, and most workers could not afford them. The dispute over medical care was one of the major sources of friction between workers and farm managers. This led, eventually, to the growth of an alternative health service for workers only, called the Workers' Sick Fund, based on mutual aid and membership fees.

The first sick fund was founded in December 1911 at the Second Convention of the Judea Agricultural Workers Organization, in Petah Tikva:

The convention confirms the vital need of a joint sick fund for the workers of Palestine and abroad, to deal with matters concerning all of them. The fund should be financed by the members' savings on the basis of mutual guarantee and help.

Infant Welfare center in a new settlement, 1950s.

The Government Press Office, Jerusalem.

Kupat Holim clinic in Petah-Tikva, 1922.

Labor Archives, Lavon Institute,

Tel Aviv.

This resolution can be regarded as the cornerstone of the workers' sick fund in Israel, later known as *Kupat Holim*, which today insures more than 75 percent of Israel's population of five million. During the years 1912-1918, three similar sick funds were established by regional worker's organizations in Judea, Samaria and the Galilee. Dispensaries run by nurses were soon opened in almost every village. Hospitalization services were provided by the Sha'ar Zion Community Hospital in Jaffa, according to an agreement with the Hebrew Medical Association, which had been founded in 1912.

In 1921, the three regional workers' organizations were merged into the General Federation of Labor, the *Histadrut*, along with their respective sick funds which became the General Sick Fund-Kupat Holim. Unlike workers' sick funds in other countries, established in the wake of the Industrial Revolution in urban working-class districts, Kupat Holim was founded first in agricultural villages, later in the cities and towns. The idea of the small clinic which enabled patients to obtain medical care close to home and to establish personal ties with their physicians has remained the model until today.

Parallel to the establishment of Kupat Holim, the Hadassah Medical Organization (H.M.O.), a branch of the Hadassah Women's Zionist

Organization of America, came to the assistance of the *Yishuv* (the Jewish community in Palestine) in 1918. Headed by Dr. Isaac Max Rubinow, the H.M.O. intended to set up a new system of health care services, based on American standards. Administered from abroad, it began to work on sanitation in general and anti-malaria prevention in particular. It opened six hospitals in the main cities, as well as outpatient clinics. Hadassah focused its work primarily on children, from birth through adolescence, including school health programs. These programs led later to the establishment of a country-wide network of maternity and child health care centers, a free public service, which continues to function successfully until today.

In 1921, according to an agreement between the H.M.O. and Kupat Holim, Hadassah financed the costs of medicines and buildings for Kupat Holim, while the latter was responsible for the practical provision of services.

During World War I, a committee for the *Magen David Adom* (the "Red Shield of David", a Hebrew version of the Red Cross,) was established, in order to care for wounded soldiers of the Jewish Legion, which fought within the framework of the British Army. The committee was active until 1920. In 1930 the Magen David Adom committee renewed its activities, focusing on emergency health services for the *Yishuv*, in which capacity it still functions today.

During the years 1922-1930, years of extensive agricultural settlement in Palestine and the establishment of many working-class districts around the larger towns, the network of Kupat Holim clinics expanded. Membership increased to 20 percent of the Jewish population of 165,000 people, among them 85 percent of the population of workers' settlements. Nevertheless, from its inception, Kupat Holim suffered from severe deficits. Membership fees covered no more than 60 percent of expenditure. An employers' health levy did not exist and few employers agreed to contribute to the costs of health services for their employees. In 1925-1927, with the immigration of the largely middle-class Fourth Aliya, the situation of Kupat Holim was aggravated even further and an inquiry commission was appointed "to examine the condition of Kupat Holim" in order to eliminate waste and

Dr. Hillel Joffe.

Dr. Joffe (1864-1936) was born in the Ukraine and came to Palestine in 1891 after completing his medical studies in Geneva. He settled in Tiberias and began practicing in the Galilee settlements. Two years later he accepted an invitation from the officials of the Baron Rothschild to practice in Zichron Ya'acov. A leader of Hovevei Zion, he accompanied Theodor Herzl on a tour of Jewish settlements in 1898. In 1907 he established a hospital in Zichron Ya'acov and a medical center for the Galilee and Samaria, with special emphasis on anti-malarial treatment. Labor Archives, Lavon Institute, Tel Aviv.

Nurses and doctors, members of the
American Zionist Medical Unit,
December 21, 1921, Jerusalem.

*Second row: Alice L. Seligsberg (7th
from right), Hadassah's representative
in the unit; Dr. Isaac M. Rubinow
(8th from right), medical director of
the unit.*

*Hadassah Medical Organization
Archives, New York.*

improve efficiency. (This was only the first in a long list of such commissions established over the next six decades.) The findings of the commission and two further commissions established the following year proposed the establishment of a National Health Authority, under the supervision of either Hadassah or the Health Committee of the *Yishuv*'s representative national council, the *Vaad Leumi*. Kupat Holim would, accordingly, be financed and supervised by that authority. In 1929, however, the civil disturbances among the Arabs of Palestine, combined with the Great Depression, resulted in the termination of the reorganization program, leaving both Kupat Holim and Hadassah to function independently. The Hadassah-Kupat Holim agreement, which had functioned well in the early twenties, broke down, and Kupat Holim decided to establish its own hospitalization system.

The first Kupat Holim hospital, the Emek Hospital in the Jezreel Valley, was opened in 1930 and its success was a turning-point in Kupat Holim policy. Until then it had focused on primary medicine, but now it expanded its activities to include hospitalization services, central urban clinics and an independent supply of medicines. Kupat Holim became a fully independent, comprehensive medical system.

During the 1930s, the Jewish population in Palestine grew to 500,000, with a large urban working class. With the arrival of hundreds of immigrant physicians from Germany, Kupat Holim activities expanded significantly. The Beilinson Hospital with a nursing school was built near Tel Aviv, and scores of neighborhood clinics were built in the large towns.

Political and social developments in Palestine during the 1930s also influenced the Jewish health services. The H.M.O. founded the Popular Sick Fund (*Kupat Holim Amamit*), as an alternative for workers who did not want to join the labor-oriented Kupat Holim. The right-wing Revisionist movement, founded by Ze'ev Jabotinsky and ostracized by the labor movement in the 1930s, founded its own National Workers' Sick Fund, taking its physicians and members out of the Kupat Holim. The great number of immigrant physicians from Germany resulted in the founding of several primary medical institutions and additional independent sick funds such as the

"The Donkey Milk Express," carrying bottles of pasteurized milk from the first Mother and Infant Welfare Station in the Old City of Jerusalem, c.1920.

Hadassah Medical Organization Archives, New York.

Children in a kindergarden in Haifa being treated against eye disease, c.1925.

The Central Zionist Archives, Jerusalem.

Maccabi Sick Fund, the Asaph Sick Fund, and the Physicians' Sick Fund. They were all competition for Kupat Holim among the upper middle classes and reduced its sources of income. At the same time, the large number of immigrant physicians from Germany who remained in Kupat Holim improved its health care services. Yet the integration of the German-Jewish physicians from central European medical schools into the centralized, socialist Kupat Holim created serious ideological problems regarding the character of the medical services Kupat Holim wished to grant its members and the position of physicians in its ranks. These problems became more pressing at the end of World War II and the beginning of the struggle for the state.

In May 1948, the State of Israel was established. Government ministries were organized and the Health Ministry took over the Mandatory Government's Department of Health. Soon after, regional health bureaus and an epidemiological service were formed. The state extended its responsibility for health services in the construction and operation of hospitals, in preventive medicine for mothers and children, and in the operation of former British hospitals. At the same time, a Military Medical Service was formed to operate military hospitals for the Israeli Defense Forces. This service, which served both soldiers and civilians, developed rapidly and established sixteen military hospitals, mainly in former British facilities. All professional positions were filled by enlisted doctors and volunteers from abroad. This service became a unique source of administrative and political power and succeeded in turning the hospitals into first rate institutions.

During the first two years of statehood the population of Israel doubled to 1.2 million people, due to mass immigration from Europe and from the Arab

countries, and within ten years, the population exceeded two million. The percentage of insured people increased dramatically to about 90 percent. Kupat Holim and the Jewish Agency, which was responsible for the immigrants' reception and initial settlement, reached an agreement whereby new immigrants would be granted automatic health insurance through Kupat Holim immediately upon arrival and at reduced rates. With financial support from abroad, the Kupat Holim expanded its services rapidly, building more hospitals and community clinics, and its status rivaled (perhaps even surpassed) that of the Ministry of Health. Other sick funds competed with Kupat Holim by opening more clinics, and in order to finance their growth,

Hadassah employees preparing for the journey to the Mount Scopus hospital in an armored ambulance, Jerusalem, 1948.

Hadassah Medical Organization Archives, New York.

they demanded an increase in government financial support. All of the sick funds received financial support from the government but refused to allow government interference in their policy-making, a situation which led to the basic problems facing the Israeli health care system today.

For reasons of financial and administrative efficiency, it was decided in 1953 to transfer all military hospital facilities to the Ministry of Health, which thus became the major provider of hospitalization services. This transfer was actually the final stage in shaping the general health system in Israel. From then on, both the Ministry of Health and the Kupat Holim each concentrated mainly on preserving its own status and vested interests.

As of 1994, Israel's population was about 5,000,000, 83 percent Jews and 17 percent non-Jews, most of them Arabs. The major part of the population lives in urban areas, and the country is considered a higher middle-income country. About 8 percent of Israel's GNP is allocated to health, similar to that allocated

by western European countries, and about 96 percent of the population is insured. Payment to the sick funds is relative to income and family status, whereas services are provided on the basis of need and not the ability to pay.

The sick funds are the major providers of health care and medical services in Israel. Today, there are four major sick funds in operation: Kupat Holim with 3.7 million members (75 percent of the population); Maccabee with 700,000 members (14 percent); the National Sick Fund with 200,000 members (4 percent); and the United Sick Fund with 150,000 members (3 percent). The Ministry of Health is the principle public health agency and the supreme body for licensing the medical and para-medical professions, as well as for implementing all health-related legislation.

Since the 1950s, preventive medicine and primary care have improved and expanded markedly, both among the Jewish and Arab communities. Over

Prime Minister Ben Gurion, greets the opening of the Hadassah Medical School on May 17, 1949.

Division of the History of Medicine, Hebrew University - Hadassah Medical School, Jerusalem.

"Renew your membership card."

Kupat Holim Poster. 94 x 62 cm.

The Central Zionist Archives,

Jerusalem.

Opposite:

"Kupat Holim opens a new clinic every

two days."

Poster by Ben David, late 1940s.

70 x 49 cm.

The Central Zionist Archives,

Jerusalem.

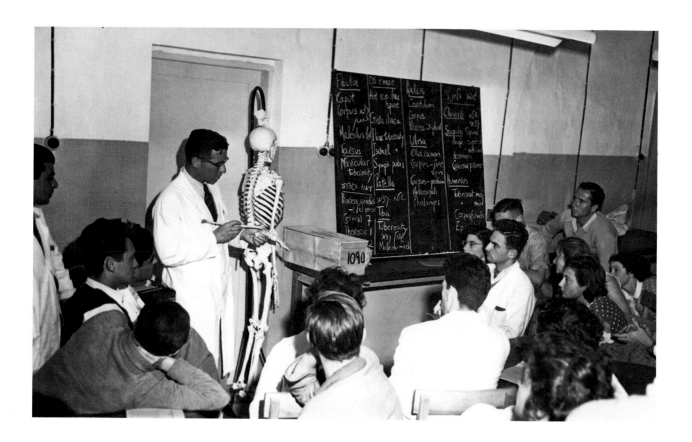

twenty general hospitals containing about 13,000 beds are presently operated by the various providers. There are also 16,000 geriatric and psychiatric beds, most of which are operated by the Ministry of Health or private bodies. There is a ratio of about 6.5 beds per 1,000 people, one of the lowest among western countries. On the other hand, the ratio of physicians to population is more than 1 to 350, one of the highest in the world. Most of Israel's 15,000 physicians are salaried public employees. The relatively high number of physicians, together with the strong primary care services, contributes to the low hospitalization rate in the country.

The Ministry of Health operates 850 free maternity and child health care centers, *Tipat Halav* ("A Drop of Milk"), which, inter alia, provide immunization for infants and children until the age of five. There are over 2,000 community-oriented primary care clinics (about 1,300 are operated by Kupat Holim).

Research at the Weizmann Institute, c.1950.
Division of the History of Medicine, Hebrew University - Hadassah Medical School, Jerusalem.

Opposite:
First anatomy class at the Hebrew University Hadassah Medical School.
Courses in anatomy were inaugurated in April 1952.
Division of the History of Medicine, Hebrew University - Hadassah Medical School, Jerusalem.

Israel has four medical schools affiliated with major universities in the country: the Hebrew University Medical School (associated with Hadassah); the Tel Aviv University Medical School; the Technion Medical School in Haifa; and the Ben-Gurion University Medical School (associated with Kupat Holim). The latter runs a special program of community-oriented medical education with an emphasis on family physician specialization. The university affiliation of most hospitals in Israel provides them with valuable research initiative. Research is also carried out in the Kupat Holim community health service network. Numerous epidemiological studies have grown out of the collaborative efforts of community clinics and hospital staff. Hundreds of physicians and support staff engage in full time research while many others pursue scientific investigation in addition to their clinical work. Every year hundreds of scientific papers are published in Israel and abroad. In 1994, for example, 1,585 scientists were involved in medical research in Israel – 948 of them hospital physicians and support staff, and 637 of them university scientists. The two Hadassah Hospitals in Jerusalem lead in the field, followed by the Sheba Medical Center, and the Beilinson Medical Center of Kupat Holim.

Major medical research is also being carried out in the Weizmann Institute of Science in Rehovot, one of the leading research centers in Israel. Biological research there was begun in 1950 when Prof. Isaac I. Berenblum of Oxford University was invited to develop its Life Science program. Ten of the Institute's twenty research departments are devoted entirely to biological and bio-medical investigations, as are groups in five other departments. The core of the Institute's Life Science work is cancer research carried out in six of its departments. The Weizmann Institute plays a vital role in the international research community. In 1994 it published 505 works in medical research.

Israel has built a substantial and comprehensive health care system. For more than eighty years the system provided voluntary health insurance for almost all of the population, based on mutual aid and social justice. In February 1993, after many years of debate, the Israeli Knesset enacted a National Health Insurance Law, structured on the existing health providers, the sick funds and hospitals, and the Institute for National Insurance. The law, providing consumers with good accessibility, became effective at the beginning of 1995. In general, the principles of the health care system are based on the old Jewish tradition of mutual aid and a strong sense of community.

~

BIBLIOGRAPHY

H.S. HALEVI, "The Pluralistic Organization of the Israeli Health Care System," *Bitachon Sociali*, 1979, 17(3): 5-49.

S. SHVARTS, "Religion, Community and Politics in the Establishment of the First Jewish Hospitals in Jerusalem During the 19th Century," *Koroth*, 1988(9)7-8.

The Health of the People is the Wealth of Society, Kupat Holim, Health Insurance Institution of Israel, Achdut Press, Tel Aviv, 1992.

The Netanyahu Commission Report: National Inquiry into the Functioning and Efficiency of the Health Care System, Jerusalem, 1990, I,II.

A. DORON, *The Health Services in Israel: The Propect of the 1990s.*

A. SHIROM, *The Evolvement of a National Health Policy in Israel, 1990-1994: The Controversy over the State Commission's Report and its Aftermath.*

E. LESHEM, *The Israeli Public's Attitudes toward the New Immigrants of the 1990s.*

Gerhard Baader is professor Emeritus of the Freie Universität, Berlin, and visiting professor at the Hebrew University of Jerusalem. His fields of study include classical and German philology, linguistics and the history of Vienna, medicine in antiquity and the Middle Ages, Jews and medicine, eugenics and medicine during the Nazi era. He is a member of the Bavarian Academy of Sciences, Munich.

Ron Barkai is professor of medieval history in the Department of History at Tel Aviv University. He is presently visiting professor at the Faculty of Philology, University of Salamanca, Spain. Amongst his major publications are *Les infortunes de Dinah, ou la gynécologie au Moyen Âge* (Ed. Cerf, Paris, 1991), and *Science, magie et mythologie au Moyen Âge* (Ed. Van Leer, Jerusalem, 1987, 1988, 1991).

Natalia Berger is a Curator at Beth Hatefutsoth - the Museum of the Jewish Diaspora, Tel Aviv. She has edited and compiled several catalogues on different aspects of Diaspora Jewry, among them *Where Cultures Meet, the story of the Jews of Czechoslovakia* (Ed. Beth Hatefutsoth, M.O.D. Publishing House, 1990).

Theodore M. Brown holds a Ph.D. in history of science from Princeton University and was a postdoctoral fellow in the history of medicine at the Johns Hopkins University Institute of the History of Medicine. He is a professor in the Departments of History and of Community Preventive Medicine and in the Division of Medical Humanities at the University of Rochester in Rochester, New York. His research focuses on the intellectual and social history of medicine and psychiatry, on American health policy and educational practice, and on the American health left.

Aaron J. Feingold is a practicing physician in Edison, New Jersey. He is the senior member of the Raritan Bay Cardiology Group and a Fellow of the American College of Cardiology. Dr. Feingold is a collector of books and objects relating to his Jewish heritage.

Peter Gay was born in 1923 in Berlin. He is Sterling Professor of History Emeritus at Yale University. Amongst his main publications are *The Enlightenment: An Interpretation*, in 2 volumes (1966, 1969), *Freud: A Life for our Time* (1988), *Freud, Jews and Other Germans*, (1978) and 3 volumes of the series *The Bourgeois Experience - Victoria to Freud* (1984, 1986, 1993).

Samuel S. Kottek, M.D., is an assistant professor and Head of the Division of the History of Medicine at the Hebrew University - Hadassah Medical School. His fields of research include medicine in Ancient Hebrew literature; Jews and medicine and pediatrics in the 18th century.

Hagit Matras is a lecturer in the Department of Jewish and Comparative Folklore at the Hebrew University of Jerusalem and author of various articles in the field of folk medicine and related areas. She has published a book on the literary works of Joseph Haim Brenner.

Daniel Nadav was born in Tel Aviv in 1940 and received his doctorate from Tel Aviv University on the politics of social hygiene in Germany which was published as a book in Germany in 1985. He is a research fellow at the Institute of German History, Tel Aviv University and chairman of the section on Medicine during the Nazi era, a division of the Israeli Society for the History of Medicine.

Shmuel Nissan, M.D., is Professor Emeritus of Surgery at the Hadassah Hospital on Mount Scopus, where he was head of the Department of Surgery from 1976-89.

He is a member of the American Academy of Pediatrics. He has done extensive research on the history of hospitals in Jerusalem.

Harriet Pass Freidenreich, a Professor of History at Temple University, Philadelphia, is the author, inter alia, of *Jewish Politics in Vienna*, 1918-1938 (Indiana University Press, 1991) and *The Jews of Yugoslavia* (Jewish Publication Society, 1979). She is presently at work on a collective biography of Central European Jewish university women before the Nazi era.

Thomas Schlich, born 1962 in Kassel, Germany, studied medicine in Marburg/Lahn and worked at the University Hospital in Marburg. He was the recipient of a scholarship of the German Academic Exchange Service and a visiting scholar at the Wellcome Unit for the History of Medicine at the University of Cambridge. Since 1992 he has been research assistant at the Institute for the History of Medicine of the Robert Bosch Foundation, Stuttgart. He has published on Jewish physicians, modern medicine and Judaism, the history of modern medicine and science (physiology, bacteriology, surgery, especially organ transplantation).

Shifra Shvarts is a faculty member of the Ben Gurion University of the Negev, in the Medical School and the Kay College of Education. A graduate of Ben Gurion University in Jewish history and health sciences, Shifra Shvarts specialized in Israel's health care system and the history of medicine and public health in Israel. Among her works are *Health Care System in Israel - An Historical Perspective* (Pennsylvania Academy of Sciences, 1994) and *The Workers' Sick Fund in Israel in the Early 20th century*, (Sigerist Circle, 1994).